Photography and Germany

exposures

EXPOSURES is a series of books on photography designed to explore the rich history of the medium from thematic perspectives. Each title presents a striking collection of images and an engaging, accessible text that offers intriguing insights into a specific theme or subject.

Series editors: Mark Haworth-Booth and Peter Hamilton

Also published

Photography and Africa Erin Haney
Photography and Anthropology Christopher Pinney
Photography and Archaeology Frederick N. Bohrer
Photography and Australia Helen Ennis
Photography and China Claire Roberts
Photography and Cinema David Campany
Photography and Death Audrey Linkman
Photography and Egypt Maria Golia
Photography and Exploration James R. Ryan
Photography and Flight Denis Cosgrove and William L. Fox
Photography and Germany Andrés Mario Zervigón
Photography and Humour Louis Kaplan
Photography and Ireland Justin Carville
Photography and Italy Maria Antonella Pelizzari
Photography and Japan Karen Fraser
Photography and Literature François Brunet
Photography and Science Kelley Wilder
Photography and Spirit John Harvey
Photography and Tibet Clare Harris
Photography and Travel Graham Smith
Photography and the USA Mick Gidley

Photography and Germany

Andrés Mario Zervigón

reaktion books

Published by Reaktion Books Ltd
Unit 32, Waterside
44–48 Wharf Road
London N1 7UX, UK
www.reaktionbooks.co.uk

First published 2017

Printed and bound in China by 1010 Printing International Ltd

A catalogue record for this book is available from the British Library

ISBN 978 1 78023 748 0

Contents

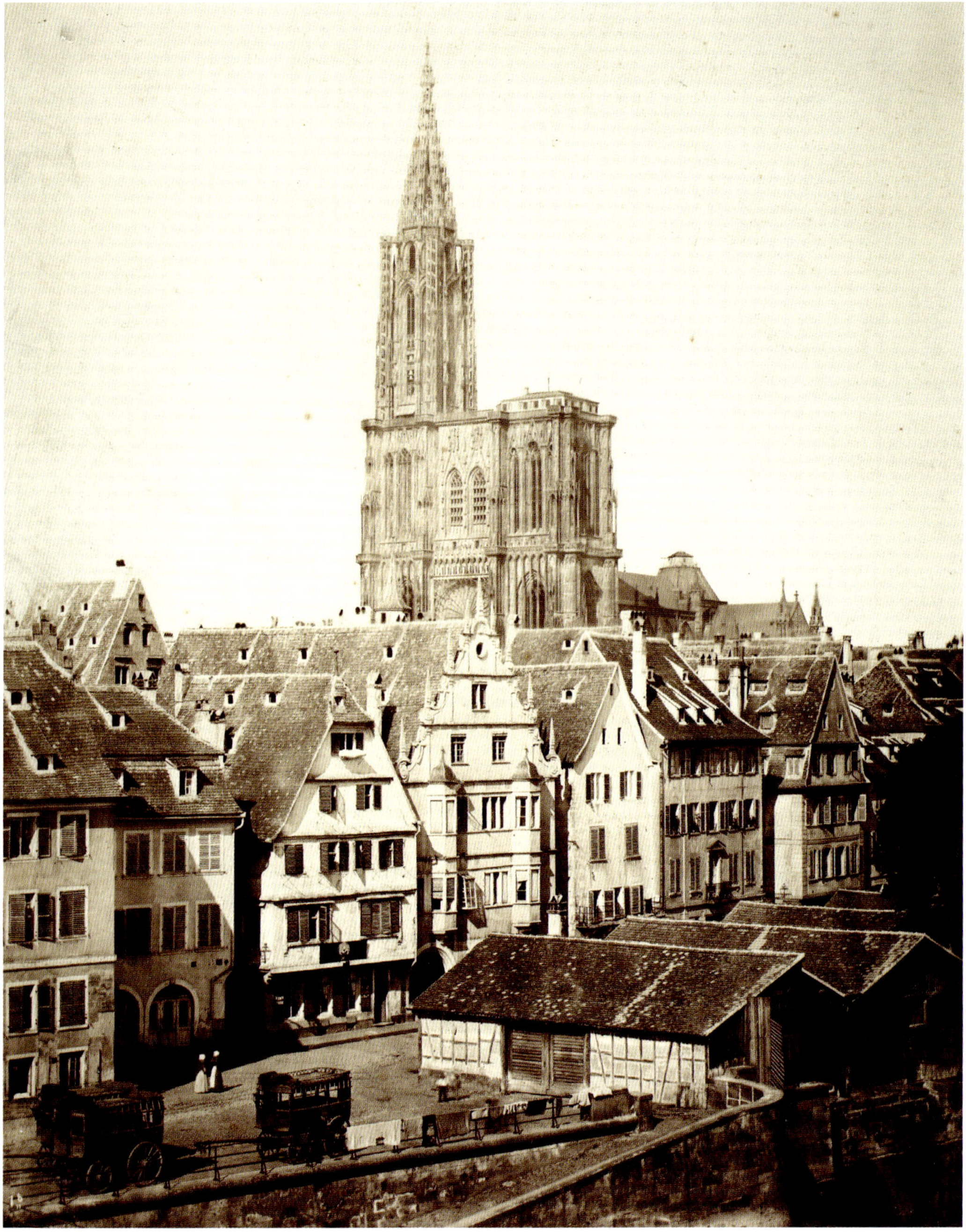

Introduction

In early May 1997, an ambitious and long-anticipated show opened at the Art and Exhibition Hall of the Federal Republic of Germany. Titled *Deutsche Fotografie. Macht eines Mediums 1870–1970* (German Photography: Power of a Medium, 1870–1970), it strove for an encyclopaedic history of the country's photography using key framing questions such as 'what is a national history of photography?' and 'does such a thing as German photography reflect a German mentality?'[1] The answers were provisional and the coverage of this enquiry was limited to the hundred years that followed unification in 1871, thereby missing the breathless march of history around the 1989 fall of the Berlin Wall. But up to this exhibition and thereafter, no institution has attempted to chronicle the longer histories of photography that can be associated with the country or otherwise categorized as German. This book attempts just such coverage by critically enquiring once more into the relationship between photography and Germany.

For many observers, the idea of photography in Central Europe evokes pioneering modernist pictures from the Weimar era or colossal digital prints that define the medium's art practice today. For others, it recalls horrifying documents of wartime atrocity. *Photography and Germany* seeks to broaden these perceptions by examining the medium's multifaceted relationship with Germany's turbulent cultural, political and social history. It shows how many of the same phenomena that helped generate the country's most recognizable photographs also led to a range of lesser-known pictures that similarly documented or negotiated Germany's cultural identity and historical ruptures. The book rethinks the photography we commonly associate with the country by discussing

1 Charles-David Winter, *View of Strasbourg*, c. 1862, albumen print.

the wider sea of emulsion it navigates and the historical context that gives it deeper meaning.

Photography and Germany correspondingly covers over 175 years of pictures, beginning with pre-photographic experiments in the light-sensitive chemicals that made the medium's origins possible, and ending with the tension between analogue and digital technologies that have stimulated the country's famous contemporary art photography. In these nearly two centuries, Germany played a central role in some of modern history's most significant events. It also accomplished a harried transition from a loose confederacy of near-feudal agricultural states to an industrialized, modern world power that unified itself not once but twice. This transformation included two revolutions, two world wars, the rise and fall of fascism, an unparalleled genocide and the redivided country's 'economic miracle' under the shadow of Cold War tensions. Photography has been inextricably linked to these events, both as a token of modernity itself and a means of documenting or even intervening in their unfolding. As this book aims to establish, the history of photography in Germany is the history of the country's troubled encounter with modernity, realized in visual form.

The underlying premise of this investigation is that there is little that can convincingly define a body of photography as German. Individual photographers and movements may have produced prints that share aesthetic values which were realized in other art forms from the country, such as a twentieth-century focus on technological subject matter that mirrors the country's famous industrial and graphic design. But it is impractical to suggest an essential German style for a medium that has been used so promiscuously across fields as diverse as science, advertising, journalism and the fine arts, areas of practice where German-based photographers have excelled. Similar uses of the medium in other parts of the world also mean that no one quality can be isolated as distinctly German. For example, the country's Pictorialist photography may have boasted the brooding character of Wagnerian opera or German fin-de-siècle literature and painting. However, similar melancholy prints were also produced at the time by members of the Stieglitz circle of American photographers. It is therefore just as difficult to designate a distinctly German photography as it is to define German identity as a whole.

The book takes this problem of designation as an important point of departure, showing not that there is a German photography per se, but that the medium was heavily employed to define what the notion of 'German' meant. Photography, for instance, played a key role in the troubled effort to forge a coherent national identity at a time of galloping nineteenth-century change. Perhaps more than other nations in Europe and elsewhere, most of which rested on broadly recognized geographic, linguistic and cultural boundaries, the area of Central Europe that became Germany leaned heavily on the medium of photography to envision what the nation was supposed to be. This task entered a particularly intense phase as the country first united in 1871 and sought to become a world power. The result was a cultural schizophrenia driven by the new nation's strong embrace of liberal economic policies and the rapid industrialization that followed, as well as the countervailing longings for a pre-industrial age in which a rural and mystically driven cultural identity was imagined as eternal, fixed. As a product of the modern age, photography in Germany intervened in this fraught project of national imagining, largely to productive ends but sometimes with catastrophic results. The book covers this history chronologically in six chapters, each of which is introduced by a representative case study that limits the material discussed to a single critical question. Set along a historical arc, the chapters highlight the medium's important role in Germany's cultural, social and political development – what I term its ongoing imagining in emulsion.

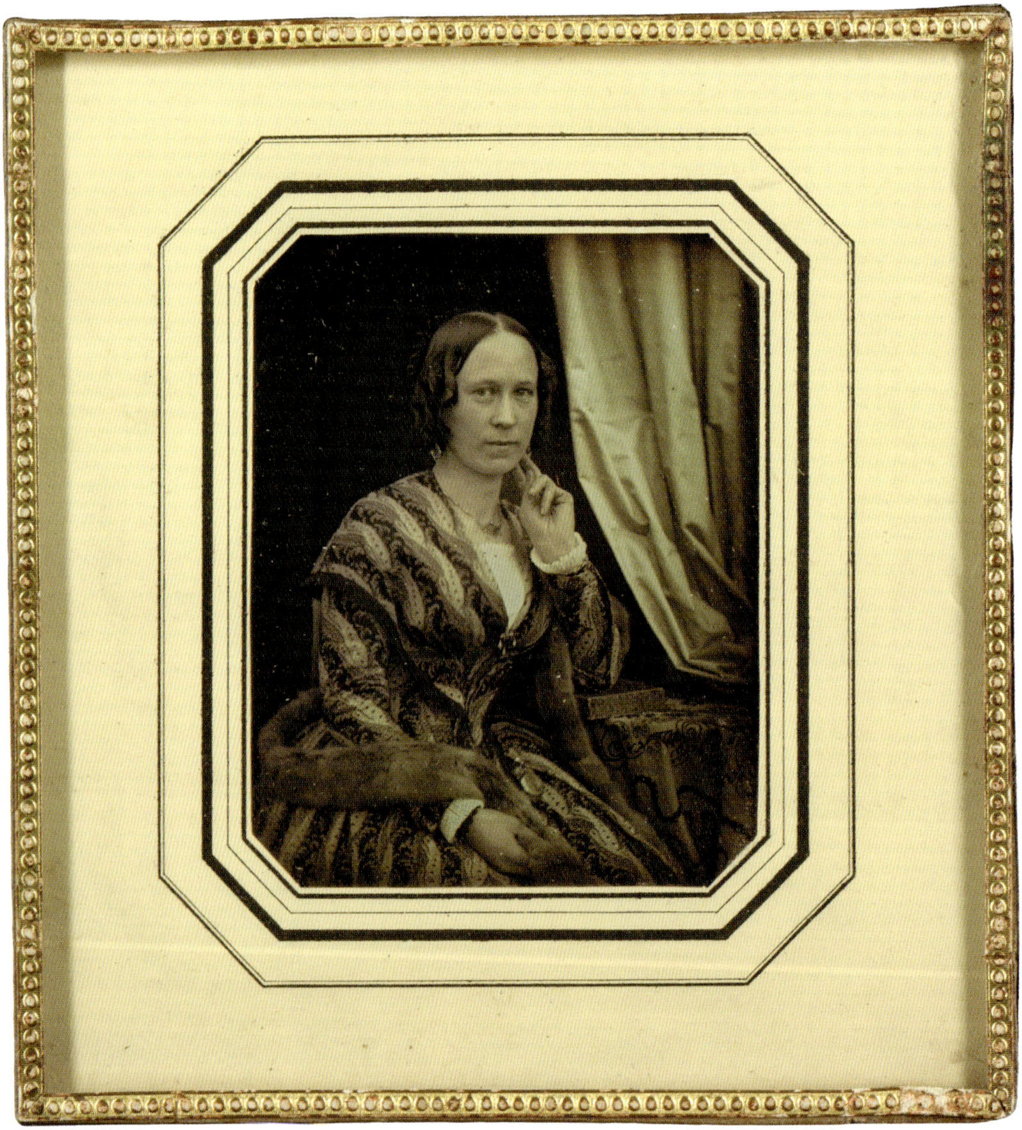

one

Belated Photography, 1839–1870

In February 1839, the painter Friederike Wilhelmine von Wunsch, resident in Paris, wrote to the Prussian king Frederick III on hearing of the photographic inventions of Louis J.M. Daguerre and William H.F. Talbot that had just been announced in Paris and London one month earlier. 'While France and England may claim the honour of this beautiful discovery,' she exclaimed, 'I am happy and proud to be able to tell his Majesty that our fatherland no longer needs to feel left behind in this glory, and that my investigations are not only older than those of my wise emulators, but have far surpassed their results.'[1] Proof of von Wunsch's experiments never surfaced – and they probably never took place. Still, her letter reveals a widespread sentiment of belatedness among German speakers, a shared sense that Germany lagged behind other European powers across a range of cultural, political and economic endeavours. These included the arts, literature, colonial conquests and – until unification in 1871 – even the project of nationhood itself.

Yet by the time modern compatriots such as Josef Maria Eder came to write the first comprehensive histories of photography in the 1880s, the medium's development in German-speaking lands had become a point of national pride.[2] Chroniclers like Eder cast photography as being, to a great extent, a *German* invention. According to their accounts, Johann Heinrich Schulze identified the light sensitivity of silver salts in 1717 and correspondingly made the first impressions by luminescence alone; descendants of Carl August von Steinheil invented the first anti-astigmatic lens in 1866, making possible consistent focus across a photographic plate; Hermann Wilhelm Vogel discovered the invaluable dye sensitization of photographic emulsion to the full spectrum of visible light in 1873, allowing an image of sky and land

2 Bertha Wehnert, *Self-portrait of the Photographer*, c. 1850, daguerreotype.

to be taken with the same exposure time; and Ottomar Anschütz perfected the split-second exposure in the 1880s, precisely capturing animals, people and objects in motion. As late as 1938, in his book *The March of Photography*, the photography chemist and historian Erich Stenger felt it necessary to emphasize these contributions and protest 'against the general belief that photography is a purely foreign [non-German] invention'. He countered that 'It was a German who produced the first image by light (Schulze), it was a German who first used the word "photography" in a newspaper (J. H. Maedler). It was a German who contributed to the perfecting . . . which led photography in colour to the achievements of today (Vogel).'[3] Though Stenger penned these words under the toxically chauvinist context of National Socialism, they ultimately represent sentiments expressed ever since von Wunsch sent her missive from Paris to Berlin. They therefore offer a key to understanding the fascinating and vexed relationship of photography and Germany.

This pride leavened with a sense of belatedness, however, ran parallel to what were in fact tremendous developments and uses of photography east of the Rhine. The reigning feelings of inferiority that generated a sense that the region had to catch up with the rest of Europe may have even stimulated these achievements, as in the larger nineteenth-century realms of technology, literature, philosophy and art, where the German lands ultimately excelled. Between photography's debut in 1839 and Germany's unification in 1871, the speakers of the language embraced the medium with a fantastic enthusiasm. From family photo studios to royal pomp, and from archaeological sites to anthropological investigations, German speakers both within the region and abroad employed photography substantially, often as a token of the modernity and national coherence that seemed to have passed them by. In this way, photography as both an innovation and a way to make innumerable images helped construct notions of Germany and the German in the modern age. This chapter discusses the first phase of this compensatory and identity-building project leading up to the year of national unification, 1871.

Defining the German Lands

When Friederike Wilhelmine von Wunsch trumpeted not just her invention but also its remarkable characteristics, including colour and split-second exposure, the king she addressed was not the monarch of Germany. Rather he was the head of Prussia, the power among German-speaking lands that had expanded substantially after the Napoleonic Wars of the early nineteenth century. Her 'fatherland [that] no longer needs to feel left behind in this glory' of France and England, therefore, did not exist, at least not as a nation state greater than her Prussian homeland. The area of Central Europe from which Germany was ultimately formed consisted instead of a league of 39 sovereign entities, most of which had entered into a *Zollverein* (customs union) in 1834. Prussia was the driving force behind this union, which specifically excluded the young power's prime German-language adversary, the Austrian Empire. In addressing the Prussian king, von Wunsch was not only reaching out to the land of her family. She was also casting her lot and that of German photography in with the power that had begun to unite Central Europe through its economic might, and that would finish the job with military force in coming decades. In this respect, she conjured a role for photography as a rallying point for national striving, and even unification.

She was not alone in this type of effort. Sixty-seven years earlier, in 1772, when the region was even more politically fragmented into tiny sovereignties, the young poet Johann Wolfgang Goethe stood before Strasbourg's grand Gothic cathedral and famously concluded that the impressive building was German (illus. 1).[4] This judgement took an exercise in intellectual gymnastics, given that no political entity named 'Germany' yet existed. But such was the challenge that partly drew Goethe to this monument in the first place. The vast structure presented him with what seemed the material expressions of a nation that existed in the past but which the modern vagaries of geography, politics and language had since diffused. For instance, Strasbourg, the capital of the Alsace, had been a part of France since 1681, though German remained the dominant tongue. This was actually typical of Central Europe's rich cultural mix prior to the nineteenth century, when German speakers were spread patchwork-like through the larger region. They even populated large portions of Russia's Volga basin far to the east and the Balkans in the south. Further enriching this mosaic were constituencies who spoke the language but were not considered ethnic Germans, such as the Jews of Hungary, Bohemia, Galicia and Bulgaria who used the tongue as their vernacular. Geography, language and government were therefore difficult criteria to use in defining what was German. But Strasbourg's cathedral sported an identifiable style, and Goethe wished to celebrate this manner of building as a purely Teutonic cultural and technological achievement of the Middle Ages. Goethe's focus on the building allowed him to define his belated nation through an idealized medieval culture that was, as he argued, coherent, pure, defiantly beautiful and enviable. What he did with medieval architecture, von Wunsch later tried to replicate with photography. In this way, the medium as a conception could join architecture, language, literature, philosophy and music to perform the cultural work of national self-imagining.

A photograph of the cathedral from circa 1862 provides a visual analogue to Goethe's argument (see illus. 1). From a beautiful nest of medieval homes, the Gothic building soars upward into the sepia-golden sun, seemingly propelled by the Teutonic architectural heritage that the half-timbering and terraced floors of the homes below mark. Yet this photograph's history actually reveals the complexity that Goethe's formulation specifically obscured. The picture was taken by Charles-David Winter, a local photographer who bore a French compounded first name and a German family name that, together, were typically Alsatian. As a proud native, he committed himself to picturing his local architectural heritage while cultivating the area's most prosperous and notable citizens as studio clientele. He entered his photographs in international competitions, but almost always those based in Paris rather than in German-speaking capitals.[5] Collected as a prized Alsatian photographer today, and famous for making some of the most accomplished early daguerreotypes in Europe, his larger output illustrates the challenges that Goethe and others faced in summoning a national culture for a diverse region. It also shows the degree to which photographs could complicate, rather than resolve, this larger picture that the famous poet had painted in his Strasbourg declaration.

Despite such potential difficulties, defining a German nation in clearly identifiable cultural terms took root through efforts such as Goethe's well before the introduction of photography. In fact, it had grown with particular strength under the Napoleonic conquest in the decades prior to 1839. During these years, running roughly from 1799 until 1815, resistance to French domination reinforced a sense of solidarity among speakers of the tongue. The philosopher Johann Gottlieb Fichte, for example, tried to apply to the German language itself the same sort of reasoning that Goethe had used for culture, and that others would apply to photography. In his *Reden an die deutsche Nation* (Addresses to the German Nation, 1808), Fichte proposed that the German language had remained uncorrupted by Latin influences and was therefore the only authentic European tongue spoken in his time.[6] Like Gothic architecture and von Wunsch's inventions, the German language itself was free of non-Teutonic corruption.

This consciousness of an idealized and unified past that had seemingly taken shape organically, mixed with an emotional – even anti-rational – sentiment, came to be associated with Romanticism. Under this movement's banner, both the modern notion of Germany and the idea of photography found their origins. Musing in this way about nation, public thinkers sought to conjure almost fantastically a common cultural identity across a region where the political and linguistic facts of a single state could not be invoked, and ethnic boundaries were hard to draw. Similarly, as the photo historian Douglas Nickel has observed, inventors and early commentators viewed photography as a distinct and identifiable medium, but born of a dynamic and evolutionary process that was nearly sublime.[7] The two ideas coalesced in the experimenters who pioneered this technology and the nations to which their glories were linked. In this way too photography could join the other arts and technologies to assist in national self-imaging.

But as Winter's photograph of Strasbourg's cathedral demonstrates, the actual complexities of culture, demographics and sovereignty made this work difficult. In nineteenth-century Central Europe, local rivalries simmered, Catholic and Protestant divisions persisted, regional identities such as the Bavarian flourished, and languages such as French, Polish and Czech remained widely spoken in areas of overlapping ethnicities. It was hard work to draw a single *Kulturnation* (cultural nation) over this region that historian David Blackbourn describes as an archipelago of jurisdictions left over from the Holy Roman Empire.[8] In frustration, historian Leopold von

Ranke asked in 1832: 'Who will be able to grasp in a word or concept what is German? Who will call it by name, the genius of our country, of the past and of the future?' As he concluded, 'it would only be another phantom to lure us on one more false road,' perhaps one signposted by Winter's architectural photographs.[9] With this sort of misdirection in mind, poet Heinrich Heine asked satirically in 1840:

> Where does the *German* begin? Where does it end? May a German smoke? The majority says no. May a German wear gloves? Yes, but only of buffalo hide . . . But a German may drink beer. Indeed, as a true son of Germanias, he should drink beer . . .[10]

These assertions, questions and jests suggest that German identity in the decades prior to unification was, as the historian James Sheehan notes, a national culture in aspiration rather than an existing entity. 'Literature, literacy, even language may make the formation of a national culture easier,' he explains, 'but they are not the thing itself.' When looking at photography's important role in this history, it is important to bear in mind Sheehan's admonishment 'not to confuse aspiration with accomplishment in building a national culture'.[11] Von Wunsch's claims and the flood of photographs that followed may provide model instances of ambition over achievement, thereby showing how photographs and the public discourse around them were put to the service of constructing national identity. But they also reveal the tensions between cohesion and fragmentation that heavily defined the German national project.

Origins and Experiments in the German Lands

Von Wunsch was not alone among German speakers to perceive the newly announced technology in national terms. It was 7 January 1839 when the astronomer and member of parliament Dominique François Arago rose before the French Academy of Sciences to report that the artist and panorama impresario Daguerre had discovered a way to fix the image of the camera obscura. Exactly how Daguerre achieved this feat remained a secret, but news of his discovery spread rapidly. Twenty days later, in Augsburg's *Allgemeine Zeitung*, the pharmacist Ignaz Paul Keller mused publically to himself in a column: 'oh, you could have made this discovery long ago, had you only thought of it.' According to Keller's account, on hearing of Arago's announcement, he immediately set about devising his own procedure for capturing the camera obscura's image. As he added, 'I am convinced that I [now] possess the same art of Daguerre.' Because he did not know if anyone else in Central Europe had claimed the discovery earlier, he generously conceded: 'For the honour of my fatherland, I happily relinquish the vanity of having my name named' in connection with this discovery.[12] Like his female Prussian counterpart in Paris, Keller did not want his fatherland to be left behind in this discovery.

Photography's early history teems with similar claimants to the invention, and their assertions are often spiked by nationalism, particularly in Europe.[13] The most famous cases are of British and French citizens who proudly claimed the medium as their country's own. The German lands turned out no differently, except that there was no unified state with which to associate these declarations. Instead they gently served Goethe's Strasbourg Cathedral function, suggesting a cultural coherence where little existed. On 2 March, for example, the *Leipziger Zeitung* reported that a physician and chemist from Dresden named Dr Petzholdt had succeeded in making Daguerre's discovery 'German property'. This patriotic aspiration was dashed when the doctor himself eventually confessed that he had not yet succeeded in making anything like 'Daguerrian light pictures'.[14]

With carefully targeted letters, Fox Talbot drew many Central European luminaries into his struggle to win recognition for his negative-positive process over Daguerre's. Munich, for example, found itself in the whirl of the international news about the daguerreotype blowing through Europe when one of Talbot's dispatches, dated 9 February 1839, arrived at the Bavarian Academy. Reacting to Talbot's note, the physicist and mathematician Carl August von Steinheil reported to the Academy that he and the mineralogist Franz von Kobell had already experimented with a similar procedure 'with useful results'.[15] A tableau of this photographic yield (illus. 3), now lost, shows that the men developed a negative-generating process quite similar to Talbot's own. One of their techniques

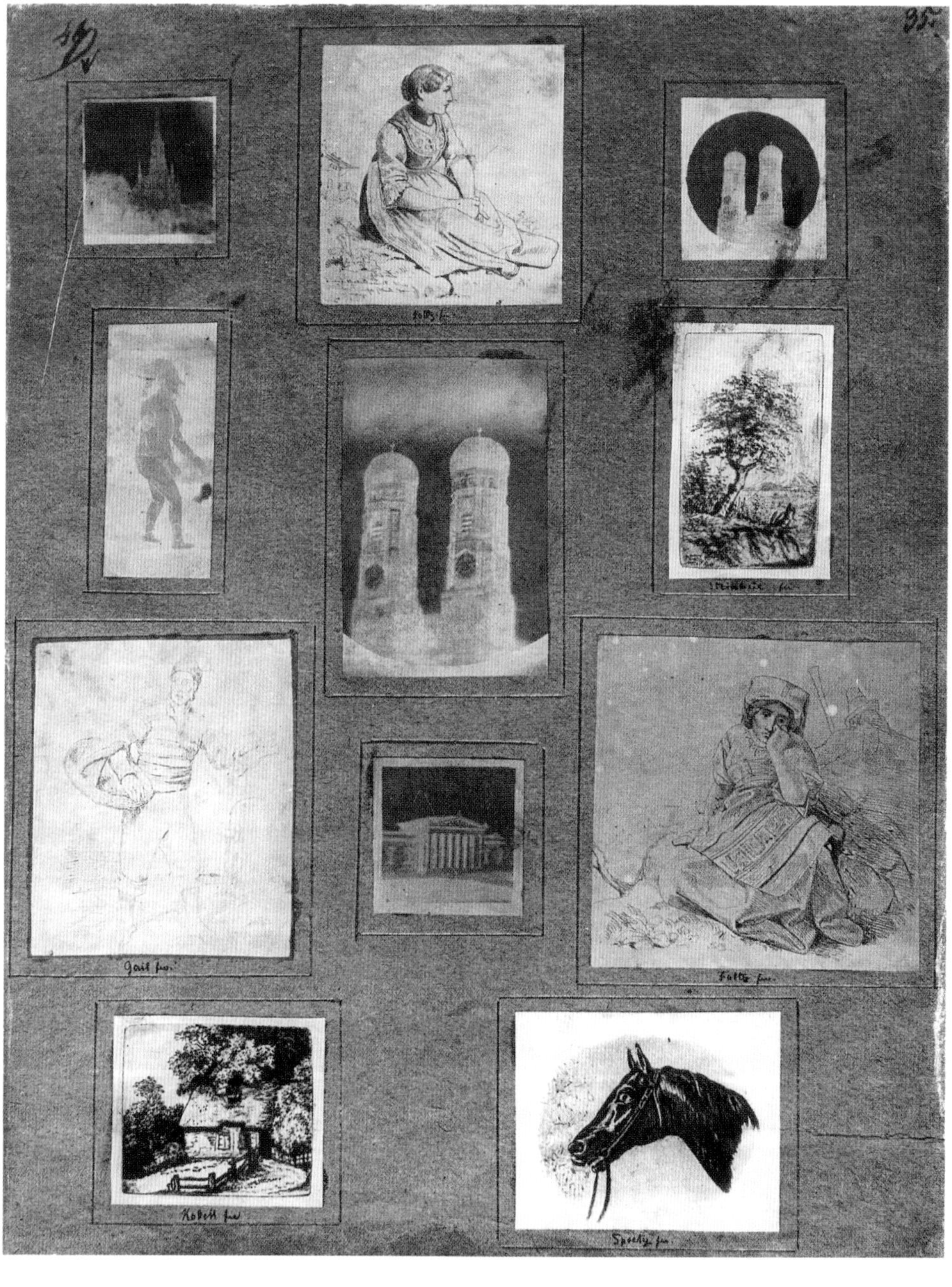
35.

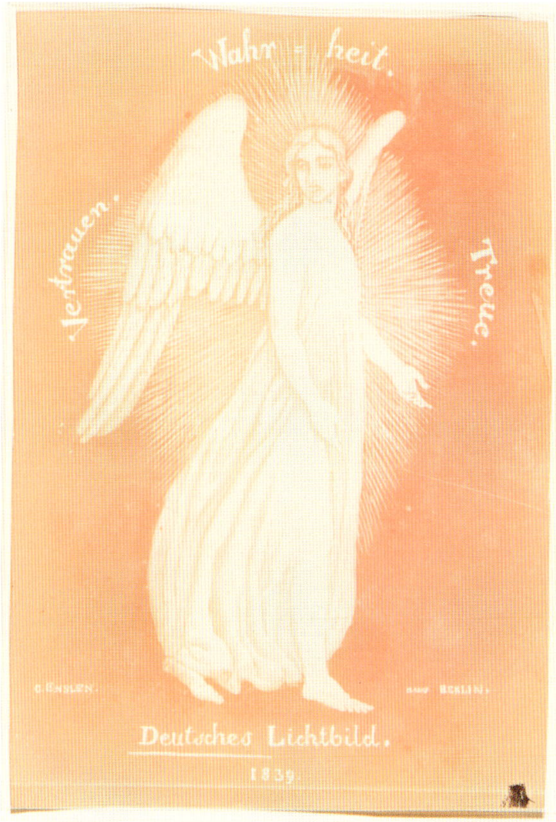

4 Johann Carl Enslen, *Allegory: Trust, Truth, Fidelity*, 1839, photogenic drawing on salt paper.

reproduced notable works of Bavarian art photo-chemically. Others used a camera to capture signature Munich landmarks: the Glyptothek, the famous towers of the Frauenkirche and the Odeonsplatz. Thus, just as one of Daguerre's demonstration pieces offered a view across the Parisian Seine, and Talbot's experiments took his Lacock Abbey home as their subject, these men were effectively stamping their photographic experiments with their locale, in this case the monument-rich Bavarian capital and its resident artists.

A further experimenter, albeit one who did not receive a letter from Talbot, followed news of the Englishman's discoveries with the goal of developing a German alternative. The eighty-year-old polymath Johann Carl Enslen devised a form of cameraless photography using light-sensitized

3 Carl August Steinheil and Franz von Kobell, *First Photographic Attempts on an Original Tableau, Munich, early 1839*, 1839, salt prints (original lost, reproduction from 1930s).

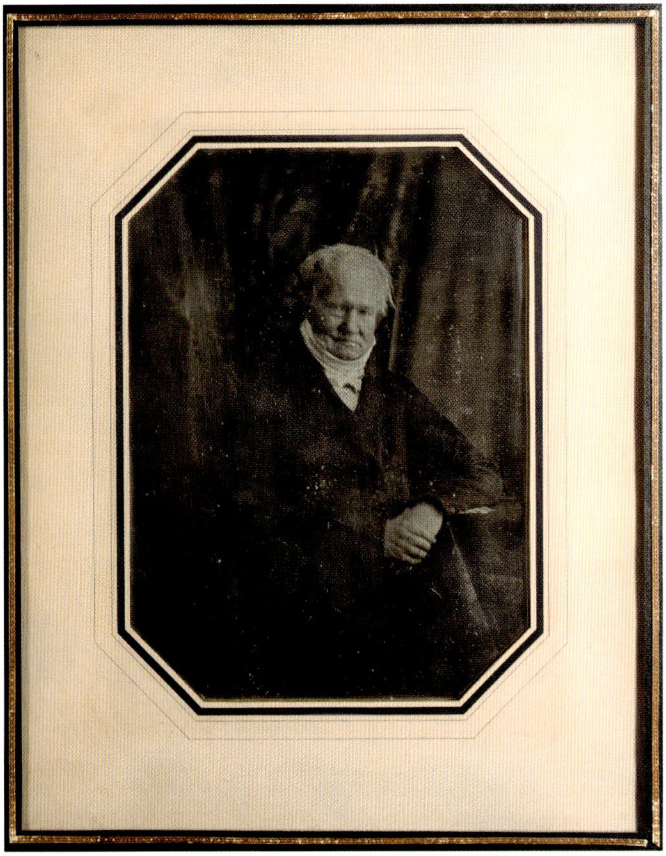

5 Hermann Biow, *Alexander von Humboldt*, 1847, daguerreotype.

paper in the spring of 1839. Surviving examples made by covering sensitized paper with objects before exposing these assemblies to light (photograms) reveal plant specimens, feathers and butterflies arranged around translucent intaglio prints. The result was often a framed composition, such as one featuring Friedrich the Great at its centre. Underneath the Prussian king runs a caption not of his name, but the term Enslen coined for his new process: *Lichtbild* or 'light picture'. Used by others such as Petzholdt, the designation stuck as a thoroughly German word for photograph until the end of the Second World War, although most people preferred the Latinized terms *Fotografie* and *Photographie*. It was the latter of these that Johann von Mädler inaugurated in print around the same time, much to the historian Erich

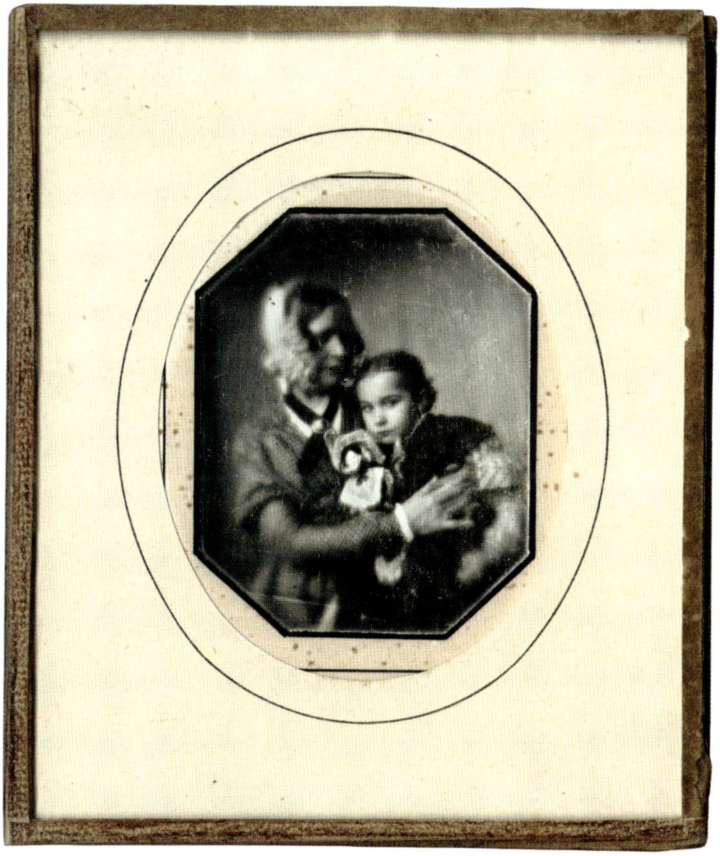

6 Carl August von Steinheil, *Elise von Steinheil with Daughter Lina*, 1840/41, daguerreotype.

Stenger's boasting pride a hundred years later.[16] Another of Enslen's sepia-brown photograms, however, stresses the German quality of his preferred word for the medium (illus. 4). Featuring a winged allegory of 'trust, truth, fidelity', the picture offers a partially underlined caption that reads '*Deutsches Lichtbild*' or 'German Light Picture' (Enslen's underlining). Not only was he nationalizing the term and the technology with this gesture. He was also identifying something specifically German about the fidelity of his photogram process to its represented objects.

Another of Talbot's letters, from late January 1839, landed in the mailbox of the naturalist and explorer Alexander von Humboldt, near Berlin (illus. 5). Von Humboldt had recently returned from an extended stay in Paris where he sat on the three-man panel tasked with judging the value of Daguerre's procedure for purchase by the French state. The other members of this board were Arago, who had announced the procedure in January and would finally reveal its details publicly in August, after the state purchased the technology, and the astronomer Jean-Baptiste Biot. Talbot had written to all three to advocate his procedure. Humboldt's inclusion for such an important task reveals the extent to which German speakers were already important players in the quickly evolving international discourse on photography.

Historians including Eder and Stenger would later foreground such German contributions by rediscovering the eighteenth-century polymath Johann Heinrich Schulze, who is attributed with having discovered the sensitivity of silver compounds to light. Eder even published a full monograph on Schulze claiming, among other things, that the letters the inventor reproduced by placing stencils over bottles filled with these compounds constituted the world's first photographs.[17] This history was surely unknown to von Wunsch, who wished to place herself squarely at the medium's origins. She must have been deeply disappointed when a new Prussian king awarded Daguerre the country's highest medal of service, the Pour le mérite, in 1842.[18]

Early Photography and Exchanges across the Rhine

While various people claimed that photography was 'German' as part of the project of creating a German nation state, the actual practice of photography and the enthusiasm for it spread quickly across Central Europe. As in other regions of the world, the daguerreotype was the first of the new procedures to flourish there. And flourish it did, with a swell of studios opening their doors from Munich in the south to Kiel in the north. Making this advent possible was the French government's decision in 1839 to purchase the rights to Daguerre's invention and offer his process to all at no cost.[19] Arago made this case before the Chamber of Deputies on 3 July, arguing in French nationalist terms that the daguerreotype deserved this honour above any other claimants. He thus roundly dismissed

> the eagerness with which foreign nations pointed to an erroneous date, to a doubtful fact, and sought the most flimsy pretext in order to raise questions of priority, and to try to take credit for the brilliant ornament which photography will always be in the crown of discoveries.

'France', he added, 'has adopted this discovery, and from the first moment has been proud that it can present it generously to the entire world.'[20]

A month later, on 19 August, Arago revealed Daguerre's secret process before a weekly meeting of the French Academy of Sciences, completing the act of nationalist magnanimousness that remains so closely associated with him. It turned out that the artist made his pictures on a copper plate that had been coated in silver and exposed to iodine fumes. The plate was developed with mercury vapours and stabilized against further exposure to light with sodium bicarbonate. Each plate was thus a negative and positive at once, visible as either depending on the viewing angle. As opposed to Talbot's negative-positive paper process, these images were not reproducible.

Even this key moment of disclosure had an attentive German ear. The young Württemberg poet and publisher Ludwig Pfau claimed three decades later to have been present at the Parisian announcement, or at least near its unfolding. According to his 1877 recollection, Pfau stood amid the crowd in the Academy's forecourt, unable to enter the crowded chamber itself, when 'finally a door opened in the distance and a few audience members bolted out . . . "silver iodide!" yelled the first one, "mercury!" screamed another, then a third insisted that sodium bicarbonate was the secret material.'[21] This squawking excitement fed the international demand for a brochure, which Daguerre published soon afterwards. The booklet outlined his procedure in detail and, by the year's end, presses from Karlsruhe, Berlin, Stuttgart and Halle, among others, published German translations. Interest in the new procedure was strong and soon it was practised in many places east of the Rhine.[22] Daguerre himself fed this frenzy at the highest levels of society in the German lands when, shortly after his procedure's public release, he sent carefully framed examples of his work to King Ludwig I of Bavaria and the Austrian chancellor Klemens von Metternich. The first of these formed a tableau of three plates, two of which showed views of Paris's Boulevard du Temple from above Daguerre's diorama. They remain the best-known examples of his work.[23]

Following quickly on the excitement around the procedure's public release, a Berlin art dealer named Louis F. Sachse began receiving cameras from Daguerre, which he used for himself and sold to others in various Prussian cities beginning in September 1839. By the middle of November Sachse had made more than six hundred plates, and in April of the following year he succeeded in making portraits. Over the same months of 1839, fellow Berliner Theodor Dörffel managed to build his own camera using Daguerre's as a model. He produced enough plates by mid-September that the businessman and archaeologist Georg Gropius could exhibit them on the 16th, making for one of the earliest photography exhibitions.[24] By 1843, the city had eighteen full-time photographers, with fewer but rising numbers in Hamburg, Munich, Cologne and even a healthy count of three in the much smaller Lübeck.[25] As in the United States, the daguerreotype remained the favoured photographic process well into the late 1860s, even after the introduction of glass-plate negative technology in the early 1850s made photography more affordable, larger in format and reproducible.

The Biedermeier Photograph

As the daguerreotype process spread through the German lands, a gentle tension between local middle-class norms and international styles played out over the resulting plates. The region was forging its look in the new medium. But this appearance was heavily determined by Central Europe's integration into the Continent's larger middle-class cultural milieu. Key to this development was the advent of portrait photography. In the summer of 1840, just as in other parts of the West, a number of inventors, photographers and lens makers in the German lands independently developed refinements to the daguerreotype that made this sort of photography possible. At issue was reducing exposure times to an interval short enough for a sitter to hold a pose reasonably easily. Austrian mathematician Joseph Max Petzval, for example, invented a lens between late 1839 and May 1840 that dramatically shortened exposure time. Manufactured by Peter Wilhelm Friedrich von

Voigtländer, Petzval's lens became *the* standard for cameras of all sorts. As these improvements spread, portraits became by far the primary subject of photography.

At this time, Central Europe was in the midst of a cultural period that later came to be known as the Biedermeier era, a term initially born of satirical writing from around 1800 that condemned the period as petit bourgeois and lacking in taste. The Napoleonic Wars that ended in 1815 and the European revolutions of 1848 bookended these decades of political suppression and cultural conservatism. These years also saw the return of Europe's old hegemonic political powers after the reactionary Congress of Vienna restored many of the monarchies that Napoleon had toppled. In the two decades before the 1839 public announcement of photography, the impact of the wars had not yet been overcome and the industrial revolution with its prosperous middle class had not yet taken root. The Biedermeier style arose when aristocratic German speakers, and later the bourgeoisie, retreated from the repressive public sphere into a simple and idealized domesticity. Curator Laurie Stein explains that this new refuge of the plainly appointed home 'can be understood as a reflection of a deep-rooted urge for order and clarity'. In turn, she continues:

> domestic space became revered as the central site for harmonious personal and family life, a place in which individual definition – in spatial, aesthetic, formal, and functional terms – became tied to the comfort, security, and informality of the home environment.[26]

The furniture, wallpaper and clothing of these spaces have since become prized for their austerity and their straightforward use of natural forms and materials, features that make the toned-down Neoclassical style of the preceding decades seem extravagant by comparison.

Makers of early photographic portraiture in Europe relished domesticity, both as the setting in which to pose their clients and the space in which the resulting pictures would be seen. This photographic genre thus suited the German Biedermeier moment perfectly. An early daguerreotype from 1840/41 by von Steinheil shows his wife and daughter in gentle embrace, a doll held between them (illus. 6). While mother Elise looks off to the right, daughter

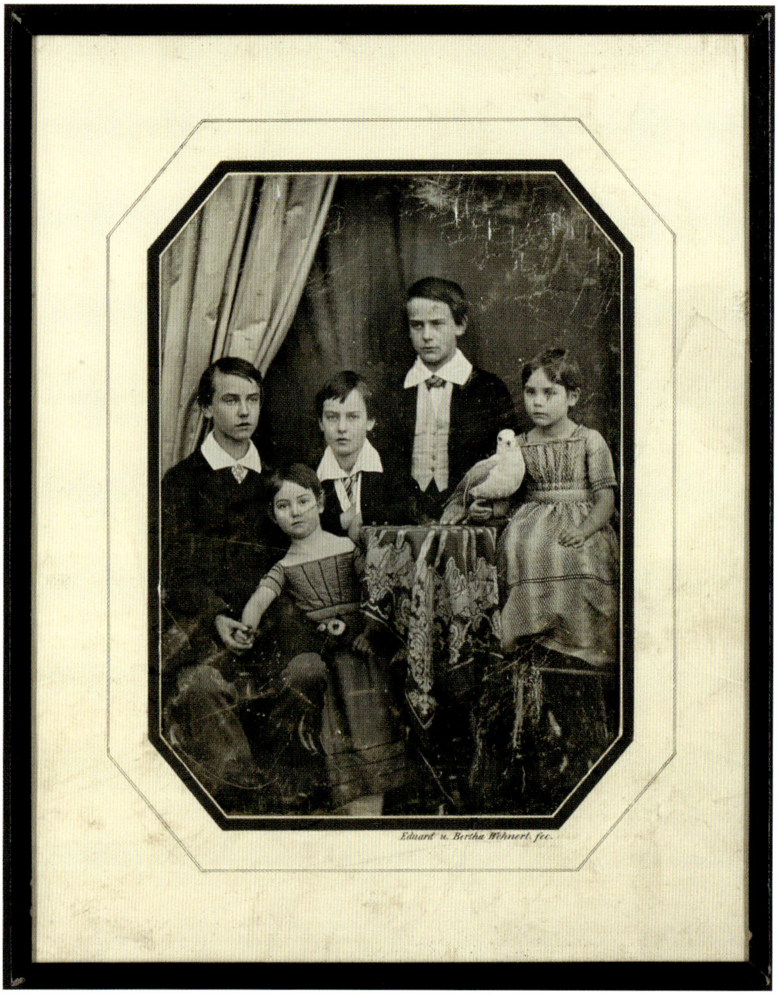

7 Bertha and Eduard Wehnert, *Group of Children with Gull*, c. 1845, daguerreotype.

Lina looks directly at us, as if we have intruded on this moment of domestic tenderness, interrupting the affection that Lina lavishes on her doll. Simple hairstyles and unceremonious clothing convey the informality of this tender moment, which is rendered a picturesque blur by the relatively long exposure time. Similarly, a daguerreotype from approximately 1845 by the famous Leipzig studio of Bertha and Eduard Wehnert shows five children (and one taxidermied gull) posed around a small living room table (illus. 7). Though

8 Carl Dauthendey, *The Photographers Bertha and Eduard Wehnert*, 1847, modern salt print from original paper negative.

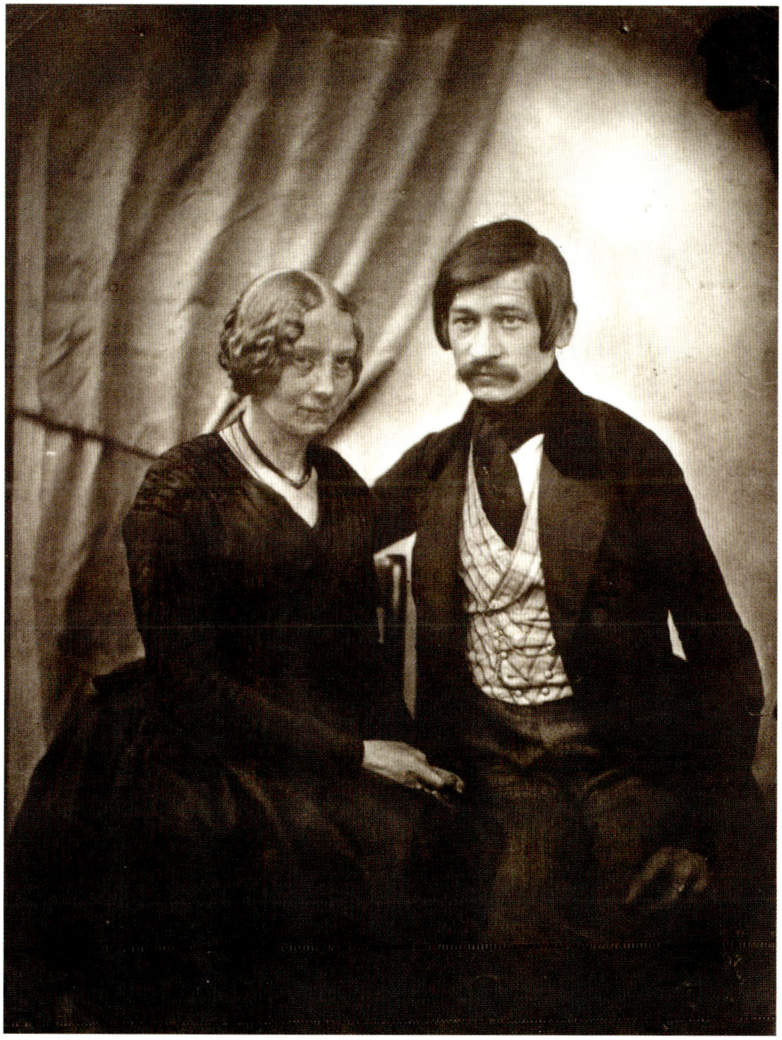

more rigid than von Steinheil's picture, the five seem just as emotionally close. The boy on the left holds the hand of the young girl, presumably his sister, while the girl on the right pulls her hand around the dove's legs. The children seem assembled for a family meeting, listening attentively to their parents.

Eduard Wehnert died suddenly in August 1847, leaving Bertha to run the studio herself, which she did with great success for another fifty years.

One can see the ill-fated Eduard in a gentle salt print taken the same year he died by the couple's friend Carl Dauthendey (illus. 8). One of the few photographers in the German lands to adopt Talbot's calotype paper process, Dauthendey closes in tightly on the pair as Eduard's right arm wraps around Bertha. Clad in a plain dress, she stares towards the camera and invites us to share the tight space between them. This space is defined by what seems to be the same close-hanging curtain before which the five children posed two years earlier. A little later, in 1850, the now-widowed Bertha Wehnert made a closely framed self-portrait using the same curtain and living room table, though this time in an opulent dress and a fur stole that announce the end of Biedermeier simplicity and a new, more prosperous era, particularly for her studio (illus. 2).

The Prague photographer Wilhelm Horn used a similar close framing for his earlier daguerreotype portraits of Clementine Wiener and Dr Siegmund Feldmann, a Jewish couple who married approximately two years after posing for the pictures shown here (illus. 9, illus. 10). As is typical of early daguerreotypes, we seem to encounter each of them in their salon as she and he sit upright, against a table, waiting to engage with guests in this bare-bones space. She stares in our direction, as if to stimulate conversation. The frames, particularly common in Central European daguerreotypes as opposed to the handheld cases used so often elsewhere, suggest that these pictures would hang on the wall of just such a salon. Their hairstyles and attire are simple. What can be identified as a typically Biedermeier German portrait style in photography also bespeaks the ethnic, religious and linguistic multiplicity of Central Europe. Horn, who was editor of the first German-language photo journal, probably

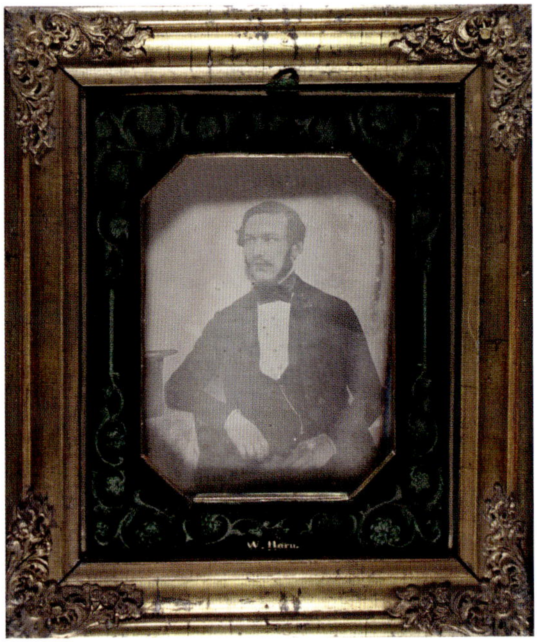

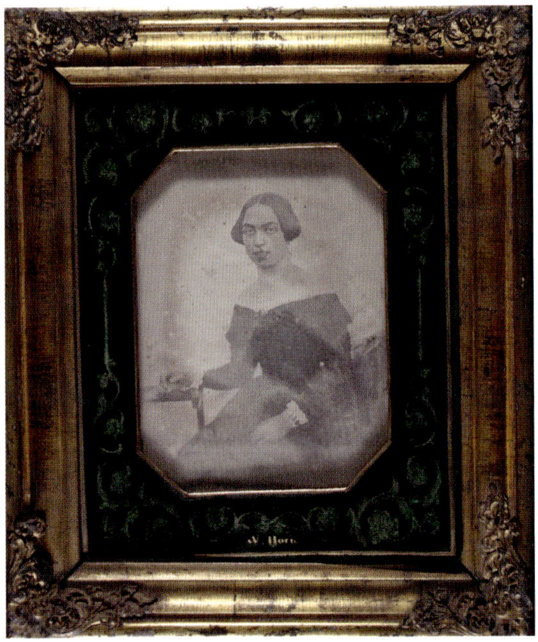

completed this commission while speaking with his clients in German. But a studio just down the street could have done the same, to identical results, while speaking in Czech.

In the decade following the daguerreotype's introduction, the German lands opened themselves to each other and to the world. The style of simplicity later called Biedermeier spread rapidly among royal residential cities as German nobles observed each other's dress and furnishings. Just as quickly, fashions in clothing and materials circulated throughout Europe among those who could afford them. The lightning spread of the daguerreotype exemplifies this mobility. Today we can identify early studio portraits from the region as representative of the German vogue for simplicity. But they also look much like other daguerreotypes made elsewhere in Europe and in North America. What makes these portraits Biedermeier is largely what makes them difficult to distinguish from their European counterparts. Photography in Central Europe was always part of a transnational traffic in taste that did as much to align the region's citizens with Europe's broader middle class as it did to stamp them as German. The daguerreotype thus became a testing ground for the levelling of Central European identity along Continent-wide middle-class norms.

Gallery of the German Nation

While early photography had been put in the service of constructing Biedermeier normalcy under repressive political conditions, in 1848 it suddenly became an agent for promoting nascent attempts at German democracy following a Europe-wide revolution. One result was a mass-produced album of images titled *Deutsche Nationalgalerie* (German National Gallery).

The first uprisings that made the year 1848 decisive for Europe's political destiny broke out in January in Milan and Sicily. Then, on 22 February, middle- and working-class partisans in Paris took to the barricades. On 13 March, Vienna toppled Count von Metternich, a recipient of Daguerre's early pictures and one of the German speakers most closely associated with the region's authoritarian rule. Revolution spread through the German

9 Wilhelm Horn, *Dr Siegmund Feldmann*, c. 1845, daguerreotype.

10 Wilhelm Horn, *Clementine Feldmann, née Wiener*, c. 1845, daguerreotype.

lands where the desire for a unified country under constitutional governance ran hot. To realize this widely shared wish, 831 delegates from throughout Central Europe first met in May 1848 for what would be known as the National Assembly in Frankfurt am Main. Feelings of patriotism surged in these months as the region paid rapt attention to the Assembly's proceedings through newspapers and fliers spinning off well-oiled presses. Some of this printed matter contained pictures of the delegates, many of them already famous intellectuals. But the artists charged with rendering these portraits had to race behind the busy delegates, catching their likenesses in rare moments of rest, including even a pause at the toilet. Under these conditions, a quick stop before a daguerreotype camera could save precious time and yield a good likeness. The two photographers most famous for having done just this are Hermann Biow of Hamburg and Jakob Seib of Frankfurt.[27]

Both men had already achieved note for their studio work. Like many early photographers in the German lands, Biow began as a portrait painter and lithographer in his Hanseatic city. But after 1841 he dedicated himself to photography. Soon thereafter he became famous for his daguerreotypes documenting the damage done by the 1842 fire of Hamburg. The conflagration itself became a rallying point for German national unity as relief streamed in from around the region. By 1847 Biow was so well renowned that the Prussian king Friedrich Wilhelm IV called him to Berlin to photograph the state's most important people in the arts and sciences. One of Biow's most famous pictures from the resulting series is his portrait of Alexander von Humboldt, made that same year (see illus. 5). Through a faint blur, one can see the scientist and explorer with a casual, almost mischievous grimace. He stares directly into the camera's lens as he gently rests his left arm on a small table. The dark drapery behind him and Humboldt's subdued inky coat emphasize his white collar, on top of which his greyed countenance rests. Within the dark ether, his head floats almost detached from his disappearing body, signalling the man's near-deified status in Prussia by these years.

From plates such as these, Biow devised the idea of a 'National Gallery' of portraits, which he probably based on the vast Walhalla that King Ludwig I had built in Bavaria, a temple-like structure housing busts of Germany's most accomplished men. With his gallery project in mind, Biow travelled to Frankfurt in early June 1848, knowing that this town now hosted the German lands' most famous professors, scientists, jurists, writers, artists and civil servants then debating at the Assembly. Seib, for his part, had also trained as a portrait painter and lithographer. He had attracted a similarly prominent clientele in his hometown of Frankfurt, making him a perfect collaborator for Biow, who entered the city as a stranger. Together, the two men photographed or sketched a great number of the Assembly delegates whose likeness they transferred to lithographs. They collected these images into a three-volume subscription publication, the *German National Gallery*.

One of the great challenges the two photographers faced was iconographic: how to pose these middle-class men as leaders of a nation-to-be, and how to make this a specifically German gallery. Seib experimented wildly. He preferred that his figures stand as if about to orate, sometimes with texts in hand (illus. 11) or in other cases with hands slipped into their jacket, in a style associated with Napoleon. Biow tried similar strategies but often relied on the old standby of the seated figure (illus. 12). Delegates posed in this manner sometimes cross their arms or let them hang as they look into the distance. In some cases he placed his men on elevated seats so that more of the body could be seen. With a new image for democracy as the goal, both photographers took the non-ostentatious photo portrait of the Biedermeier era and ginned it up with poses signalling intellectual and oratorical prowess. Under the new political climate, leaders were to be men not born into privilege but self-made, in control of their own destinies and capable of unifying the country. The lithographed portraits specifically drawn from the photographs, the majority of which appeared in the second volume, stick close to the originals but correct for blurring and wayward hairs or rumpled clothing. Their rendering of sharp light,

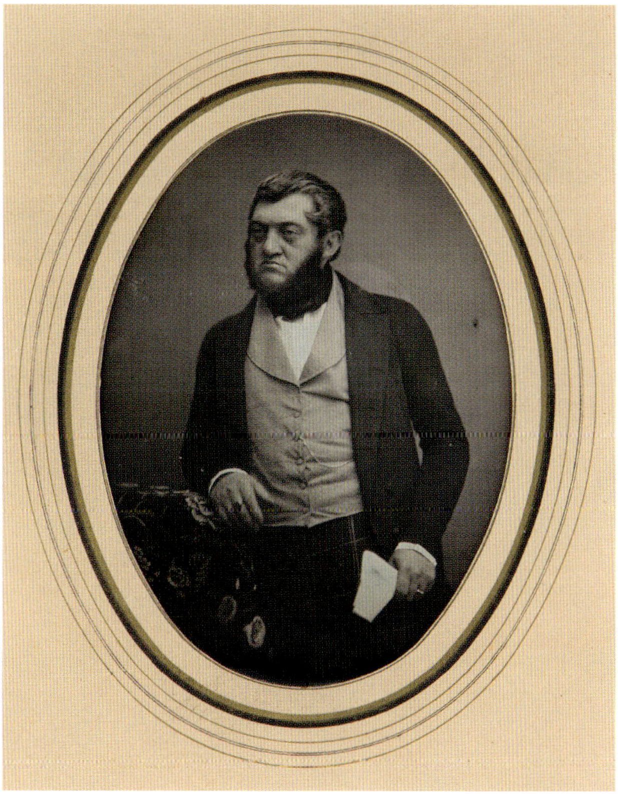

11 Jakob Seib, *Portrait of Georg von Vincke (1811–75), Member of Parliament from the 13th Westphalia Electoral District*, 1848, daguerreotype.

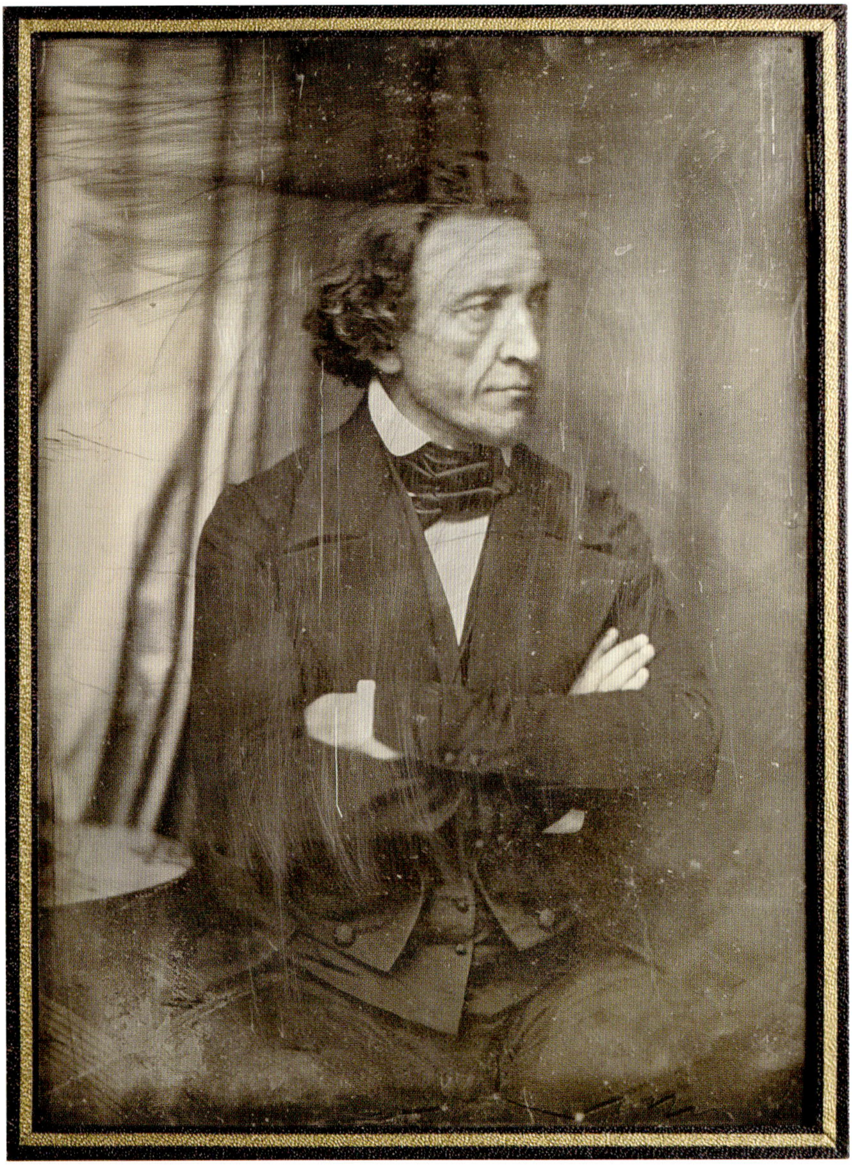

12 Hermann Biow, *The Doctor and Jurist Paul Hermann*, 1848, daguerreotype.

particularly on the bright foreheads, signals the origins of these pictures as daguerrotypes.

But for all the work put into this iconographic experimentation, very little remained that was specifically German about the members of the *German National Gallery*, much as in other Biedermeier-era portraits. Instead it was the men's role in history or in their existing celebrity that granted them this patriotic status. The portfolio's first volume foregrounded the portraits of Ernst Moritz Arndt and Friedrich Ludwig 'Turnvater' Jahn, who both played prominent roles in the independence wars against France, the conflict most responsible for generating the patriotic fervour that re-emerged in 1848. As with Biedermeier daguerreotype portraits, it was the European middle-class decorum of these men, rather than such things as regional costume or Alpine backdrops, that qualified them as august members of the *German National Gallery*.

This levelling served another purpose as well. Not long after the Assembly opened in May, it became clear that differences of religion, regional affiliation and political inclination left the delegates impossibly split on fundamental questions. Would the unified country be a monarchy or democracy? Should it include parts of Austria that spoke German or be led by Prussia as a smaller state without the Habsburg Empire? Factions met in various cafés around town and debated in the Paulskirche (St Paul's Church), where the Assembly officially met. The standard look that Biow, Seib and others gave the delegates masked these differences with a homogeneity that might suggest a consistent, unified nation. A non-photographic representation of these men that more accurately reflected the discord appeared in the title print of Henry Ritter's 1849 satirical booklet *Der politische Struwwelpeter* (illus. 13). Riffing on Heinrich Hoffmann's famous 1845 children's picture book *Der Struwwelpeter* (Shockheaded Peter), the unkempt title character of Hoffmann's stories becomes here a grotesque figure sporting the heads of the Assembly's many different constituencies. The visible discomfort of each head, crowded hydra-like atop a single body, and the slapdash patching of coats of arms on the figure's jacket, show that no unification was possible with such divergent identities and discord.

The following year, the Frankfurt parliament dissolved in failure and Prussia emerged as yet more powerful. One can track the great distance from

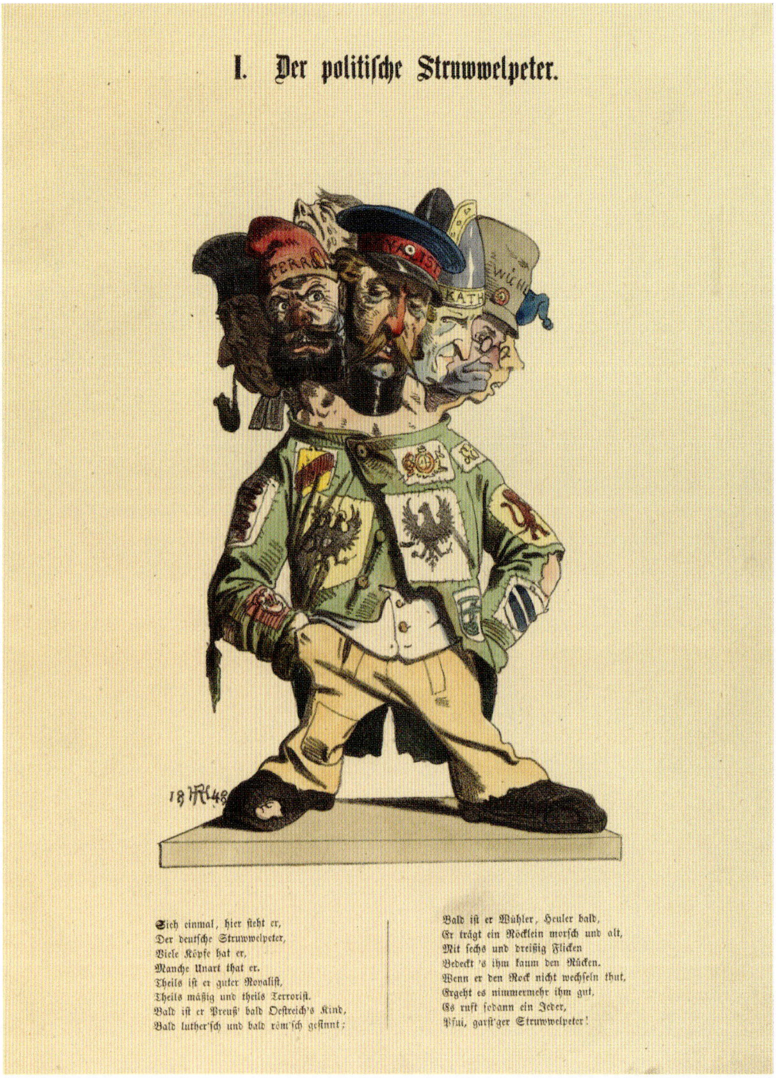

13 Henry Ritter, 'The Political Struwwelpeter', in his 1849 *The Political Struwwelpeter: An Attempt at the Unity of Germany*.

the ideal of unified constitutional governance and the reality that followed the failed National Assembly in a 1863 photograph of the Fürstentag (Diet of Princes) by Joseph Albert, the First Photographer to the Bavarian Royal House (illus. 14). This grouping of the region's monarchs intentionally recalls the Imperial Diet of the Holy Roman Empire, which regularly assembled in Frankfurt from the medieval era to the early nineteenth century. But rather than the prominent self-made men of the Frankfurt

14 Joseph Albert, 'Group Portrait after the Final Meeting, Frankfurt am Main, 1863', albumen print from the 1863 portfolio *Assembly of the German Princes in Frankfurt am Main in August*.

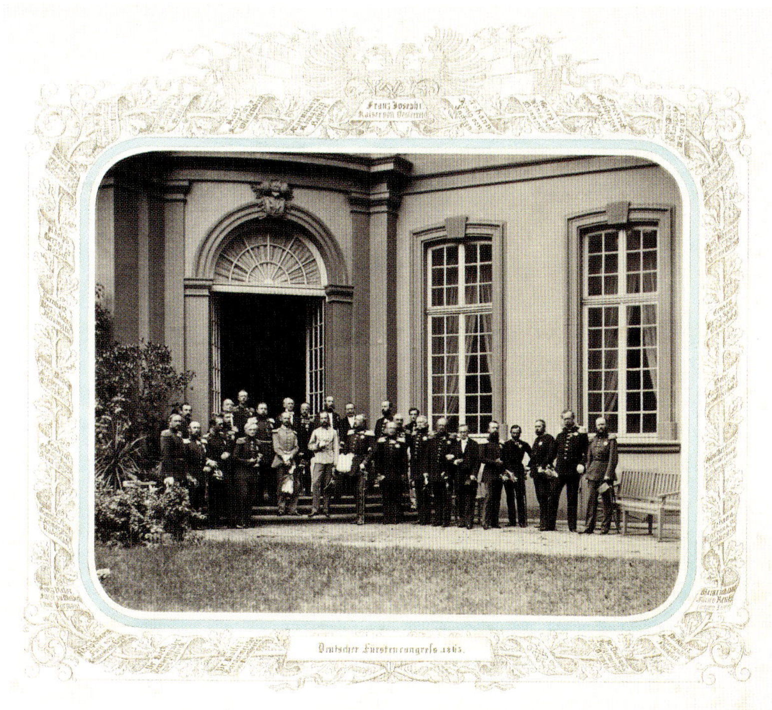

Assembly, one sees an impossibly large crowd of hereditary monarchs, most wearing similar military garb. Their discussion proceeded under the sign of absolutist rule. The corresponding group portrait offered a reactionary counter-image to Biow and Seib's *German National Gallery*. In the relationship between photography and Germany, two very different national images now circulated in an ongoing battle between democracy and Prussian-led absolutism. It was the latter that went on to dominate the German nineteenth century.

National Landscapes

While the portraits made in these early years may have predominantly defined the German along the lines of a modern and urban European norm, many of the landscape and city views produced in these decades laboured to

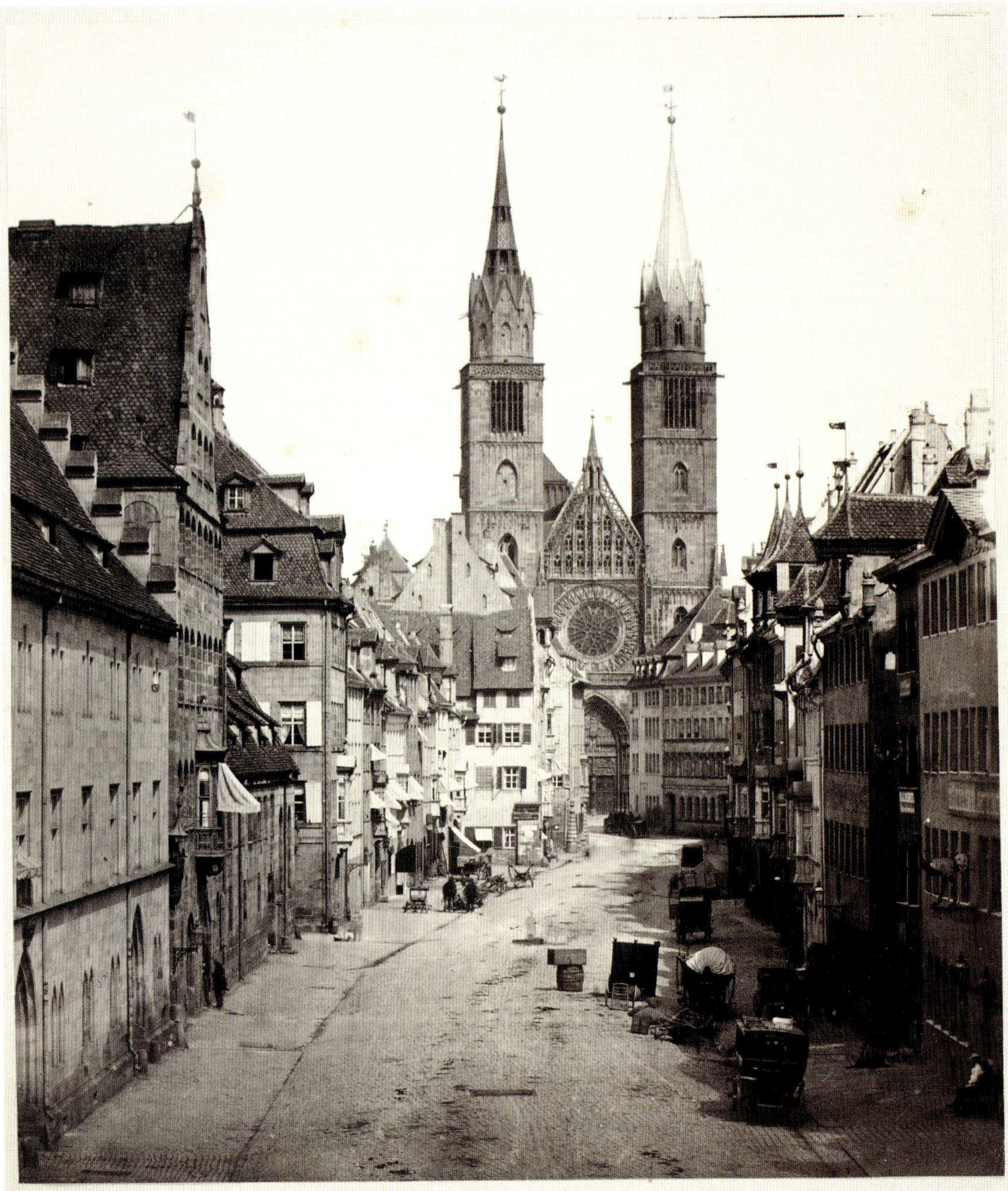

reveal an identifiable national character from local distinctions. Of course, Charles-David Winter's views of his Alsatian city Strasbourg show the difficulty of distilling a single national identity from photographs. But other prints from this period participate more felicitously in the sort of conjuring that Goethe had earlier plied. For example, the optician and painter Georg Schmidt from Nuremberg became one of the most important photographers of his city's architecture in the mid-nineteenth century. His *Karolinenstrasse with a View of the Lorenzkirche* from 1862 (illus. 15) operates much like Winter's print. Beginning with a cobblestoned foreground, the viewer's eye travels down the meandering street as medieval buildings each showcase a signature roofline of dormers, often accented with tall gables. At the road's end, the Gothic St Lorenz Church completes the composition's vertical thrust, racing upwards with stone masonry, sculpture, glass in filigree and columns. Like Winter, Schmidt was an avid recorder of his city's unique charms. And these bore a clearly identifiable style, one that Goethe had earlier pronounced as German.

Not coincidentally, outside Nuremberg's walls, Schmidt's pictures found an audience ever better prepared to perform the famous poet's national conjuring because, unlike Strasbourg, this Frankish city was increasingly being acclaimed as one of the best expressions of German cultural identity.[28] By the late eighteenth century, this home of the Renaissance artist Albrecht Dürer had become a forgotten provincial city with a population of 42,000, less than half of its earlier 90,000. But with an increasing sense of nationalism in Central Europe, writers began to praise its past achievements. The Berlin-based philosopher of the enlightenment Moses Mendelssohn declared Nuremberg a cultural capital in 1785. Nine years later, the Romantic writer Wilhelm Heinrich Wackenroder waxed poetically about the town's German medieval and Renaissance charms. In his 1797 treatise *Herzensergießungen eines kunstliebenden Klosterbruders* (Outpourings from the Heart of an Art-loving Cloister Brother), Wackenroder wrote of how he had recently wandered Nuremberg's crooked lanes, eyeing 'with childlike love [its] old-fashioned houses and churches, on which the firm trace of our old art of the Fatherland [*väterländische Kunst*] is pressed'.[29] In 1842 the Baedeker tour guide of the town recognized this sentiment and declared that 'no other German city offers through its outward forms such a vivid and markedly distinct picture of the importance of the medieval city. No city has preserved these forms

15 Georg Schmidt, *Karolinenstrasse with a View of the Lorenzkirche*, Nuremberg, c. 1862, salt-paper print.

more faithfully.'[30] The identifiably German style of Strasbourg's urban form could now be found in a town far more directly associated with Teutonic cultural achievements.

Set in amber as if modernity had passed it by, Nuremberg became the capital of an imagined German nation defined by an old indigenous culture. In this context, Schmidt's picture of the famous Little Goose Man Fountain (Gänsemännchenbrunnen) helped establish a shorthand for the *gemütlich* or homey, cosy and unhurried town, and by extension, Germany's cultural basis somewhere in an idealized medieval past. It would be no accident that this same fountain appeared in the opening shots of Leni Riefenstahl's infamous propaganda film *Triumph of the Will* of 1934. The National Socialists, having seized power one year earlier in 1933, staged party rallies in Nuremberg to associate their still tenuous legitimacy with the city's timeless authenticity. The fountain, around which Riefenstahl's camera circles, helped visualize that link.

As with Strasbourg, however, photographs of Nuremberg could mean different things to different audiences, particularly when framed through a foreigner's camera. Léon Gérard was one of the many Frenchman of the mid-nineteenth century who travelled Europe with his large camera in tow, taking pictures that might appeal to audiences back home. In 1857 he spent time in Nuremberg, showering his camera's attention on the city's fairy-tale-like scenery. But the resulting pictures may have as much to say about contemporary France as medieval Germany. The French Prefect of the Seine Baron Haussmann had already begun the radical rebuilding of Paris, leading photographers such as Charles Marville, Charles Nègre and Henri Le Secq to document the French capital's medieval quarters before their destruction. Nuremberg for Gérard may have been an admirable holdout against modernity's crushing march. Moreover, Paris had already become suspect in the minds of many French citizens as too modern, too rife with class conflict. This famously led the Barbizon painters to escape to the countryside, where they could find an authentic civilization unspoiled by the ravages of industrialization and open class conflict. Nuremberg seemed to offer just this refuge, although by the 1850s the region of Frankish Bavaria in which it sat had already seen heavy industrialization.

Gérard's pictures compensate by showing no people and scarcely a sign of modernity. His view of the city's Kaiserburg (Imperial Castle, illus. 16)

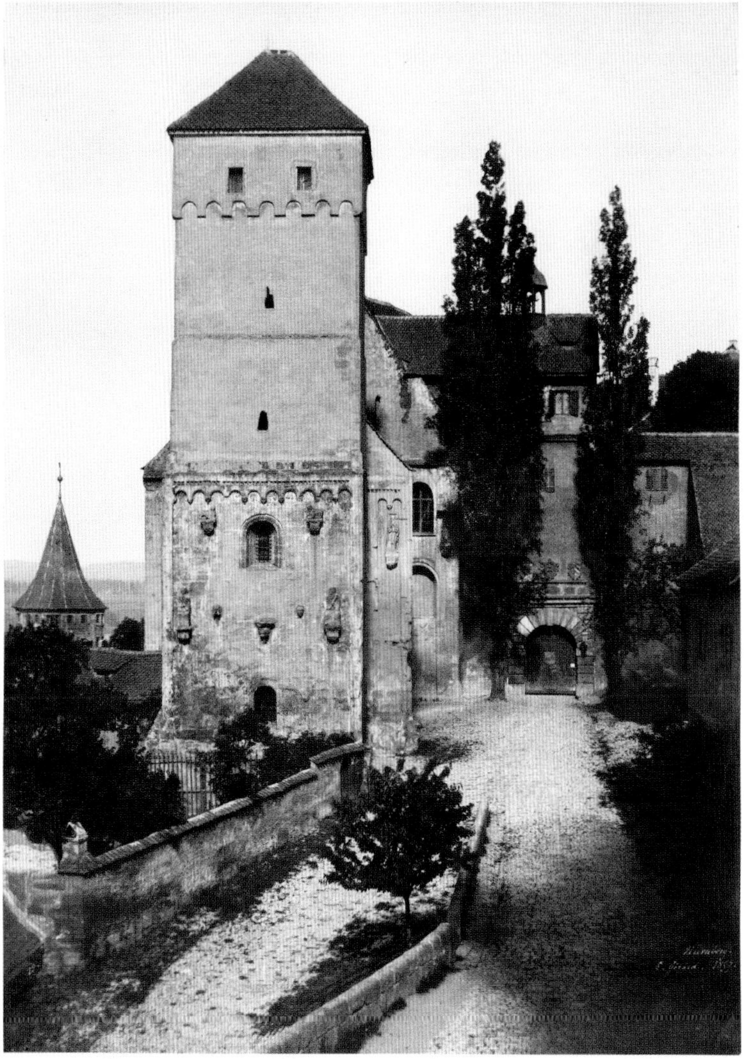

16 Léon Gérard, *The Heidenturm* ['Heathen Tower'] *and Kaiserkapelle* ['Imperial Chapel'] *within the Kaiserburg* ['Imperial Castle'] *Walls, Nuremberg*, 1857, albumen print from a paper negative.

could have been composed with another technology any time in the centuries before exposing his plate. Here was the pre-modern simplicity that France was busily ploughing under. Germany, seemingly stuck in an agrarian past, had managed to preserve such heritage.

The famous British photographer Francis Frith offered much the same in his 1864 *Gossiping Photographer on the Rhine*. Conceived as a casual first-person – even spiteful – version of a Baedeker guide for British tourists, this early photo book heaped attention on the many ruins along the famous river while complaining of current-day Germans as oafish, ignorant, drunken and immoral. In what would become a nineteenth-century British travellers' cliché, he compared the glorious past to the current ignobility. Correspondingly, his photo of Rheinfels and St Goar (much like his view of Ehrenbreitstein) offers a sweeping view of the river and town, with the ruined castle perched majestically above (illus. 17). As his text explains:

> Rheinfels, by far the most extensive ruin on the Rhine. It is, perhaps, more poetic than picturesque – more suggestive of incident than beauty;

17 Francis Frith, 'Ehrenbreitstein', albumen print from his 1864 *Gossiping Photographer on the Rhine*.

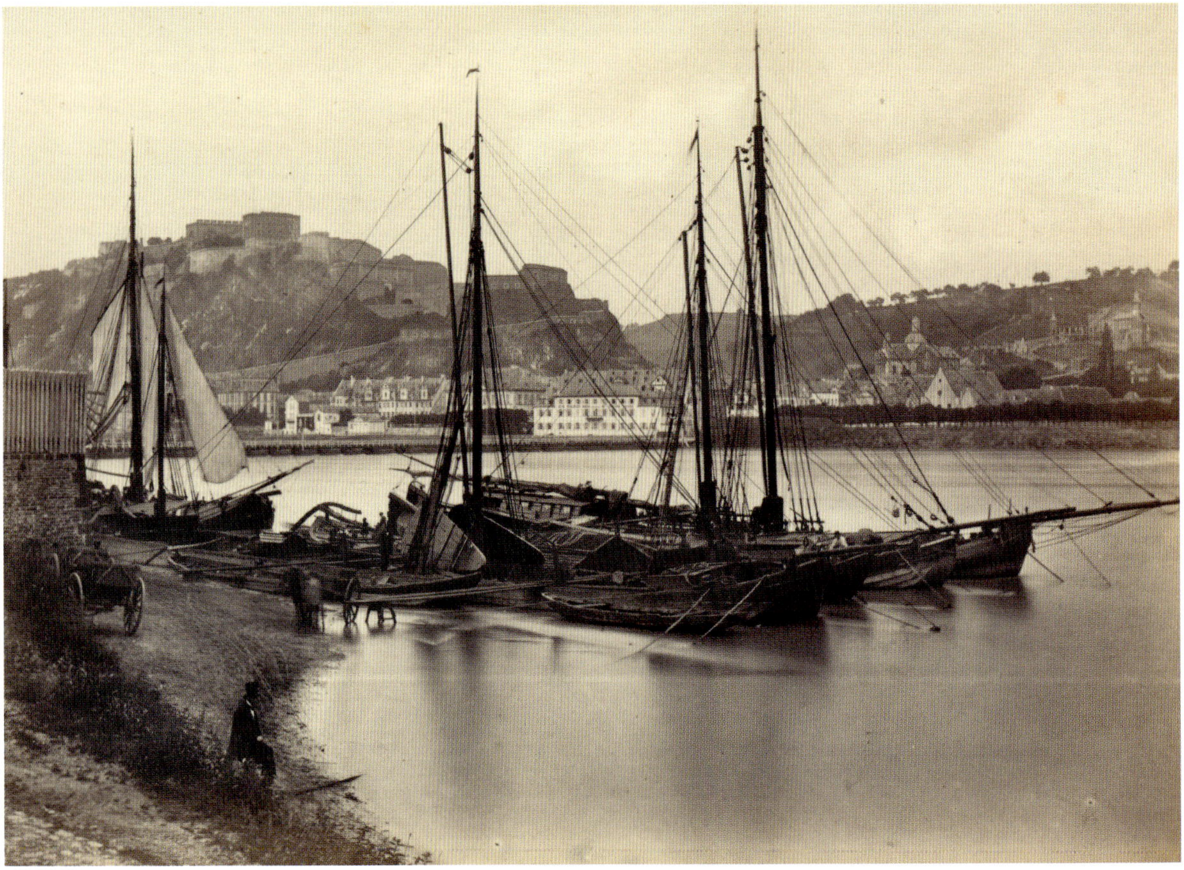

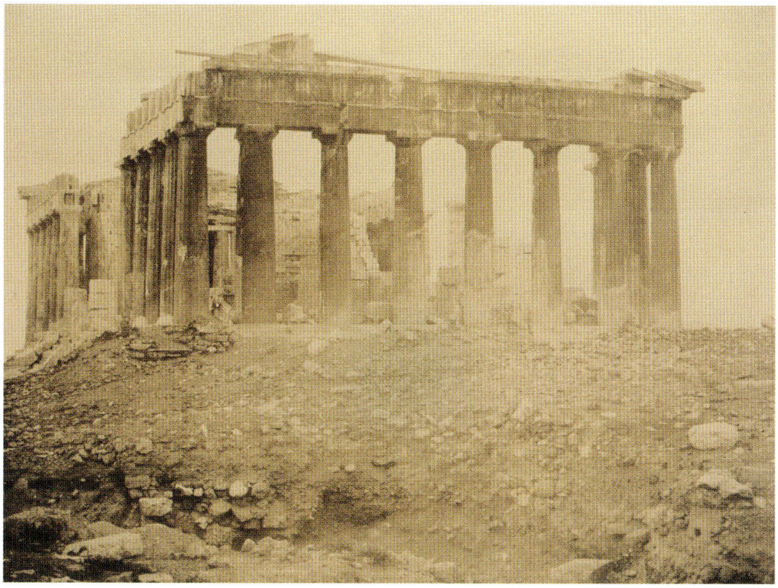

18 August F. Oppenheim, *The Parthenon – East Front and Southern Side – Athens*, 1853, salt print.

> yet in situation it is magnificent, and its present *period of decay* is the golden one . . .[31]

But contrasted with this medieval beauty in splendid ruin, which the locals scarcely appreciate, is the contemporary German cuisine: 'I loathe German cookery, and abhor a *table d'hôte*. I had rather have one solitary "plate" in a little dark box in London, than pick about for an hour and a half, with the "host" of people strictly uninteresting'.[32] For Frith, who unlike Gérard acknowledged that there was such as thing as contemporary Germany, the region offered decay both in the best and the worst of ways.

German speakers engaged in their own travel as well. In fact, it is no coincidence that the Baedeker family, famous for their tour books, was German. If early photography became the means to construct and idealize Germany, it was also the case that German speakers, like other Europeans, travelled abroad and engaged in their own acts of photographic ethnography. August F. Oppenheim of Dresden, for example, travelled to France, where he learned the useful wax-paper negative process from its inventor, Gustave Le Gray. This negative-positive procedure, built on Talbot's calotype, produced unusually sharp negatives. They could be developed well after exposure and made to produce multiple prints, a great plus for travel photography. By 1852 Oppenheim was in Spain capturing famous sites. In 1853, he photographed the many ruins of Athens, which he assembled into an award-winning published volume. His salt print of the Parthenon shows the ruin towering above a sea of strewn rocks toward a hazy sky (illus. 18), not unlike Frith's picture of the Rheinfels and Ehrenbreistein.

A volume of photographs that did not see publication or award was assembled for a specific set of eyes, King Carol I of Romania, born Prince Karl of Hohenzollern-Sigmaringen in 1839, the year of photography's public announcement. In 1866 he was elected emperor of Romania after the country freed itself from Ottoman rule. The new German-speaking monarch began his reign by touring the country to acquaint himself with its distinct customs and locations. The Transylvanian photographer Carol Szathmari, famous for his photographs of the Crimean War, accompanied the new emperor on this trip and produced at its end the *Rumanian Album* (1866), a series of prints meant to further familiarize Carol I with the country. These pictures, carefully

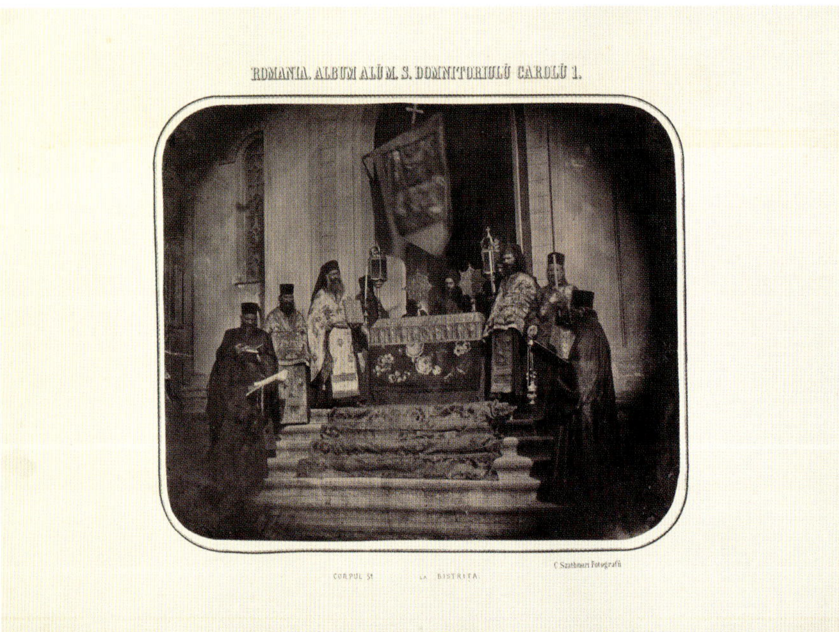

19 Carol Szathmari, 'Shrine with the Remains of St Grigorios Dekapolities in Bistriţa [Romania]', albumen print from his 1866 *Rumanian Album*.

realized with glass negatives, catalogue ethnic groups, famous locations, architecture, national treasures and Orthodox Christianity. 'Costumed Group in Campulung', for instance, stresses the unique folk clothing of these carefully posed figures while 'Shrine with the Remains of St Grigorios Dekapolities in Bistriţa' offers priests decked out in sumptuous robes before a gilded reliquary (illus. 19). These were images meant to train German eyes to see Romania, and they did so with a surfeit of trappings specifically chosen for their visual appeal and their distance from the Central European familiar. Defining the German would in part involve describing the foreign.

Unification Wars

What Goethe, growing public will, the National Assembly and the Fürstentag were unable to achieve, Prussia's armed forces completed with military battles. By cleverly manipulating France into declaring war on Prussia in 1870, chancellor Otto von Bismarck successfully rallied vast constituencies of German speakers outside his Prussian-led Northern Federation to his cause. In a matter of months, the country's forces overran French troops, besieged Paris and won a clear victory in what is now known as the Franco-Prussian War. The Prussian king Wilhelm I was proclaimed emperor of nearly all the German majority states excluding Austria. There was now a united German nation ruled under one constitution, albeit smaller than had it included Habsburg-ruled areas and Switzerland. In this conflict, and the two Prussian-led wars preceding it, photographs recorded the aftermath of battles.

These images were not disseminated widely, given that the public found itself far more interested in lifelike battle paintings produced by artists such as Wilhelm Camphausen. Photographers on the French side of the Franco-Prussian War, by contrast, carefully documented the destruction that Prussian troops wrought on besieged cities such as Soissons, St Cloud and Strasbourg. For French audiences, a destroyed building in St Cloud taken by the studio of French photographer Numa Prosper Blanc de Lebarthe (Numa Blanc et Cie) was Germany, the fragmented walls and collapsed floors a mark of the new empire's mindless and violent militarism (illus. 20). Even if unified politically, Germany could not be defined by single characteristics. As in

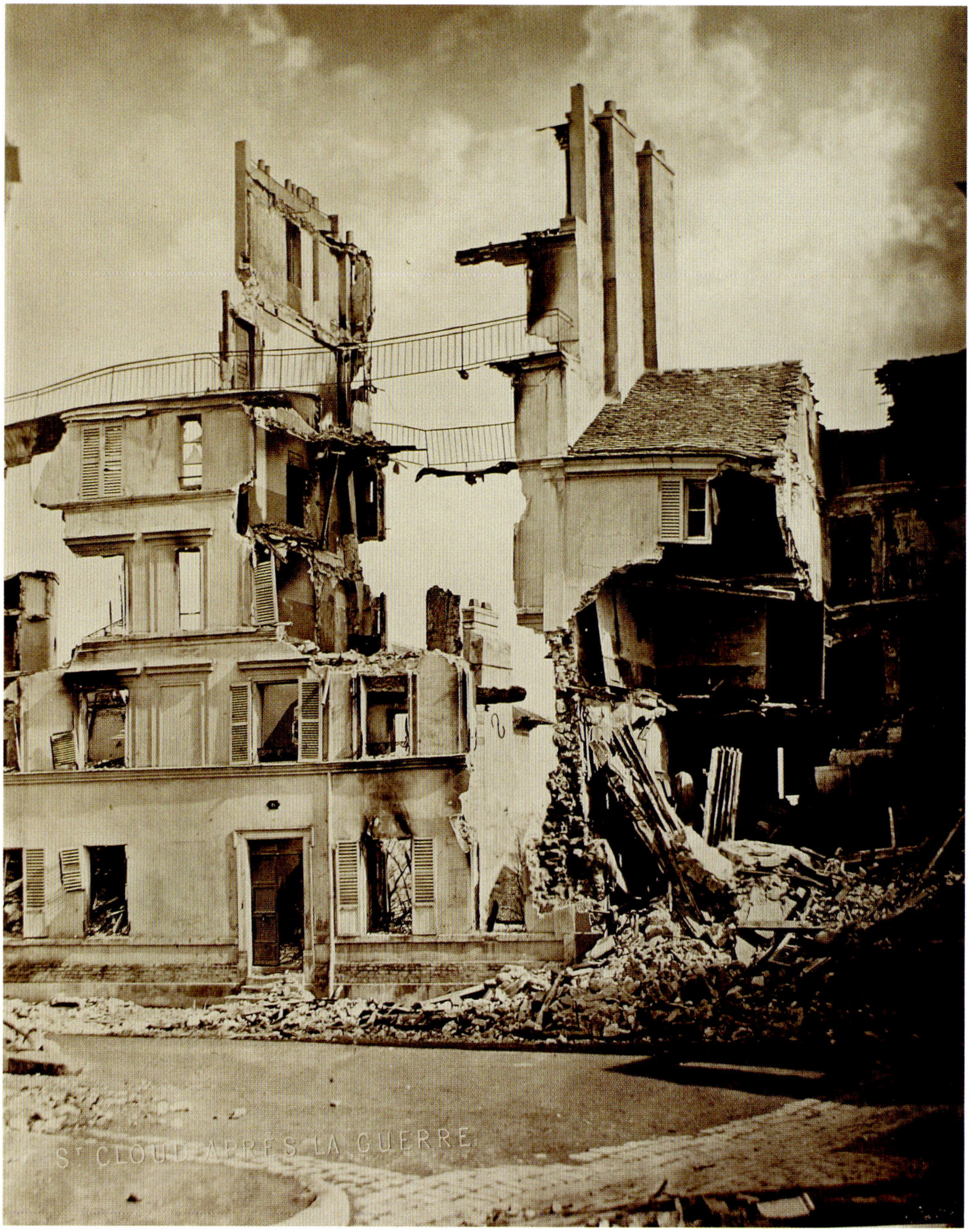
ST CLOUD APRES LA GUERRE

20 Numa Banc et Cie, *Place de l'Hôpital after the War, St Cloud*, 1870/71, albumen print.

the decades before this moment, the middle-class norm was both European and German, the image of democracy vied with another of absolute rule, and visions of national landscape were at once authentically German and reflective of France's lost medieval past. Though now a nation, Germany remained a diverse and conflicted country that photographs could at best show as unified but often revealed as fragmented.

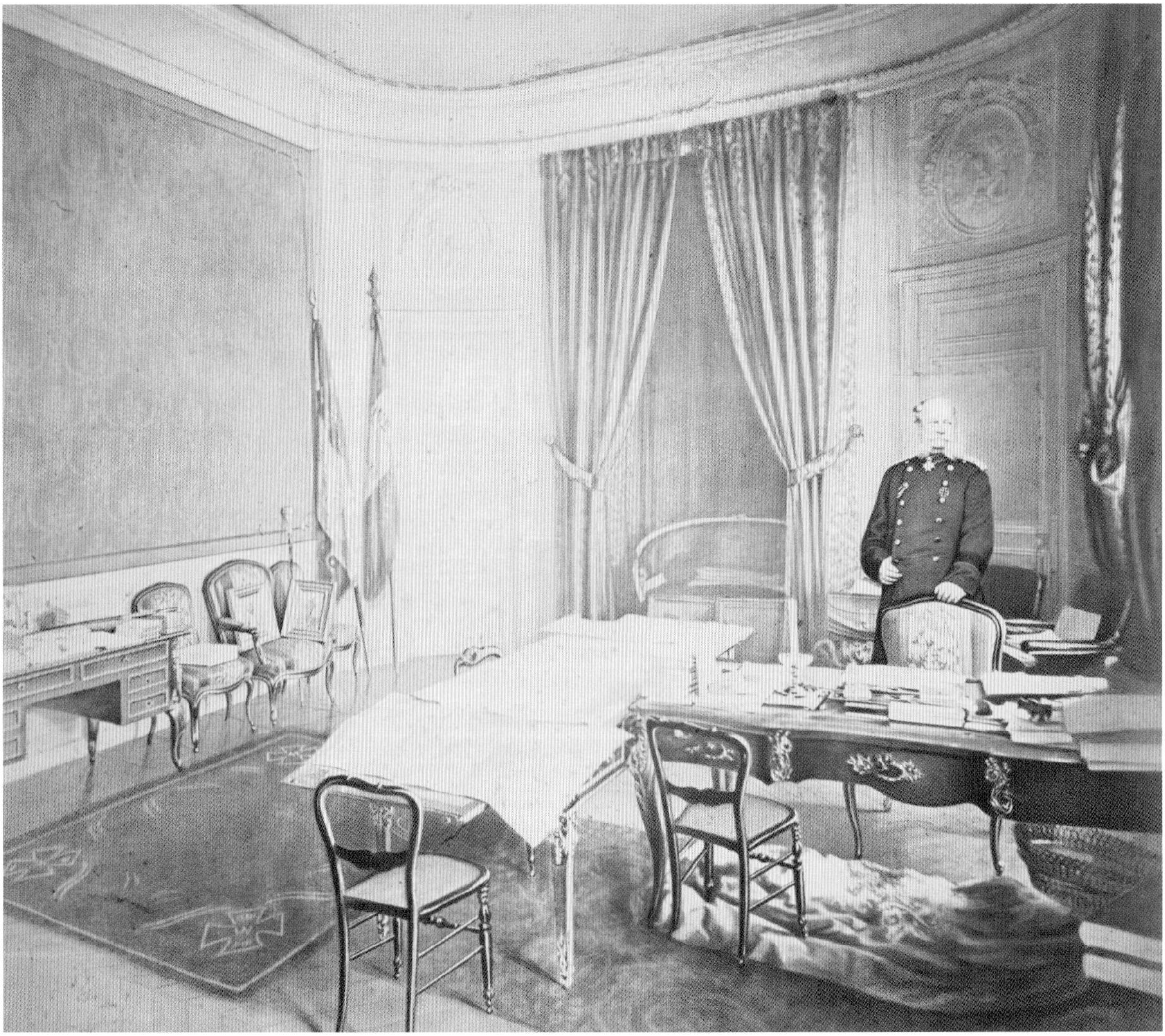

two

Photography and Nation, 1871–1918

On 18 January 1871, the German Lands officially united when a group of key Central European princes declared the Prussian king their kaiser (emperor) of a newly unified country. What had been an expressed desire for a nation state at least since the days of eighteenth-century German Idealism had now become a reality, albeit without Austria's participation. Paradoxically, this highly significant and patriotic event took place not within the country's newly drawn boundaries, but far away at France's Versailles Palace, where Prussian forces then besieging Paris were headquartered. Nationalist fervour had been running high since Wilhelm I's armies soundly defeated French forces in the primary battles of the Franco-Prussian War. And now the many raised hands of princes who declared Wilhelm I their leader expressed that same enthusiasm, which chancellor Otto von Bismarck had cleverly marshalled into national unity. But what exactly did this inaugural and soon-to-be mythologized moment look like?

There were no cameras present. But remarkably enough, a portfolio of 56 photographs documenting the event miraculously went on sale later in the same year. These prints, assembled quite literally by Berlin-based Heinrich Schnäbeli, visually betray the often curious relationship between photography and the newly cobbled-together nation. Titled *Proclamation of the German Empire in the Palace of Versailles on 18 January 1871*, the portfolio purported to show this grand event and the moments leading up to it (illus. 21). Schnäbeli had created these pictures by assembling existing photographs of the kaiser, Prussian soldiers, the Versailles Palace interior, pieces of furniture and various knick-knacks into seamless compositions. Today we use the word photomontage to designate this mode of transfer, manipulation and

21 Johann Anselm Heinrich Schnäbeli, 'Wilhelm I in His Study at Versailles', albumen composite print from the 1871 *Album of the Proclamation of the German Empire in the Palace of Versailles on 18 January 1871*.

reproduction. But at the time it was the result of a complicated process called composite printing, which involved making negatives of the appropriated images and then exposing each, often one at a time, to a large sheet of light-sensitized paper. While cumbersome, the process allowed Schnäbeli to depict the quickly moving events that bulky cameras and slow exposure times could not capture, had they been present.

One of the portfolio leaves, titled 'Wilhelm I in His Study at Versailles', is compositionally awkward, as one might imagine of the difficult composite printing process (illus. 21). But this inelegance is also a product of the assertive national conjuring that Schnäbeli, much as Bismarck, had employed. A veritable nationalist potpourri, the picture features the king-cum-emperor, complete with a heavily retouched Iron Cross medal, and a large array of chairs, maps and carpets. One of these floor coverings even sports multiple Iron Crosses, lest Prussian militarism get lost in the dense mix. Just as important are the two flags at the left. These were the banners of the prestigious Garde Mobile, which the Prussians had captured from the French in the course of the war.

Schnäbeli's picture is in essence an assembly of nationalist fantasy. Like the other leaves in his portfolio, it is clearly manipulated to today's eyes and thus inauthentic as a historical document. Yet it answered the need to envision what this moment looked like, doing so with an image technology that seemingly bore a more faithful witness to historical events than painting or drawing ever could, at least according to some observers at the time. The imperial family was certainly convinced. It embraced the portfolio and hung some of Schnäbeli's leaves in the Babelsberg Palace near Berlin.[1] This chapter is about just such efforts to envision the new nation and, in turn, what those endeavours did to photography. The resulting pictures, much like *Wilhelm I in His Study at Versailles*, demonstrate that visions of unification could be as constructed as the German nation itself, and the fissures and seams just as retouched and off-scale. Yet both creations could be accepted as natural and authentic.

The stakes for both the medium and the country were quickly escalating in importance. Through the years following unification, photography offered visions of German history, its present and its myth, just as it had in previous decades. But the medium was now becoming more easily reproducible and was correspondingly being disseminated to its public on an industrial scale, as was already the case with Schnäbeli's 1871 portfolio. Pictures such as his began playing a significant role in directing public perception of the world outside one's immediate experience and provoking responses in the form of further photographs. Through the overlapping epochs known as the *Gründerzeit* (Founding Period) and the Wilhelminian Era (dominated by Kaiser Wilhelm II), the medium came to saturate the everyday lives of the country's citizenry. The 1882 refinement of halftone printing by the Bavarian native Georg Meisenbach, for instance, allowed an image technology principally restricted to photo studios now to expand into mass formats such as periodicals and books. Similar advances led to the mass-produced carte-de-visite and picture postcard, the second of which had found its first great use during the Franco-Prussian War. Soon photographs became the pictorial ground over which perceptions of the nation where forged and contested by makers and consumers in vast numbers. The medium was becoming an important technology of collective imagination, continually advancing and finding use in fresh ways as the nation found its footing. The result was an endless stream of strange and captivating pictures that awoke a fascination with photographic technology, particularly as an aid to human perception.

Photographic Presence and Absence

Schnäbeli's conjuring involved reaching into the mechanics of photographic printing and, much as Walter Benjamin would later write of the cinematographer, working deeply in reality's tissue.[2] Other strategies of national imagining did not involve foregrounding the mediated quality of photography quite so heavily, although Schnäbeli's manipulations were probably less visible to the contemporary eye. Instead, the majority of pictures plying national themes passed themselves off quite easily as transparent visions. This was the case for an important picture taken at the long-belated inauguration of Cologne's cathedral.

The event unfolded on 15 October 1880, when Wilhelm I visited the city to celebrate the completion of its famous and vast Gothic structure.

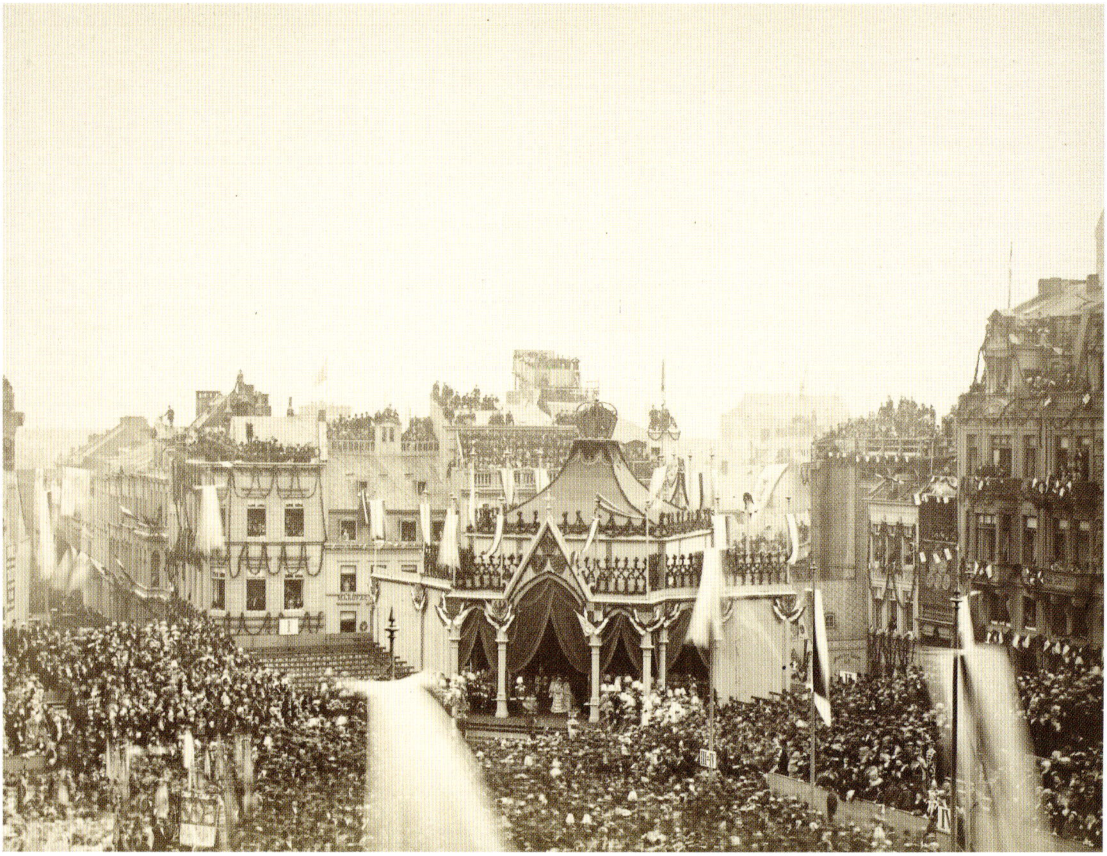

An albumen print by local photographer Johann Heinrich Schönscheidt beautifully documents the inauguration's pomp and splendour (illus. 22). This picture, however, is just as striking for what it omits without any resort to composite printing: Catholicism. Shortly after the German states unified under Protestant Prussian rule in 1871, von Bismarck forcefully legislated against what he perceived as the Roman Catholic Church's rising political power. Consequently, the 1880 print from Cologne may showcase the empire's imperial and military hierarchy, but it shows neither the cathedral's archbishop, who had fled into exile, nor the local clergy, who refused to attend.

22 Johann Heinrich Schönscheidt, *Festival Tent of Kaiser Wilhelm I at the Roncalliplatz during the Inaugural Ceremony of the Cathedral, Cologne, 15 October 1880*, 1880, albumen print.

The Schönscheidt picture makes this absence clear. Shot from a position somewhere on the cathedral itself facing the event, it focuses on an elaborate neo-Gothic tent festooned with flags, coats of arms and tracery. Underneath this curious enclosure, which was capped with a colossal crown, stand the kaiser and his wife, the Kaiserin Augusta, both clad in imperial finery. All faces turn intently in the couple's direction, even those behind the tent without a direct view. Yet there is a visible range of empty seats. The crowd may be packed tight before the tent, on balconies and even along the roofline, where constructed loggias team with spectators despite their precarious position in the sky. But a section of bleachers just to the left of the tent marked with the Roman number 'I' is demonstrably empty. Might this have been the space where clergy was supposed to have sat? Even if not, its vacancy amidst a densely crowded and attentive audience signals a significant absence nonetheless, a tear in the national fabric that the cathedral and the kaiser were otherwise supposed to mend. The photograph may have attempted to capture this carefully staged moment of national celebration. But in the process, it accidentally caught a sign of the country's fragmentation.

As the print demonstrates, visions of national unity and pride did not have to arise through direct intervention in the printing process. A strategic vantage point for the camera, clever titling and the arrangement of real conditions could summon the same sort of message of unity that direct manipulations had in 1871. With Catholicism's absence from this picture, the kaiser and the cathedral could symbolize a unity untroubled by the actual religious, political and social divisions that this photograph obscured, and that were probably more representative of the experience of Germany in 1880. In cases such as these, conjuring worked as a filter over the photographic field.

Picturing Identity

The constituents whom those members of the clergy would have otherwise represented in the photograph were the majority of Rhinelanders who identified with the Church as much as, or more than, with the unified Germany. Or more fundamentally, they would have represented the one-third of Germans who were Catholic. Many participated in an increasingly secular modern society that had abandoned old-style Christian customs. But as the Roman Catholic Church seemed to assert itself politically in the mid-nineteenth century, Chancellor von Bismarck publicly called the institution's allegiance into question and, in 1872, he began pushing legislation in the Prussian regional parliament that mandated government authority over the Church's internal affairs, including the appointment of bishops. In the resulting *Kulturkampf* (Culture Battle), legislative onslaughts provoked widespread clerical defiance, which in turn led to imprisonments, exile and confiscation of Church property. Much of the Catholic population even outside the Prussian state (which included the Rhine region) felt besieged by this aggression.

As an unintended consequence, this constituency identified even more strongly with its religious affiliation. Separate Catholic societies formed, along with Catholic grocery cooperatives, Catholic worker associations and even Catholic sports groups. In essence, a parallel civil society took shape that dramatically expanded on the existing network of parochial schools and other Church institutions. Photography allowed self-identified members of this milieu, as such parallel cultures came to be called, to picture themselves as a coherent group. Descendants and veterans of one of the many Katholische Arbeitervereine (Catholic Employee Associations, illus. 23) that had formed in these decades recreated a nostalgic example in the 1920s. Sitting for a portrait in the Weimar era that harked back to the 1880s, they are dressed in their old-fashioned formal best. The men brandish their four flags, which sport religious figures, and foreground their drums, which they would have beaten when parading through their town of Rees, due north of Essen. The nineteenth-century groups such as these consisted of lay members who worked to relieve the stresses of Germany's rapid industrialization and of the *Kulturkampf*, and to foster connections between workers and local parishes. Another Katholischer Arbeiterverein from around the First World War drew itself from a non-German constituency, namely Polish Catholics who had been migrating to Berlin in significant numbers since the eighteenth century. Distinct by ethnicity, language and religion – particularly in the heavily Protestant Berlin – these members would assemble before a camera in similar finery to brandish a flag with their name in Polish and the Polish national coat of arms.

These pictures lie well within the mainstream middle-class standard for such group portraits. They differ only in detail, for example, from a portrait

23 Unattributed, *Anniversary Party of the* KAB [*Katholische Arbeitnehmer-Bewegung*, 'Catholic Employee Association'] *in the* KAB *District Union in Rees* [Nordrhein-Westfalen], *July 1927*, 1927, format unknown.

24 Julius Braatz, *Plenipotentiary of the Bundesrat* [Federal Assembly Council], 1889, most likely albumen print.

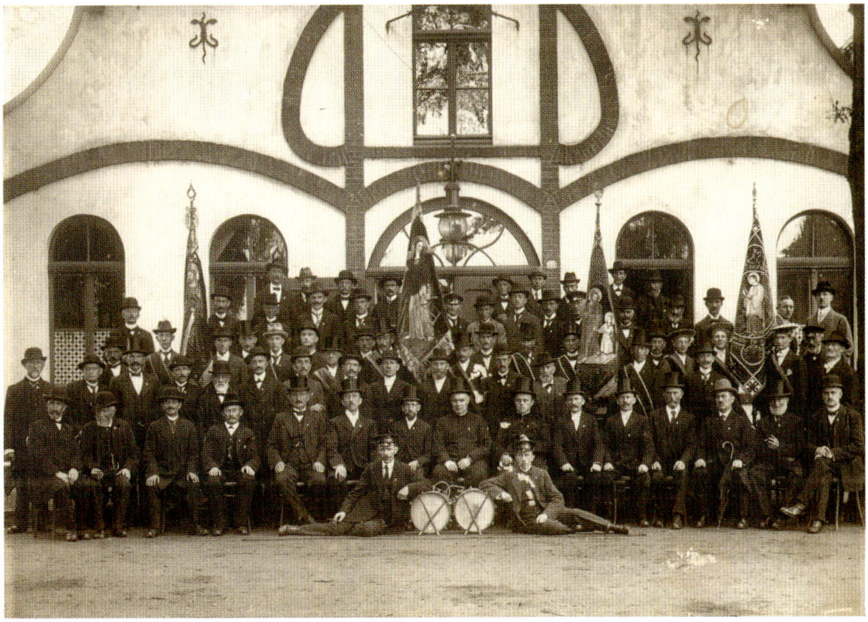

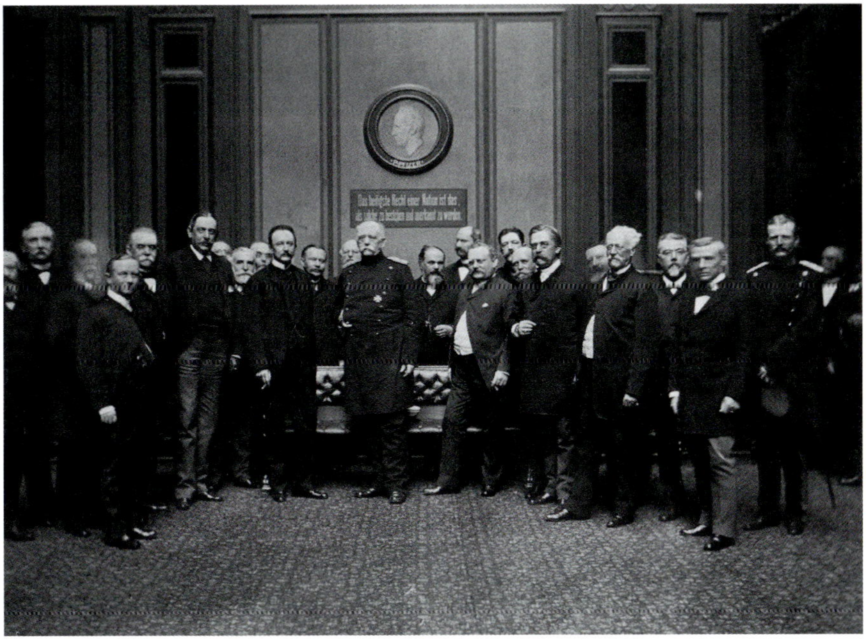

of the politicians largely responsible for the anti-Catholic legislation that stimulated the formation of this milieu. A picture from around 1880, taken in the Reichstag (the German parliament building), shows Bismarck and his party allies in formal attire and, thus, not unlike the Katholische Arbeitervereine (illus. 24). They are nearly indistinguishable even from the Social Democratic members of parliament, whose party and constituency suffered even more severely from punitive anti-socialist laws that Bismarck pursued not long after beginning his anti-Catholic campaign. These portraits demonstrate that members and leaders of parallel societies could use the camera much like others citizens in Germany. But it also suggests that public schools, obligatory conscription and other elements of imperial culture were Germanizing even those people who felt apart from the enterprise.[3] There developed, in other words, a widely accepted baseline of common culture and self-perception centred on the empire's middle class, which was the later nineteenth-century inheritance of the Biedermeier.

Dream Visions and Counter-identity

Other groups employed photographic technology in far more fanciful ways or simply rebelled against this neo-Biedermeier baseline. A Katholischer Gesellenverein (Catholic Journeymen Association) from the southern city of Lindau (illus. 25) appears in a postcard from around 1900 as eight figural groupings montaged – which was possible by this time – onto a grassy berm overlooking their medieval island town on the Bodensee (Lake Constance). All but one of these parties cluster around a table and hold the implements of their sociability: musical instruments, beer steins, ledgers and more. At the compositional centre stands a maypole with denominational signals of affiliation that bring the men together as an identity group in this imaginary space. In its strange mismatch of scale and lighting, the postcard makes the anti-Catholic vision of Bismarck and the subsequent rallying of these constituents into support groups pictorially explicit as a social and pictorial construction.

25 Unattributed, *Katholische Gesellenverein* [Catholic Journeymen Association], *Lindau* [Bavaria], c. 1900, postcard.

Other groups used photography to convey distinctly different appearances. The *Lebensreform* (Lifestyle Reform) movements that began

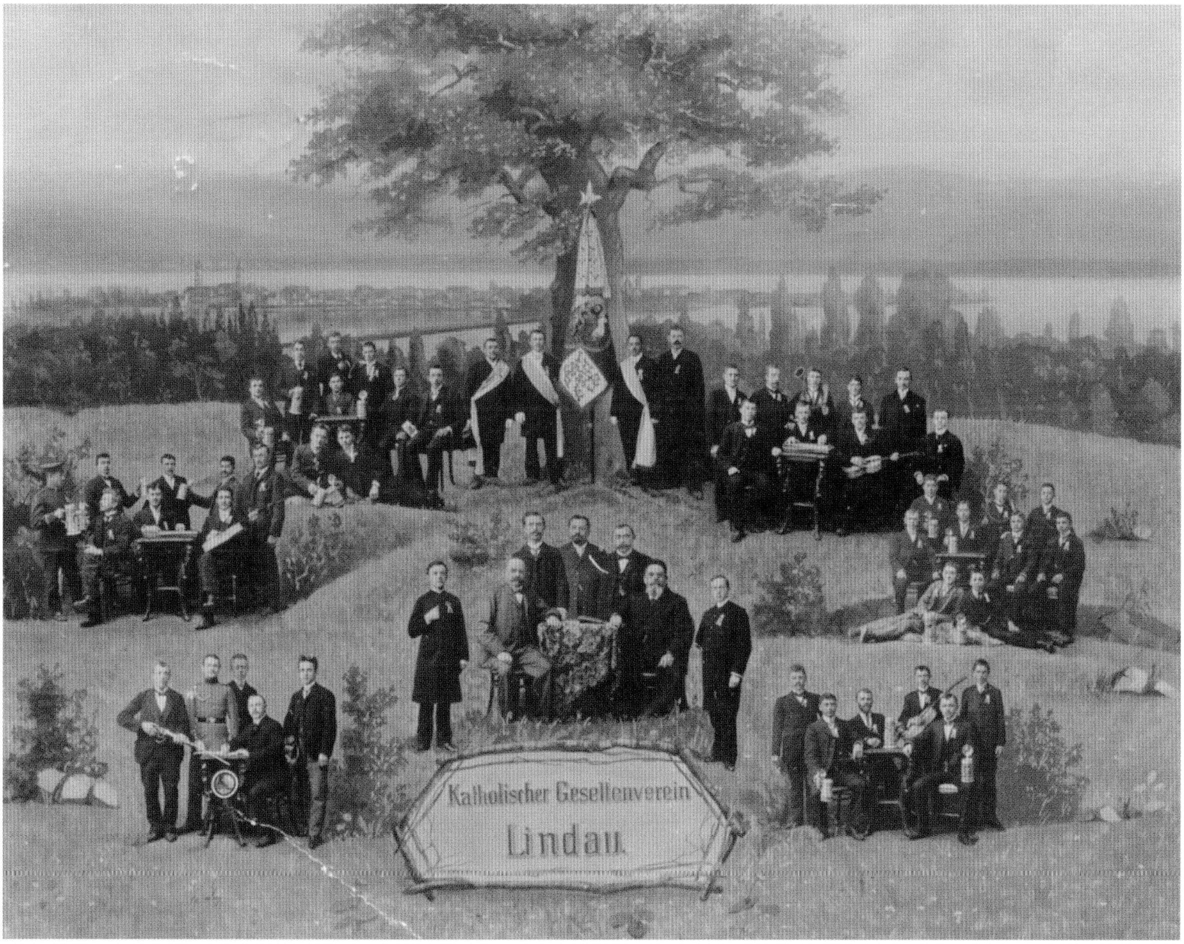
Katholischer Gesellenverein
Lindau

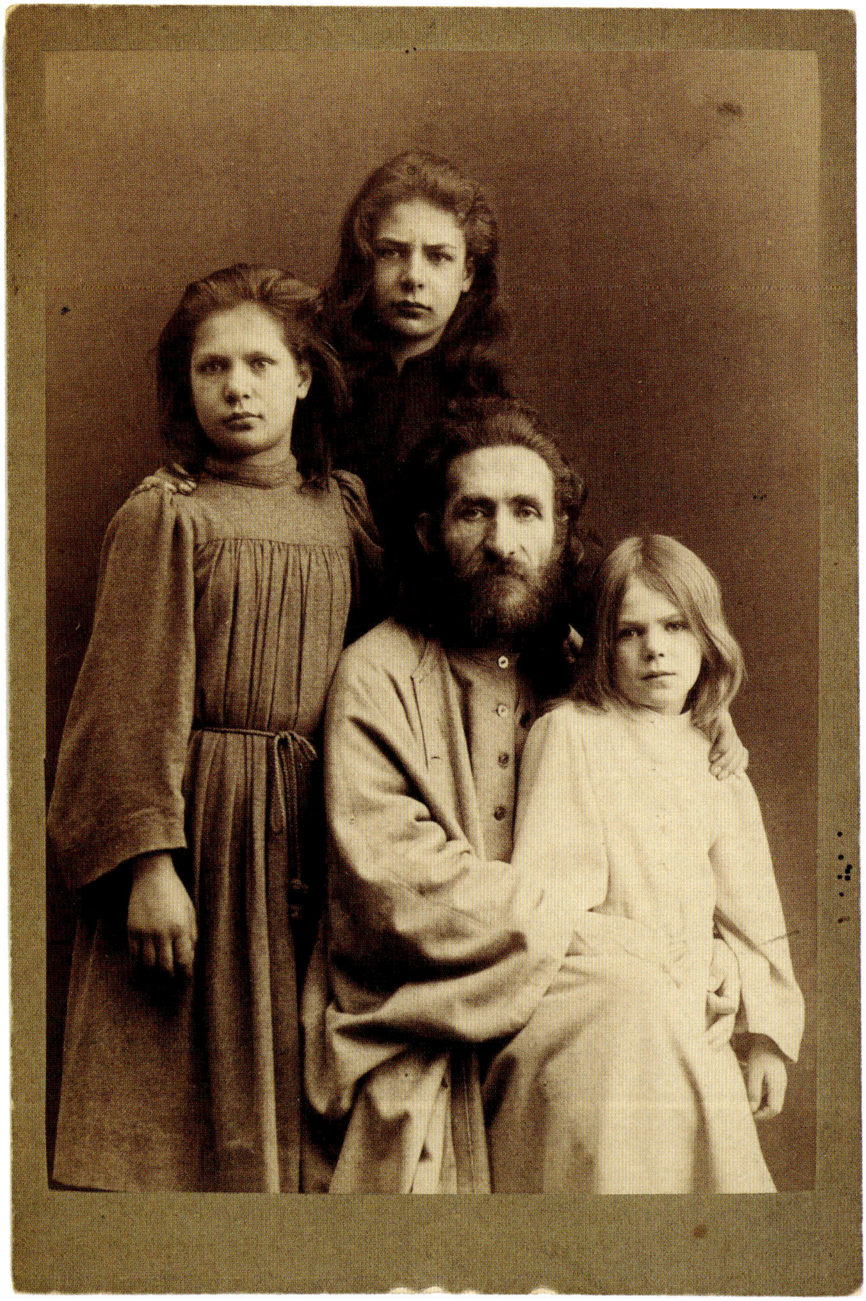

to take shape around the time of unification were keenly aware of the role appearances could play in protesting the German imperial norm. This reaction generated back-to-nature advocates, sexual-liberation champions and teetotallers, among others, who raged against the consequences of quick-paced industrialization. In their eyes, growing poverty, urbanization and materialism were ultimately the consequences of modernity itself. In response, they built rural communes and pursued homeopathy, nutritional reform, clothing reform and nudism. It was the last two of these movements that purposefully availed themselves of photography to spread their message.

The artist Karl Wilhelm Diefenbach, for instance, was a master before the camera, most likely because he trained as a painter in Munich. He gravitated to homeopathy after natural means seemed to cure him of a typhoid infection and, in 1881, he left the Catholic Church to begin a free religion based on his understanding of nature as uncorrupted. Ascetically clad in a tunic and sandals, he wandered Munich's streets preaching the benefits of vegetarianism, fresh air, free sex and nudism. The 'Kohlrabi Apostle', as he was mockingly called, regularly posed for portraits to help press his message, such as one with his children (illus. 26). Easily mistakable for a 1960s hippie, he gazes from behind his lush hair and beard as he draws his children closely to his side. This makes for an expression of warmth generally unlike the Wilhelmine norm. More broadly, pictures such as these were made in conscious opposition to the German imperial standard that the Catholic and socialist portraits followed. Various slivers of Germany's fragmented society, therefore, took forceful and creatively independent control of photography to pursue their unique self-presentation for themselves and, in many cases, wider audiences.

The *Jugendbewegung* (Youth Movement), which also span off from the *Lebensreform* phenomenon, drew from middle-class urban youth in the late 1890s who wished to throw themselves into the countryside and, frequently, rid themselves of clothes to ease that immersion. They effectively popularized the *Freikörperkultur* ('free body culture', or nudism) that was already part of the reform movements by founding periodicals such as *Deutsch Hellas*. Like many others, this magazine published photographs of young people frolicking through German forests, often in poses drawn from ancient statuary, as the title *Hellas* would suggest. But this was specifically

26 Unattributed, *The Painter Karl Wilhelm Diefenbach with his children Helios, Stella und Lucidus*, late 19th century, most likely albumen print.

a contemporary German envisioning of ancient Greece, one engaged with debates on nineteenth-century morals, as much as the nude utopia of antiquity. 'Moralizing and shame are inseparable from man,' *Deutsch Hellas* lamented in one issue. 'We must ask ourselves what is more natural, the naked or the clothed person?'[4] The photographs published in each issue answered this question in favour of the nude, so comfortably set in the contemporary countryside. Here was an extremely self-conscious use of mass-printed photography to convey an emerging identity in contrast to the Wilhelmine norm, and to reach a wide audience of adherents.

27 Baron Wilhelm von Gloeden, untitled classical nude, c. 1900, likely gelatin silver print.

This escape from prudery also expressed itself in the fine art photography of Baron Wilhelm von Gloeden and his cousin Guglielmo Plüschow, who both moved not to the German forest but to Sicily to seek out a natural Greek ideal. These gay men may have been fleeing not only the disappointments of urban modernity but the homophobia of their Prussian homeland. In von Gloeden's carefully lit and posed pictures, scarcely pubescent nude boys cuddle and kiss each other. In less erotic scenes, a subject stands alone with an amphora held in his bent arm, or next to fluted columns, all to evoke the homosocial ancient Greek past and the desire that brought von Gloeden to envision it (illus. 27). Such images related as much to Germany as to Sicily, given that they arose from Teutonic wish images of antiquity first generated by the influential Johann Joachim Winckelmann in the eighteenth century and given new life by the discontent arising from Central Europe's rapid modernization in the empire. Von Gloeden sold his work internationally on the art market and even made a living from these proceeds after losing his German fortune. Prized widely in their day, his carefully composed pictures participated in the rising fashion for art photography known as Pictorialism. They also influenced how foreigners viewed the German fascination with the past and, more specifically, how European gay men could picture their desire under the legitimizing fig leaf of antiquity.

The Monarch of Unity

The kaiser himself, standing under the odd neo-Gothic tent at Cologne Cathedral's inauguration in the Schönscheidt picture, was also a grand

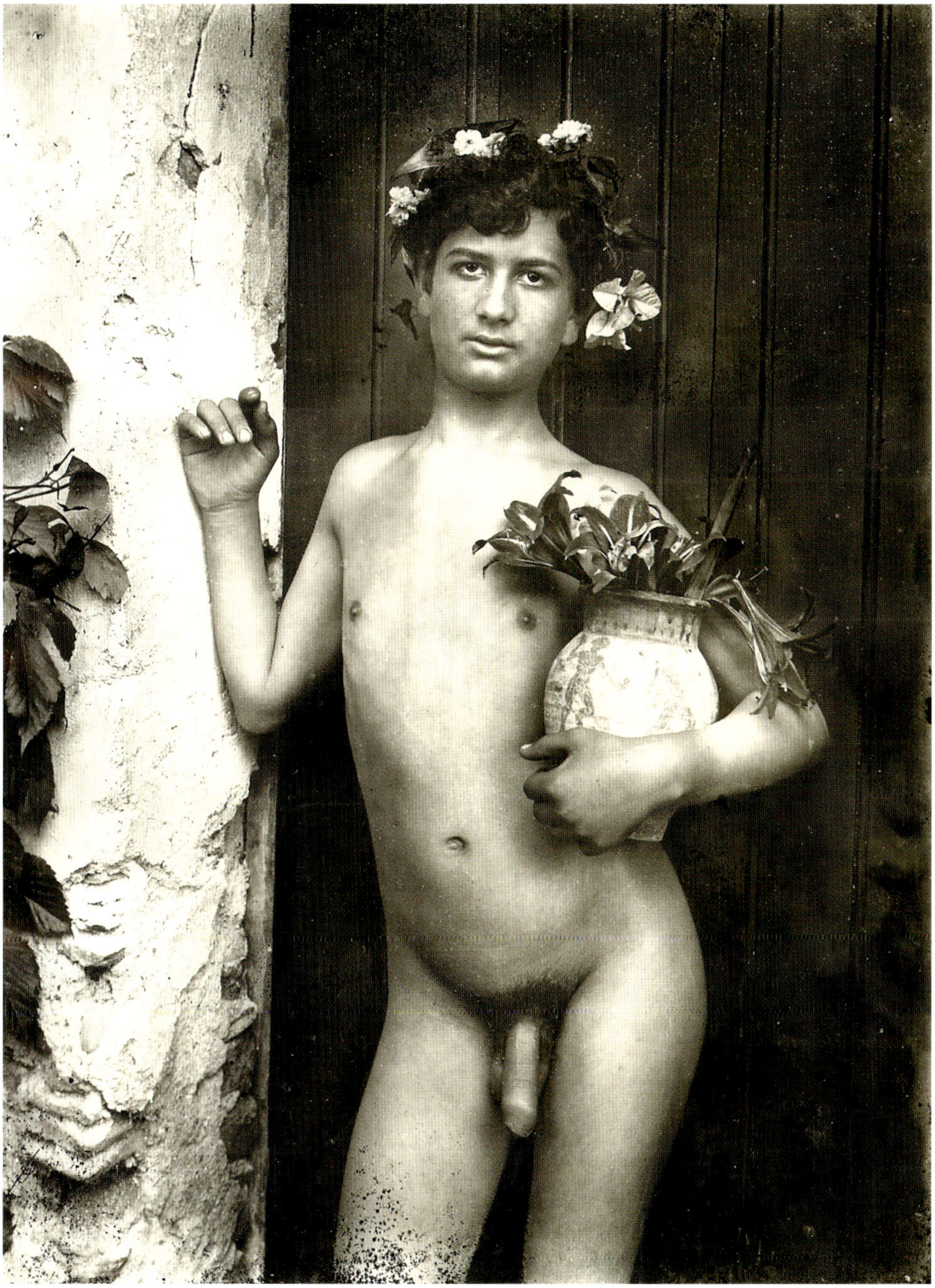

catalyst of photographic invention. Much like the famous church itself, his increasingly proliferating image was to symbolize the new country and embody its diverse regions and peoples. The same held true for other European royals such as Queen Victoria, whose ubiquitous image performed a similar service. But the new kaiser combined the mediated presence of Victoria with fresh national unification and far greater political power (at least on paper), making the German monarch's pictorial presence all the more important in active national imagining.[5] It was the modern photographic form of the carte-de-visite that first served as the agent for this mass imagining.

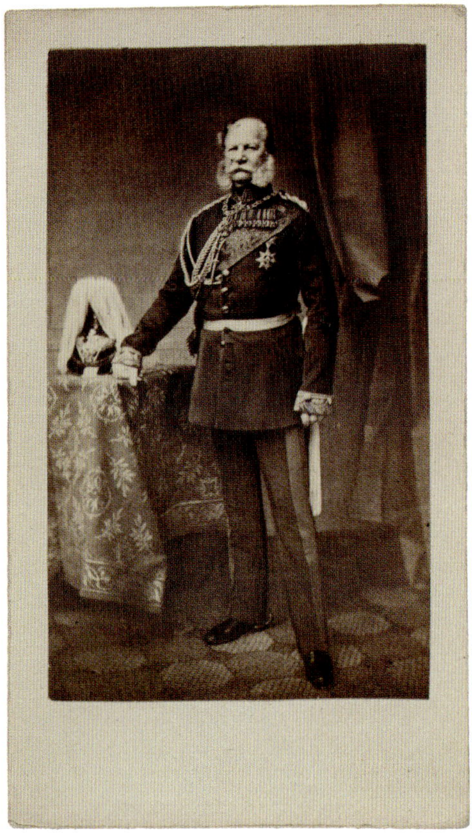

28 Unattributed, carte-de-visite of Kaiser Wilhelm I, c. 1880, albumen print on paper and card.

Patented by its French inventor André-Adolphe-Eugène Disdéri in 1854, this portrait format used the same wet-glass negative process that had superseded the daguerreotype and calotype around 1850. But Disdéri's purpose-built camera enabled eight separate exposures on a single negative plate. The resulting small-format pictures were far more affordable than full-plate portraits, and they were easier to reproduce on a mass scale. Sitters could be cycled through photo studios as if on a conveyor belt, shuffled before ready-made backdrops and props before receiving their picture at the studio's exit. This led to a conformity that helped establish the middle-class look and that one found even in portraits of consciously separate Catholic or socialist associations. Just as importantly, one contact print made from a negative plate sporting eight exposures of the kaiser, for instance, vastly multiplied the number of reproductions that could be produced. These images flooded Europe's rising consumer culture, allowing collectors to amass pictures of family, friends and celebrities in albums, which they might share with loved ones and visitors. The carte-de-visite inaugurated the Europe-wide phenomenon of the photographic souvenir, a frenzy that the picture postcard and the illustrated magazine would later overtake. Wilhelm I's rise to emperor took place in the midst of these developments and made him, much like famous actors and personalities, a natural focus for modern fan culture and memorabilia. This constituted a personalization of national memory that well-stocked private vendors were eager to feed.[6]

The imperial house under Wilhelm I participated in this pictorial culture by granting approximately 120 studios the status of *Hofphotograph* (court photographer), generally on the basis of each one's felicitous pictures of the kaiser and his family. The results were carte-de-visite studio pictures that resembled the staged portraits that the average studio at the time made for its clients (illus. 28). In one example, the emperor poses with his gloved right fist on a table next to his plumed martial helmet. An image of potent imperial power and masculinity, he juts his left foot forward and arches his back as his protruding chest proudly displays multiple medals and drooping swag. Meanwhile, his signature sideburns flutter like the curtain behind him, which gathers at its middle as it parts for the monarch. Carte-de-visite copies of this picture reached millions of consumers.

Some *Hofphotographen* produced standard-sized pictures, known as cabinet cards, intended for the kaiser himself and distributed by his court to close associates and government and military officials. This is probably true of the studio photographer Wilhelm Kuntzemüler, whose portraits of Wilhelm I in military costume became iconic in the 1880s. These pictures could be transformed into cartes-de-visite by private entrepreneurs, or broadly disseminated in other ways, such as with woodblock printing, or even transferred onto stained glass for installation in offices and homes.

These pictures made the new kaiser's visage a significant presence in the citizen's public and private life. They could also signpost the owner's devotion to the monarch and country, particularly if delivered directly by the kaiser himself. In 1876, a high-school student named Nicolaas von Cammenga wrote directly to Wilhelm I with a specific entreaty: to have the ruler return a photographic portrait. 'Until now', the student explained, 'I have had a photograph of Your Majesty hanging in my room, but a [store-bought] picture – as Your Majesty no doubt knows – never has the same charm as one received from the hand of the person in question.'[7] Cammenga added that he had always maintained the 'dearest wish' to devote his life to emperor and Fatherland, expressing sentiments that connected this desire for a photograph of – and touched by – the kaiser, to his fidelity to the country united just five years earlier. The young man's petition provides an example

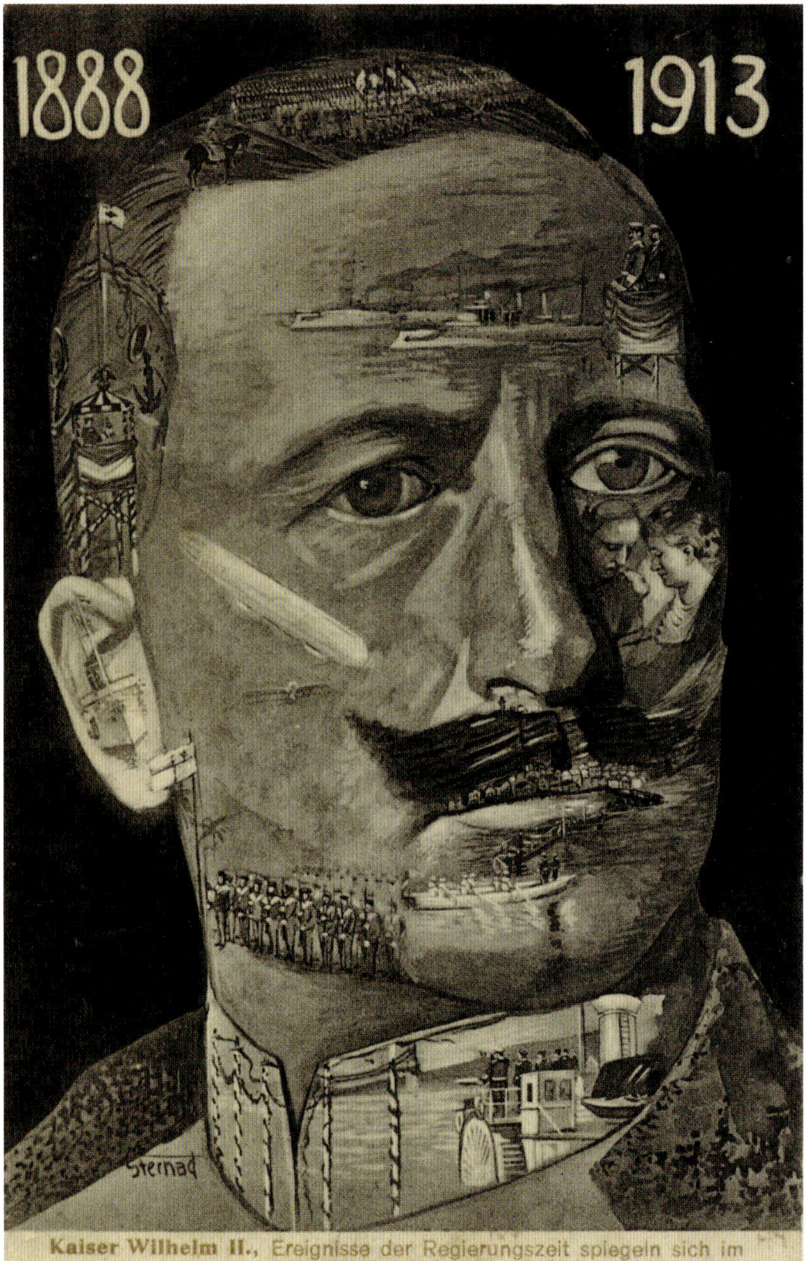

Kaiser Wilhelm II., Ereignisse der Regierungszeit spiegeln sich im Antlitz des Kaisers. (Erklärung umseitig)

of the burgeoning fan culture in which mass-produced photographs had begun playing such an important role, and the degree to which this new phenomenon broke down old social barriers in Germany. In earlier epochs, a common subject would not request something from a monarch without offering a gift first, and usually through well-placed intermediaries who might filter out the entreaty. But the democratization of access that this new fan culture promoted now stimulated Cammenga's letter. This licence, in turn, encouraged him to seek the 'charm' that he wished to sense embedded in the kaiser's portrait, an aura added by the monarch's personal dispatch. The picture could then help Cammenga feel more fully bound to his Fatherland, given the print's amalgamated physical and pictorial access to the monarch, the figure who embodied the nation most publicly.

This infrastructure of public photography, fan culture and added charm played an even greater role under the reign of Wilhelm II – grandson of the first kaiser and the son of Friedrick III, who sat on the throne a mere 99 days before succumbing to throat cancer on 15 June 1888. More than his father and grandfather, Wilhelm II faced a frequently deadlocked Reichstag and a growing cynicism about the perceived failures of the young country's constitutional system. German scholars of constitutional law at the time proposed that Wilhelm II bypass the Reichstag to forge a direct connection to his subjects as a *Volkskaiser* (people's emperor) and rule effectively by plebiscite. As Martin Kohlrausch, scholar of the Wilhelmine monarchy, has summed up: 'these writers believed that only an "integrator", a political force ideally identical to the monarch and ruling through plebiscitary means, could realize the social integration of an increasingly fragmented German society.'[8]

The new emperor, notorious for his strong personality and hard-headedness, took up this role of 'integrator' and directly approached his subjects by employing a combination of bombastic speeches, copious travel for leisure and to visit his subjects and a stress on the symbols of militarized monarchy. Photographs of the monarch creatively combined visual expressions of this self-conscious approach to rule. One litho-photographic postcard perfectly symbolizes this role of the *Volkskaiser* (illus. 29). Composed of photo-lithographic fragments, the picture depicts the ruler as the mirror image of the nation, his head and collar reflecting the achievements of his

29 Emil Bieber (the Imperial house photographer), *Kaiser Wilhelm II: Events of His Reign Reflect Themselves in the Kaiser's Face*, 1913, postcard.

25 years of service. His chin and moustache show his 1890 acquisition of the North Sea archipelago Heligoland, and his collar the 1895 opening of the North–East Sea Canal. These achievements were seemingly the products of his direct appeals to the public. Here they constituted the modern country as much as the kaiser's increasingly self-fashioned public persona.

Like his grandfather, Wilhelm II sat for court photographers and thereby helped build a body of official images, which were then copied into various formats and sold by private firms. Though not systematic, the kaiser and his imperial house fashioned an instantly recognizable look of severity and pomposity that effectively became a brand. Pictorial signs of this grim authority included a stern unsmiling face and moustache edges retouched to absurd heights.[9] Reproductions of this earnest countenance could be imaginatively transformed in a process best described as commercial rebranding. For example, a postcard from 1907 captioned *Grandfather's Darling* recycles a photograph of the dour kaiser, seated in formal eveningwear, with another photograph of his grandson Prince Wilhelm, settled on the monarch's lap (illus. 30). The two may adhere visually, but they are light years apart emotionally. The original picture of the toddler prince appeared, among other places, on a postcard from 1907 with the caption *The Youngest Hohenzoller*. The original closely framed shot revealed a gentle smile, allegedly provoked by the photographer performing tricks behind the camera.[10] In turn, the postcard publisher who montaged young Wilhelm onto his grandfather's lap simply disregarded the kaiser's intention to be seen as awe-inspiring and worthy of reverence. Instead, the person responsible for this montage realized that consumers preferred to consume the family as a spectacle of an ideal middle-class family, rich in domestic sentimentality, and the model for their own studio portraits. Such pictorial inventions reimagined the imperial embodiment of the nation as a gregarious grandfather rather than a remote heredity monarch, as the palace preferred.

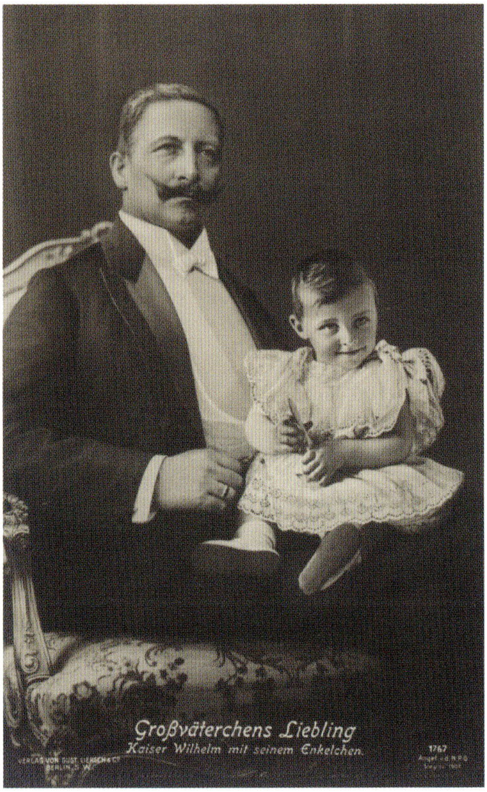

30 Gustav Liersch & Co., Berlin, *Grandfather's Darling: Kaiser Wilhelm with His Little Grandson*, 1907, postcard.

We might expect that such obvious manipulations hoodwinked consumers into perceiving that what they desired was what reality offered. But the 'doctoring' of photographs had long been a part of middle-class life in the West, particularly at photo studios.[11] Outside the photo salon, Germany – as other European countries and North America – saw a booming industry in photographic amusements of which these pictures were merely representative. As in the case of *Grandfather's Darling*, they largely appeared on picture postcards, 90 per cent of which were photographic by 1900. Most were lightly humorous, poking fun at modern life and sexuality and openly playing with the tenuous link that photography seemingly maintained with the reality it represents.[12]

Enlisted soldiers took a direct role in exercising this sort of photographic imagination. Before handheld cameras and rapid exposure times, photographs of soldiers in battle were exceedingly difficult to capture. Even when photographic technology caught up with the speed of modern combat, soldiers often languished in dull or even degrading moments that were unfit for the glory-seeking camera, leaving military personnel with few 'suitable' photographic records of their service. Entrepreneurs, such as the maker of the image shown here (illus. 31), compensated by mass-producing fanciful lithographic panels showing a soldier's clean and strong body charging, shooting or standing to attention. Often sold at photo studios near barracks or battlefields, these compositions merely required a military man to pay a small fee and have his portrait taken. A quick cut and paste by studio assistants attached the subject's head to the bravely charging body, personalizing the mass-produced composition. Handwritten additions complete the process by noting the cavalryman's regiment number and company on the coat of arms, as seen here under the tableau. Portraits of the kaiser and other royalty generally floated above, displaying the national hierarchy into which the soldier fitted and that he served. Printed in cabinet-card format, these pictures graced tables or walls in the family home, satisfying fantasies of war cultivated by traditional battle paintings while also giving even the most idle soldier a starring role in grand scenarios, all with a testimonial assist from photography. Here was a 'memory of my service',

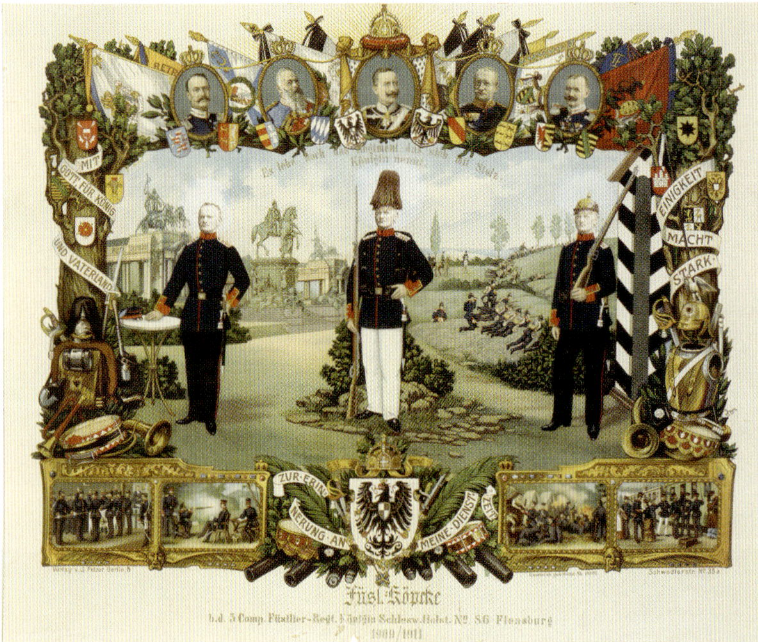

31 Verlag J. Pelzer, *In Memory of my Period of Service – Rifleman Köpcke*, 1909–10, mixed media.

as these were often called in Germany, that made a soldier and his family proud.[13] They also show the degree to which consumers of studio photography directly participated in the sort of conjuring that appeared in the kaiser images and other amusing postcards.

In addition to joining in making these fanciful pictures, German audiences also consumed similarly manipulated photos on a mass level every 1 April, when many of the nation's illustrated periodicals published their photographic *Aprilscherze* (April Fool Jokes). The high-circulating *Berliner-Illustrirte Zeitung* (Berlin Illustrated Magazine), or *BIZ*, in particular stressed the iffy testimonial force of photography in their hoaxes, such as a 1904 jest showing the famous animal trainer Carl Hagenbeck guiding his exotic charges through the Brandenburg Gate (illus. 32). Pictures such as this one, both here and in other periodicals, were published without commentary. But the subsequent issues would run excited features on how audiences were duped by the hoax of the previous week or, even better, how other readers had suspected some of the straight photos in the same early April issue of being fakes. Though the jokes and the follow-on commentary spoke in the language of humour, they were teaching earnestly serious lessons about the mixed delight and hazard of photographic mediation and the degree to which photographs might enable overly credulous readers to accept what they saw as fact. More consciously engaged with this problem of veracity than fantasy postcards and military service montages, these features cultivated a consciousness about photographic mediation that built on the earlier body of kaiser images.

Moreover, they did so on a vast scale. The *BIZ*, for instance, circulated one million copies a week by 1920 and availed itself liberally of halftone printing technology. This image process arose from a number of key developments in three different countries, beginning with Fox Talbot's early experiments

32 Unattributed halftone print, 'A "Photographic" Record of the Entry of the Hagenbeck Zoo through the Brandenburg Gate', 1904, from the 1927 celebratory publication 50 *Years of Ullstein Verlag, 1877–1927*.

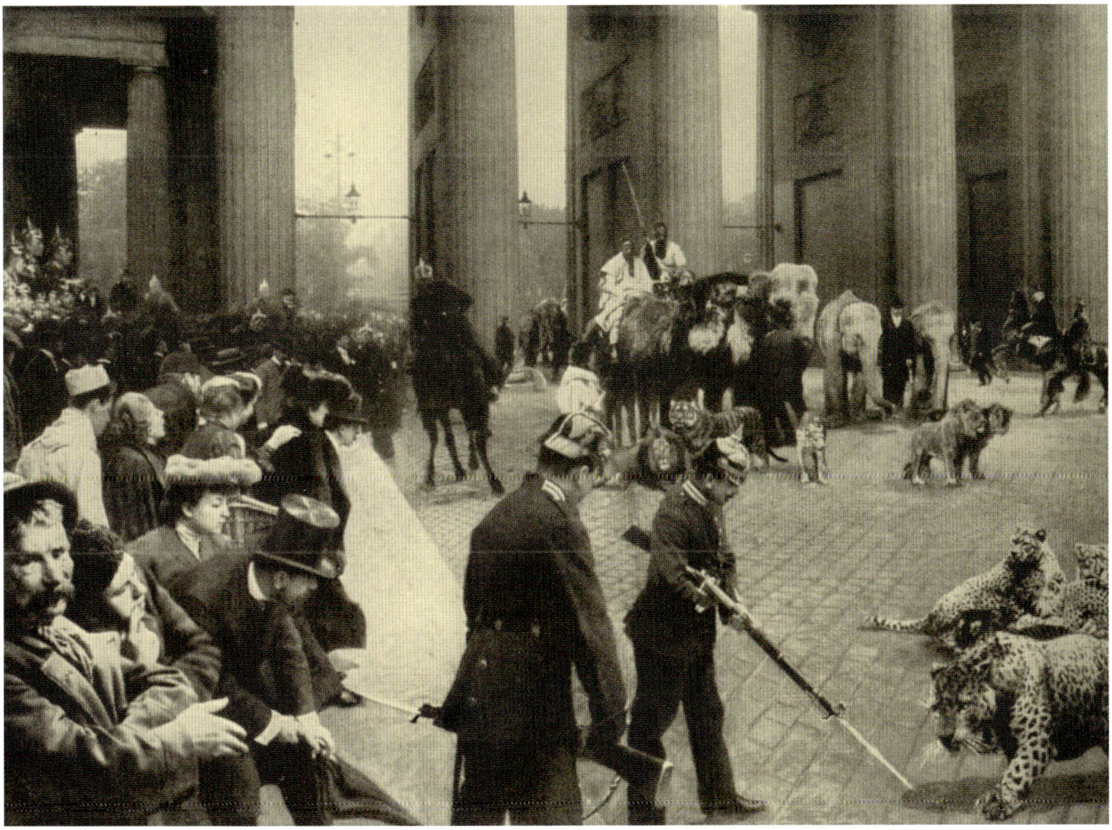

in reducing a photograph's subtle tonal range for easier mechanical printing and, in 1881, Philadelphia resident Frederic Ives's use of screens to distil that range yet further into dots of varying size. Ives's technique produced the illusion of a photograph's pictorial subtlety from tiny specks of black ink of varying size, which was then easy to reproduce mechanically. One year later, Munich resident Georg Meisenbach made this process commercially feasible by using two screens of lines, turned at right angles to each other, to cheaply reproduce the photograph as an even finer array of dots on a standard printing plate. One year after that, Germany's first illustrated magazine, the Leipzig-based *Illustrierte Zeitung*, availed itself of Meisenbach's invention in printing its first photographic image. Its choice of subject was quite stunning: a gilded and jewel-encrusted ornament of such complexity that it pushed the halftone's fidelity to its limits and cultivated the fascination of the magazine's readers. Despite this success, it was only in the mid-1890s that audiences learned to accept the halftone image over the customary woodblock engraving, leading to an explosion in the use of this photographic technology. The *BIZ* used it extensively by 1900, leading other German magazines and weekly supplements to adopt it as well. By the First World War, most photographic images consumed by Germany's population appeared in magazines, making the news and popular culture an increasingly visual affair that the *Aprilscherze* light-heartedly critiqued for millions of readers. Masses of Germans were being asked to become conscious of the role photography played in their daily perception of the world.

Technology and Vision

As photography began to saturate everyday life, several technological advances enabled the medium to picture previously invisible things and phenomena, thereby demonstrating new forms of perception to a broad audience. In Germany, photographer Ottomar Anschütz took advantage of the sensitive dry-plate photographic process, first introduced by Englishman Richard Maddox in 1871 and perfected in 1878. Working from these developments, he devised a camera around 1882 that could capture the fleeting instance. This was around the same time that Eadweard Muybridge, a Briton in the U.S., and Étienne-Jules Marey, in Paris, began perfecting 'chronophotography': instantaneous shots made – and then shown – in sequence, or arrayed as multiple exposures on a single plate. Anschütz observed and followed on their developments carefully.[14] But more than these men, Anschütz paid close attention to the quality of each shot. His pictures thereby defined the early aesthetic of the snapshot, to much popular acclaim. His enlarged photographs of galloping and jumping horses, which he made available to the photo trade press in 1882 and personally showed to the kaiser, earned the admiration of the *Photographische Mitteilungen* (Photographic News), which declared them far superior to Muybridge's earlier silhouette-like images.[15] His shots of military manoeuvres, complete with dust clouds thrown up by the action of horses and men, appeared as halftone prints in an 1884 issue of the *Illustrirte Zeitung*, making his new technology a mass-public affair.

Such instantaneous pictures of Germany's fighting men became so popular that other photographers purchased cameras designed by (or after) Anschütz before rushing into military manoeuvres to photograph for the new illustrated press. A satirical paper from 1900 quipped on this burgeoning photo genre closely associated with Prussian militarism (illus. 33). Titled 'Instructions before Battle in the Future', the feature shows a field peppered with soldiers and cameramen in equal number, and with devices even aimed from balloons. The colonel facing his men commands: 'People, stay alert in combat. Consider that there are hundreds of cameras aimed at you!' By this reckoning in the popular *Meggendorfers humoristische Blätter* (Meggendorfers Humour Sheets), the camera's appeal had guns switched out for lenses and bravery replaced with vanity. Correspondingly, the second in command checks his appearance in a pocket mirror as the cameraman in the foreground holds aloft a Goerz Anschütz Patent Camera, which Anschütz designed in the late 1880s. The surge of military footage that this satire provoked had fed the country's militarist fascination and ultimately become the seed of Germany's press photography apparatus, a system that boomed in the Weimar era. It also touched on the growing anxiety among soldiers and citizens alike that cameras could be observing them from anywhere.

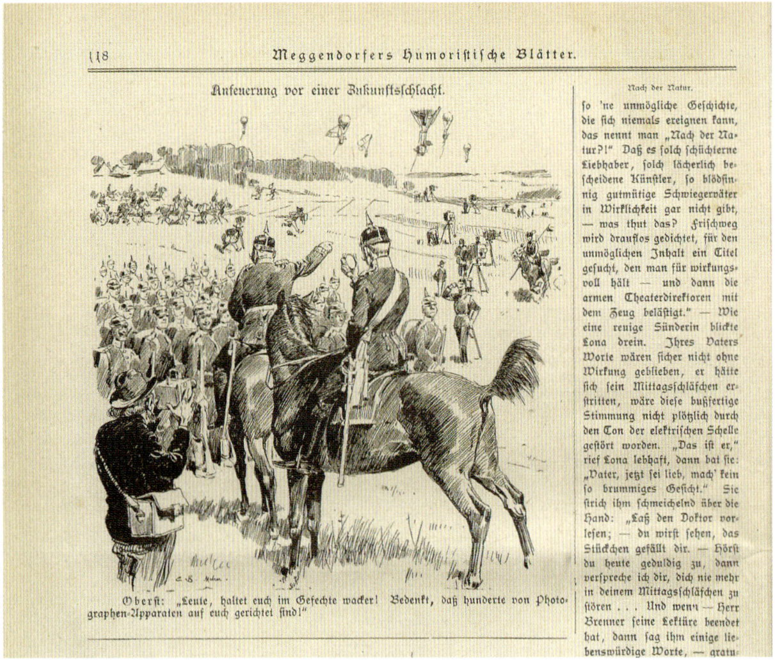

118 Meggendorfers Humoristische Blätter.

Anfeuerung vor einer Zukunftsschlacht.

Oberst: „Leute, haltet euch im Gefechte wacker! Bedenkt, daß hunderte von Photographen-Apparaten auf euch gerichtet sind!“

Nach der Natur.

so 'ne unmögliche Geschichte, die sich niemals ereignen kann, das nennt man „Nach der Natur?!“ Daß es solch schüchterne Liebhaber, solch lächerlich bescheidene Künstler, so blödsinnig gutmütige Schwiegerväter in Wirklichkeit gar nicht gibt, — was thut das? Frischweg wird drauflos gedichtet, für den unmöglichen Inhalt ein Titel gesucht, den man für wirkungsvoll hält — und dann die armen Theaterdirektoren mit dem Zeug belästigt.“ — Wie eine reuige Sünderin blickte Lona drein. Ihres Vaters Worte wären sicher nicht ohne Wirkung geblieben, er hätte sich sein Mittagsschläfchen erstritten, wäre diese bußfertige Stimmung nicht plötzlich durch den Ton der elektrischen Schelle gestört worden. „Das ist er,“ rief Lona lebhaft, dann bat sie: „Vater, jetzt sei lieb, mach' kein so brummiges Gesicht.“ Sie strich ihm schmeichelnd über die Hand: „Laß den Doktor vorlesen; — du wirst sehen, das Stückchen gefällt dir. — Hörst du heute geduldig zu, dann verspreche ich dir, dich nie mehr in deinem Mittagsschläfchen zu stören . . . Und wenn — Herr Brenner seine Lektüre beendet hat, dann sag ihm einige liebenswürdige Worte, — gratu-

33 C. B. Mohn, 'Instructions before Battle in the Future', woodblock print illustration in a 1900 issue of *Meggendorfers Humoristische Blätter*.

Though instantaneous shots of military manoeuvres made him famous, Anschütz achieved his greatest coup in 1884 with striking photographs of animals caught in action, such as a series of enlargements showing a stork caught mid-flight around its nest, feeding its chicks (illus. 34). These – at the time – unbelievable prints struck many viewers as the opening to an invisible world. The Austrian chemist and physicist Ottomar von Volkmer noted that they were 'the most delightful genre pictures that one can imagine' and that they 'convey the natural history of the stork better and more powerfully than my own rambling description ever could'.[16] Such pictures cultivated a new sense that photography was vastly expanding sensorial perception, revealing far more than the eye could ever see or that the mind might anticipate.

Within the German context, this perception not only supplemented the ongoing fascination with the military, but played with the anxiety over religion in an increasingly secular world. Another satirical drawing, from the humour journal *Simplicissimus*, proffered a pious priest capturing a floating demon with his modern handheld camera (illus. 35). Below the image, the well-fed clergyman is quoted as saying: 'Why didn't I think of this earlier! With a single good snapshot I can overturn the entire Enlightenment!' The notably anti-clerical journal was proposing what a reactionary priest might anticipate from the invisible word revealed by the new camera. More than ever, broad audiences in Germany were becoming aware of the medium as a technology, as much as an image form.

More wondrous still was an accidental discovery in 1895 by the German physicist Wilhelm Conrad Röntgen. While experimenting with the passage of electricity through a cathode ray tube, Röntgen noticed that fluorescent material in his laboratory began to glow in the dark. Upon further experimenting with this mysterious and invisible 'x-ray' emanating from the tube, he saw that it would expose a photographic plate, except where certain

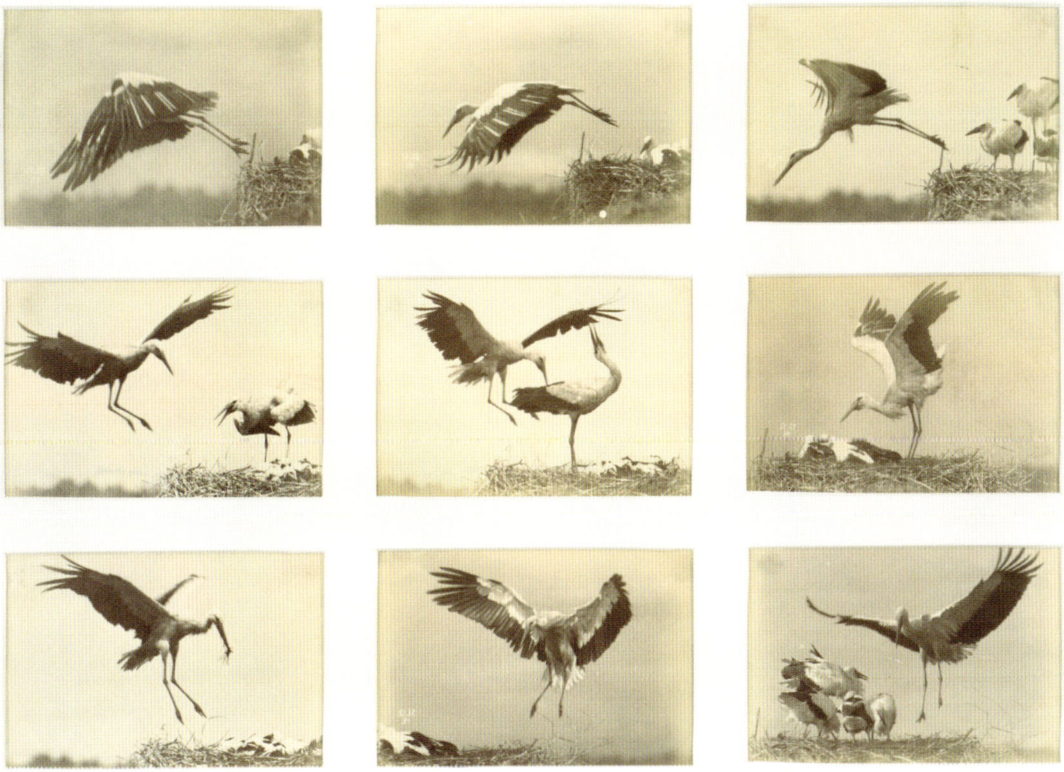

34 Ottomar Anschütz, *Storks*, 1884, celluloid paper print.

objects had blocked the emissions. Bones in a hand would absorb a high percentage of the rays, whereas the skin around them took in far less (illus. 36), as he famously demonstrated with an image of his wife's hand. In this case, her bones and the ring on her finger obscured the rays over the plate's long exposure. This process resembled the photogram, a cameraless process that involves covering a sensitized sheet of paper or film with objects and then exposing the assembly to light, a process later taken up by interwar avant-garde photographers. But this was not visible light, and the process involved penetration as much as obscuring. Yet it seemed to enhance human vision in much the same way Anschütz's snapshots had, and it was quickly deployed as a medical diagnostic tool. Already in 1897, doctors on the military fields in the Balkan wars were using it.

The knowledge that invisible rays could expose photographic plates and reveal hidden worlds seemed to affirm the validity of spirit photographs, which captured floating visions of the dead. Soon, occultists devised photographic procedures to capture 'v-rays' emitted by the brain ('v' for vital), 'n-rays', 'y-rays' and even 'xx-rays'.[17] Just as importantly, the same determination to record the invisible encouraged spiritualists, bearing the

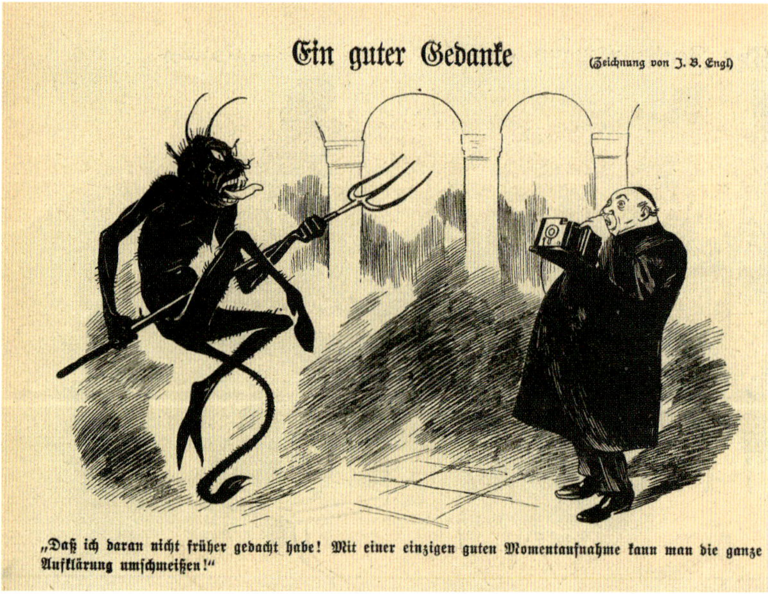

35 J. B. Engl, 'A Felicitous Idea', lithographic illustration in a 1904 issue of *Simplicissimus*.

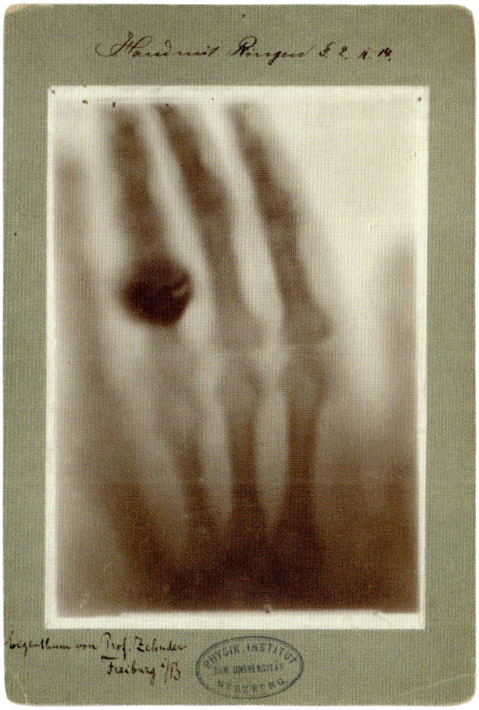

36 Wilhelm Conrad Röntgen, *Hand with Rings: X-ray by Wilhelm Röntgen of his Wife Bertha Röntgen Hand, December 22, 1895*, 1895, x-ray photograph.

imprimatur of science, to bring their cameras to seances, where they hoped to record visible phenomena as well, such as ectoplasms, apparitions and floating objects. One of the most famous of these para-scientific photographers was Albert von Schrenck-Notzing. This physician, who was deeply interested in paranormal phenomena, filled the séances of his favourite mediums with banks of cameras and magnesium flashes to record the materializations which he believed these women forged through contact with spirits (illus. 37). In one shot from 1912, he captured Eva Carrière with a felt-like materialization on her head and a luminous apparition between her hands, the second of which was probably a manipulation made to the image's negative. Schrenck-Notzing travelled widely and played a large role in cultivating this international movement in paranormal photography.

Alongside Röntgen, another German scientist profoundly influenced photography – Hermann von Helmholtz. This giant of research devised a theory of human vision based in part on his ophthalmoscope, which he designed in 1851. His device, which became a standard diagnostic device for eye doctors, allowed him to see inside the human eye and understand such things as depth perception and peripheral vision. In the 1880s, the English doctor and amateur photographer Peter Henry Emerson proposed that photographers should follow on from Helmholtz's ideas and ape natural human vision with their cameras, producing pictures that were focused at the centre and blurred at the sides. The photographs that Emerson went on to make inspired many followers, who generally overlooked the science that inspired these pictures and clung instead to the hazy aesthetic and rural subject matter of these visions. In the German context of the *Reformbewegung* and *Lebensreform* movements, this approach resonated with great force, particularly among middle-class amateurs who saw the explosion of photographic images made possible by dry-plate technology and halftone printing as vulgar.

The Dresden-born medical doctor and amateur photographer Heinrich Kühn, for example, took diffuse images of the countryside where prosperous

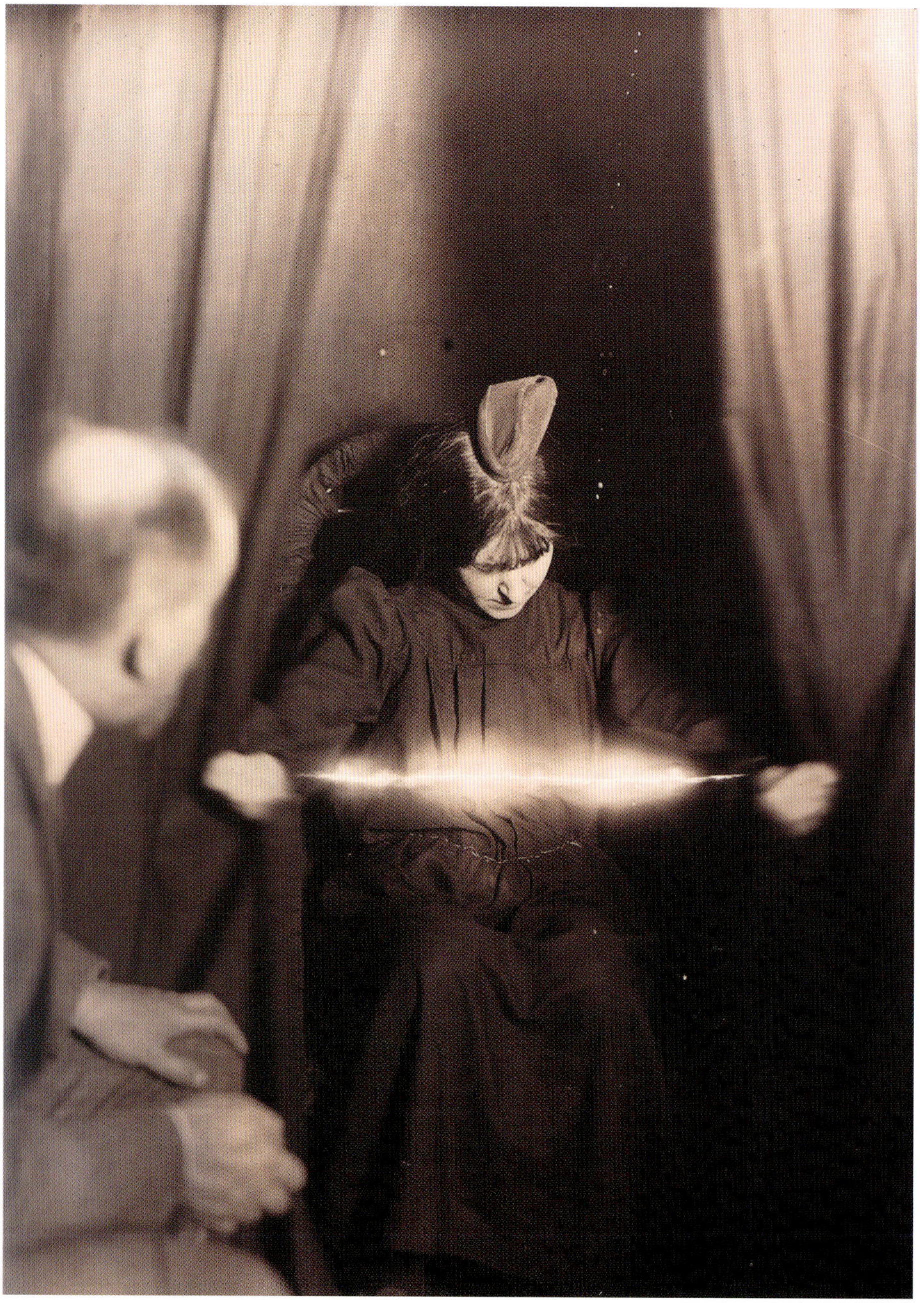

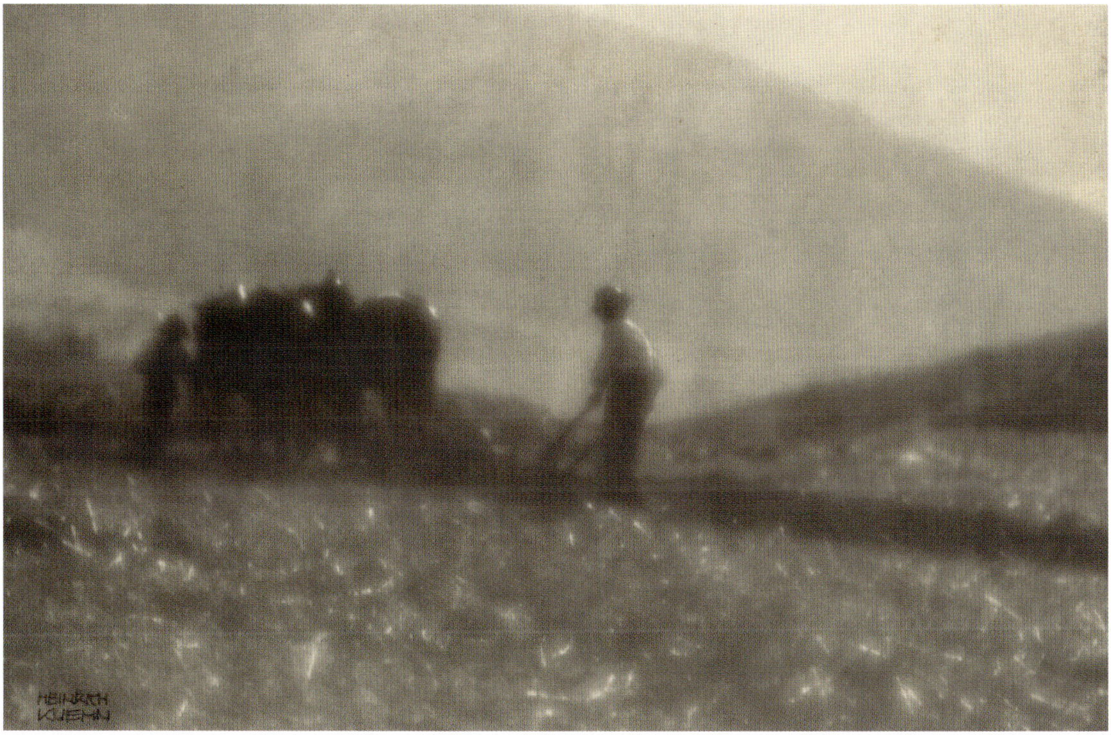

38 Heinrich Kühn, *The Plougher*, c. 1904, platinum print on parchment paper.

37 Albert von Schrenck-Notzing, *The Medium Eva C. with a Materialization on Her Head and a Luminous Apparition between Her Hands*, 17 May 1912, gelatin silver print.

children played and peasants farmed. His *The Plougher* (illus. 38) has a blurred man driving a plough nearly disappear in a glistening field seemingly composed of scratches rather than straw. To escape a chronic illness, Kühn moved to Austria, which many Germans at the time saw as having preserved the quieter and more rural Teutonic traditions lost in the north to rapid industrialization. His internationally popular works spread this dreamy vision of a lost past, a nostalgia about the landscape summed up with the word *Heimat*, roughly translated as homeland.[18] Despite this retrograde focus, however, Kühn was committed to advancing the technological progress of art photography. He contributed significantly to the platinum and gum printing technique that made his images so textual and atmospheric, and to the autochrome process developed by the Lumière brothers in France. He also made alliances with like-minded photographers in France and England, becoming a member of the Linked

Ring in London and the Photo-Club de Paris, both important associations of art photographers. His own Das Kleeblatt (Trifolium, or Cloverleaf) association included his two German collaborators Hans Watzek and Hugo Honnenberg, who both published their pictures in the American journal *Camera Work*. They too focused on the rural German landscape as a refuge. Yet the relationships they plied demonstrate a distinctly international and modern component of the movement, fully embedded in global trade and travel.

Representative of this exchange across national borders was a key participant in the Pictorialist movement, the American Alfred Stieglitz. Born in New Jersey, he travelled to Berlin where he studied with the chemistry and photography professor Hermann Vogel, who contributed regular columns in English to the important American journal *Philadelphia Photographer*. Stieglitz became, like Vogel, deeply committed to the aesthetic possibilities of photography's new technologies. He generated atmospheric pictures typical of the Pictorialists and at other times he snapped sharply focused visions. His famous *Sun's Rays-Paula, Berlin* (1889) experimented with these advances to see how advanced dry-plate emulsions, complete with Vogel's dye sensitizing of emulsion to the full spectrum of visible light, enabled the strips of light and the darker recesses of this Berlin apartment to be recorded (illus. 39).[19] For this American photographer of German-Jewish parents, his ancestral home already realized the collaboration of science and art that Emerson was concurrently theorizing in England. In the realm of contemporary art photography, Germany became an international participant with its nationally inward visions of *Heimat*.

Similar advances in photographic technology made possible the depiction of less luxurious Berlin interiors far from the countryside's purity, specifically in the city's notoriously sprawling slums. The disappointments with Germany's flash industrialization, which had provoked numerous reactions to modernity, were best represented by this vast social failure. Particularly by the 1880s, changes in the agricultural economy coupled with new job possibilities in the big cities brought rural migrants flooding into Berlin's slums and its dense, unhygienic *Mietskaserne* (tenements, or literally rent barracks). One of the largest medical insurance groups, founded after landmark health reforms pushed by Bismarck in the 1880s, inaugurated an annual survey of these

39 Alfred Stieglitz, *Sun's Rays – Paula, Berlin*, 1889, gelatin silver print (printed c. 1930).

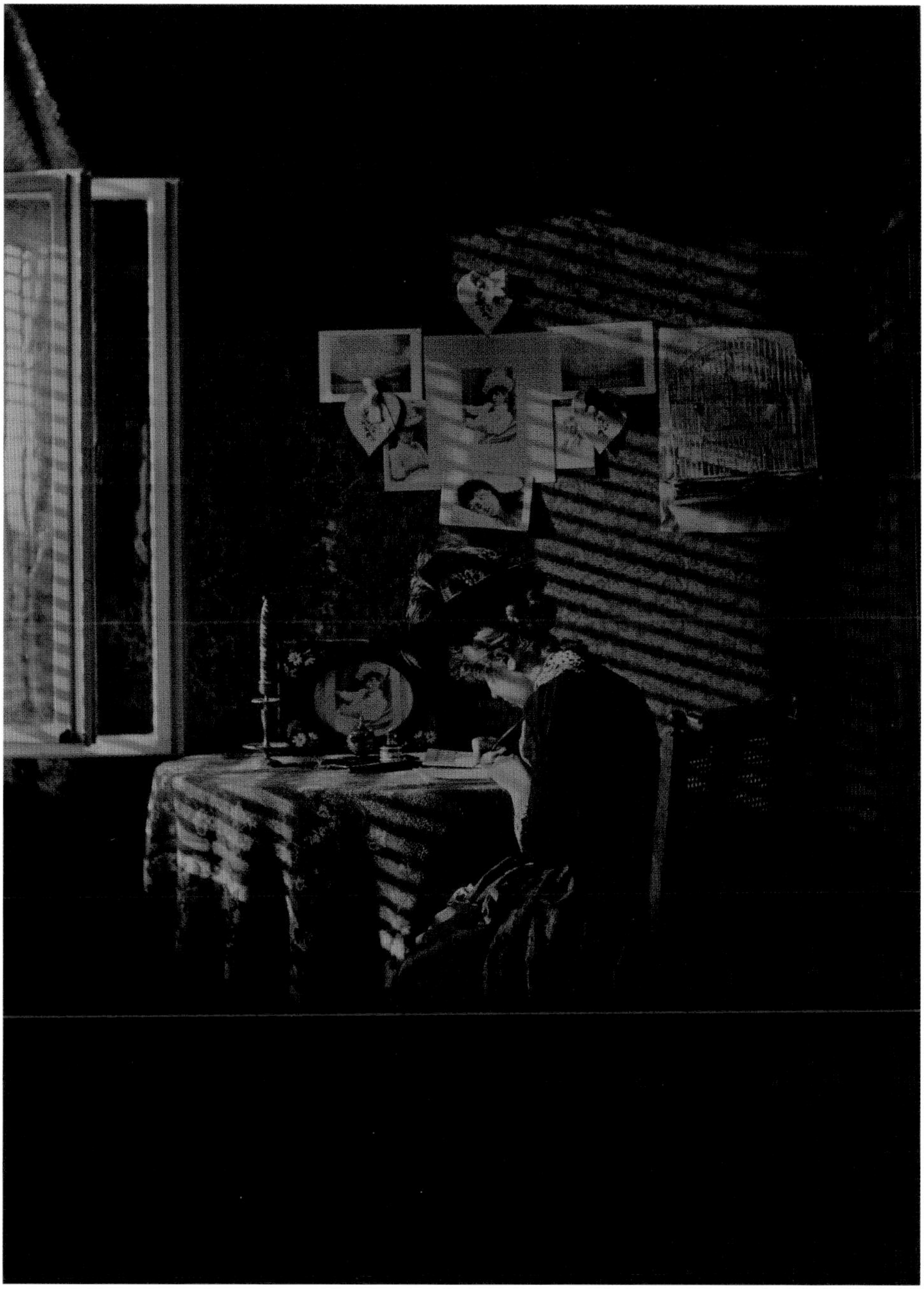

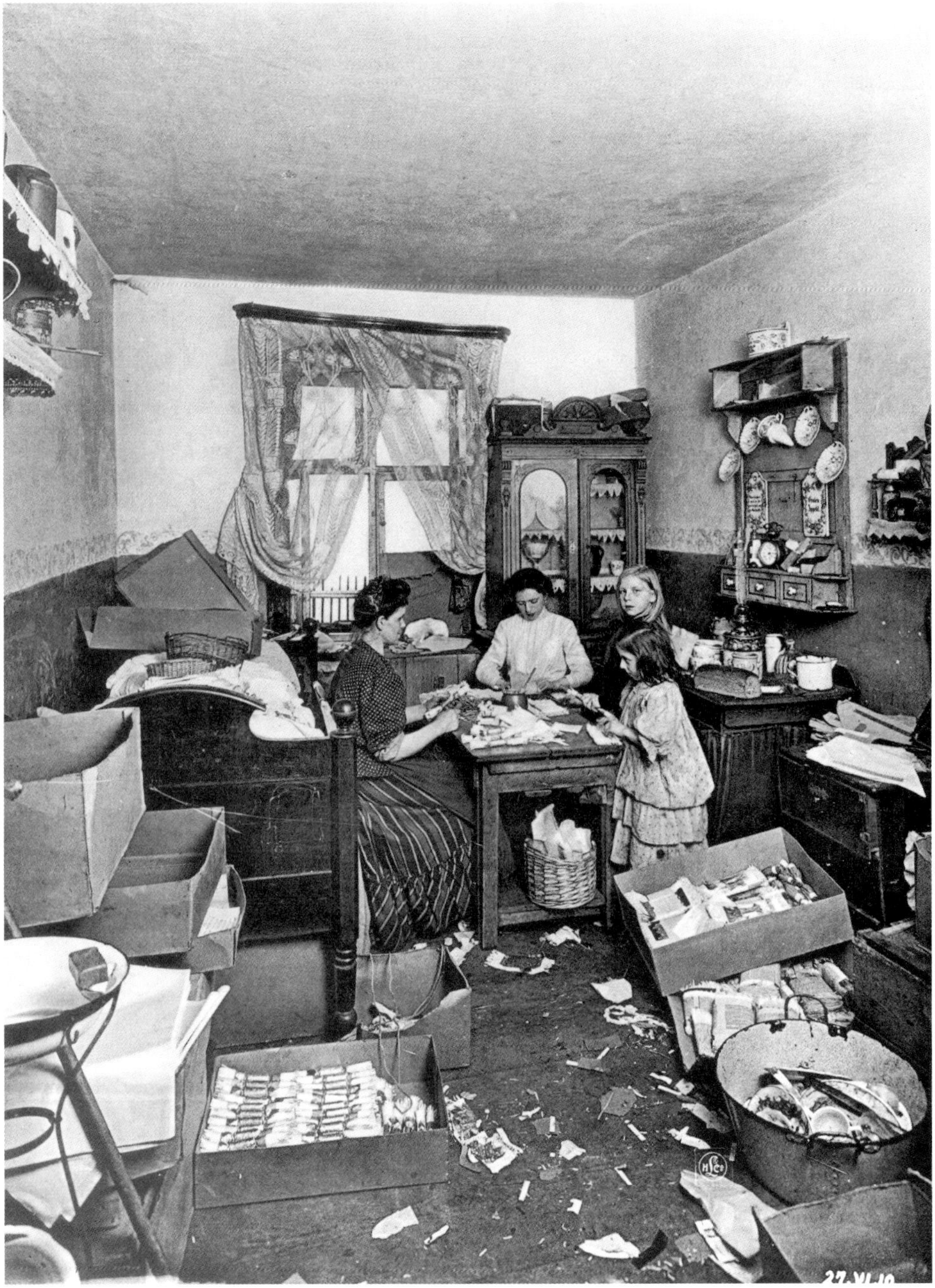

conditions just before the turn of the century. Known as *Unsere Wohnungs-Enquête* (Our Housing Survey), it was meant to illuminate the grim living conditions suffered by so many of the company's impoverished clients. In 1903 the survey introduced photography to its pages because, as Albert Kohn, director of the insurance company and its survey explained, 'we believe that some things can be better represented in this way than by the pen.'[20]

Kohn wanted the photographs, which were all taken by the same Berlin-based photography firm, to be an objective expression of the conditions expressed by the tables and statistics filling his annual survey. But observers at the time found the pictures shocking. Kurt Tucholsky, then the culture critic of the Social Democratic Party newspaper *Vorwärts*, found in one of these pictures 'filth, disorder, dirty air' (illus. 40). He focused his castigation on one picture in particular, which showed adults and their children manufacturing party poppers in their cramped space. In the left foreground of this 1911 photograph, there lies a nearly completed box of poppers. A trail of leavings leads right and back towards the family's female members, who perform their labour of manufacturing these novelties on a small table at the centre of the composition. On the left is a chaotic bed, on the right another table. As one school-age child looks toward the camera, another – younger – one stands at the work table, her gaze frozen, either by the intrusion of the camera or by the numbing burden of her ongoing tasks. This was essentially a counter image to that forged by the Reformbewegung and Germany's Pictorialists, a troubling vision of the social and economic ills that had provoked a nude escape to the *Heimat* and to an ancient, desire-infused Sicily.

More shocking still were other muck-raking images from the same year of 1911 showing the direct corporeal costs of Wilhelmine laissez-faire economic policies (illus. 41). One horrific picture in particular was shown along with many others like it at a ghastly exhibition staged during a wood worker's union congress in Berlin. It shows a mangled hand missing many digits, set against a black ground. This and the *Enquête* pictures were meant to shock contemporary Germans out of their complacency and to fight for meaningful changes in housing and labour policies. They also proposed that the idealizing vision of rural *Heimat* simply carried no currency for a vast population of contemporary compatriots. Increasingly, photography was being made and disseminated for its power of persuasion. These images in

40 Heinrich Lichte & Co, 'Berlin SO, Manteuffelstrasse 64,' halftone illustration in Albert Kohn's *Unsere Wohnungs-Enquête im Jahr 1911* (1912).

Unfallgefahren und Unfall=schutz in der Holzindustrie ::

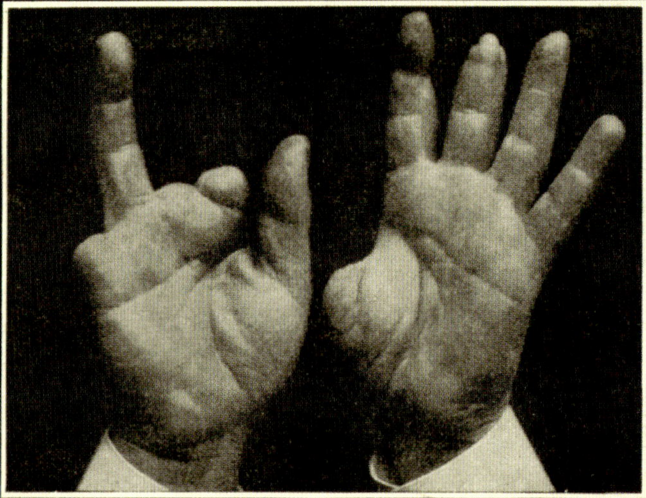

„Im Namen der Hinterbliebenen unserer Berufskollegen, die die Ma=schinen erschlagen, der Tausende von Kollegen, denen sie ihre gesunden Glieder zermalmt . . . erheben wir unsere Forderungen."

:: :: Berlin 1912 :: ::
Verlagsanstalt des Deutschen Holzarbeiter=Verbandes G.m.b.H.

41 Title page halftone illustration in the 1911 Proceedings of a Conference on 'Accident Risks and Industrial Safety in the Lumber Industry'.

particular showed the brutal economic fragmentation of the country along class lines, and the appearance of an overlooked population of poor people who seemed far from the ideal German. Amid these competing photographs of what the empire was and what it looked like, and amid the *Aprilscherze*, amusing montages, client-ordered manipulations and x-ray imagery, the country's population was finding occasion to become deeply aware of how the medium operated on perception. The coming epoch forced that awareness as never before.

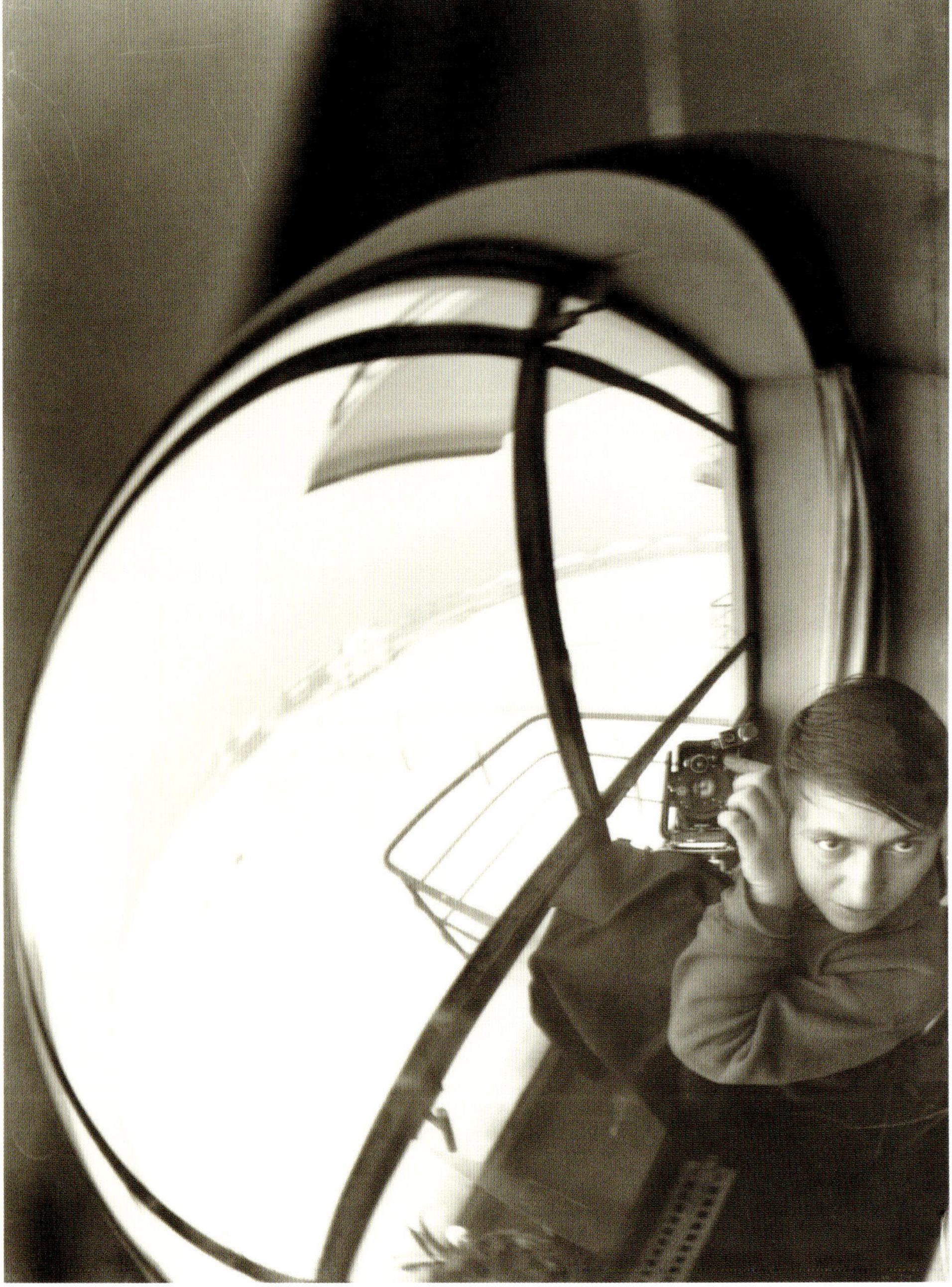

three

The Weimar Era and Photo-consciousness, 1919–1932

In 1931, the radical-left magazine publisher Willi Münzenberg levelled a complaint against his competitors that applied just as well to his own serials. By employing 'a combination of several pictures with their captions and accompanying text', he lamented, 'a skilful editor can reverse the significance of any photograph and influence a reader who lacks political sophistication in any direction he chooses.'[1] Münzenberg's misgiving about a photograph's inherently unstable yet persuasive mode of communication, especially before image-hungry audiences, typifies the medium's ambivalent reception in Germany's first republic. The late Wilhelmine era's fascination with photographic technology had already fed the broad recognition that photography was becoming the dominant form of modern image making. Now, after the First World War's traumatic disruptions, prints began rolling off innumerable handheld cameras and finding copious space in the illustrated periodicals and books that readers enthusiastically consumed. Many greeted photography as a sign of Germany's full entry into modernity, such that the medium and the veneration for it exploded, typified by the command 'Stop Reading! Look!'[2]

But with this great omnipresence and reception came the recognition that photography's representational power was treacherous. One could use prints in both laudable and misguided ways. Many photographers and critics in the Weimar era may have seen the medium as a talisman of modernity itself, a technological means of perception that could advance Germany beyond ossified modes of envisioning itself in the world. But these lessons

42 Marianne Brandt, *Self-portrait of Marianne Brandt taken in her Atelier in the Bauhaus, Dassau, Reflected in a Sphere*, 1927, gelatin silver print.

in modern perception could serve reality and fiction equally, or they could simply feed shallow commercial spectacles even as they cultivated some of the world's most exciting movements in modernist photography. Alongside this heady flood of emulsion, a tremendous corpus of essays, lessons and exhibitions encouraged the growing public to get into the game and explore photography's power for themselves. The Weimar era became a time of potent photo-consciousness, of a reflexive aesthetic concern for photography based on an indecisiveness about the medium's value and its ability to tell the truth. This self-aware hesitancy reflected the country's broader cultural, political and economic insecurities in the modern age.

Post-war Revelations

The war effort that began with the guns of August in 1914 fell apart on 3 November 1918, when sailors in the German north mutinied against their officers. Their rebelliousness spread like fire through a country that had been starved under a British shipping blockade, toppling what had essentially become a military government and leading to the kaiser's abdication. The proclamation of a parliamentary democracy followed on 9 November. Although broadly welcomed at first, this transformation was not smooth. A contributor to an advertising journal concerned with public perception wrote in late December:

> In the last few weeks so very much has occurred. First: the seemingly unshakable order collapsed overnight. Now: utopias of the latest moment stand erected and secured. And not only have the forms of politics and the constitution of the economy changed. No, all our thoughts and intentions are seized by the revolution. Now what we suddenly feel is that: everything is in motion, everything flows, we have emerged from a sudden and unmediated upheaval of all being.[3]

The German Revolution of 1918–19 made the country's first republic possible and seemed to signal a bright new future. For many, the first months of democracy brought ecstatic hope.

But violent measures taken by more extreme elements on the political Left and Right set a pattern of action and reaction that made this democracy a continual and frequently savage conflict. In fact, the era was given the name Weimar because its constitutional assembly had to meet in that more peaceful city rather than the violent Berlin. Powering these tensions were the period's subsequent tribulations, such as the assassination of high-level politicians Matthias Erzberger and Walter Rathenau, multiple failed putsches, devastating hyperinflation cresting in 1923, and parliamentary paralysis along with chronic unemployment, both exacerbated by the Wall Street collapse of 1929. The golden twenties of the Weimar era were years of hope, progress and enthusiastic experimentation, particularly in the cultural realm. But they were also characterized by deep economic despair and political tension. During the period, continual battles received a helping hand from the persuasive and often misleading use of photography before a credulous public, as Münzenberg's admonishment about illustrated periodicals suggests. But just as important for the medium's destiny in Germany was the rising public discussion *about* this persuasiveness, and the broader idea that photography could direct human perception like no other medium aside from film.

A book written in 1915 by the renowned poet and editor Ferdinand Avenarius demonstrates that, even if the vicissitudes of Weimar accelerated the interest with photography, discussions about it were already well under-way during the Great War. In that year he began opining on the subject with a volume about the problem of photographic deception among Germany's adversaries. His book was part of a broader campaign against anti-German *Hetzpropaganda* (hate propaganda), with Avenarius focusing on foreign newspapers and illustrated periodicals that had falsely offered photographic evidence of German atrocities (illus. 43). One of Avenarius's examples reproduced a Russian picture postcard from 1905 and its reissue a decade later by the French periodical *Le Mirror*. With the help of a caption in the newer version, the postcard's mother and child killed in an anti-Semitic pogrom read instead as the dead of Lodz, left by retreating Germans. The caption's French text sardonically explains: 'As in Belgium and France, the champions of *Kultur* have given the inhabitants of Russian Poland an accurate picture of German domination.' Leading German voices had in fact repeatedly declared

Diese Linie bezeichnet die untere Grenze des in „Le Miroir“ abgeschnittenen Streifens mit der Schrift.

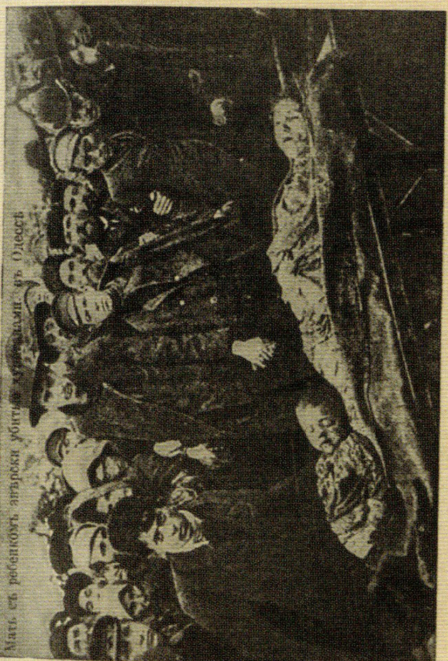

Etwas vergrößerte Wiedergabe einer Postkarte, die von russischen Juden nach dem Odessaer Pogrom von 1905 verbreitet wurde. Die Aufschrift besagt: „Mutter und Kind von Banden grausam erschlagen zu Odessa.“

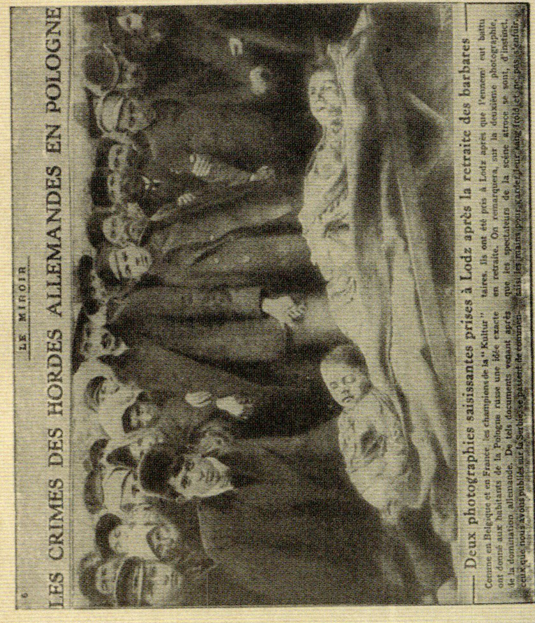

6 LE MIROIR

LES CRIMES DES HORDES ALLEMANDES EN POLOGNE

Deux photographies saisissantes prises à Lodz après la retraite des barbares

Comme en Belgique et en France, les champions de la "Kultur" ont donné aux habitants de la Pologne russe une idée exacte de la domination allemande. De tels documents venant après ceux que nous avons publiés sur la Serbie, se passent de commentaires. Ils ont été pris à Lodz après que l'ennemi eut battu en retraite. On remarquera, sur la deuxième photographie, que les spectateurs de la scène atroce se sont, d'instinct, saisi les mains pour garder leur sang froid et ne pas s'enfuir.

Dasselbe russische Pogrombild als Dokument einer deutschen Schandtat in Lodz, erschienen als großes Bild in „Le Miroir“ von Mitte Februar 1915 und in anderen illustrierten Blättern aller Erdteile. Beweis der bewußten Fälschung: Der Streifen mit der russischen Aufschrift oben ist von der Postkarte weggeschnitten.

Überschrift: „DIE SCHANDTATEN DEUTSCHER HORDEN IN POLEN.“ — Unterschrift. „Zwei ergreifende Photographien, aufgenommen zu Lodz nach dem Rückzug der Barbaren. Wie in Belgien und Frankreich haben die Vorkämpfer der „Kultur“ den Bewohnern von Russisch-Polen eine klare Idee von deutscher Herrschaft gegeben. Solche Dokumente nach denen, die wir bereits aus Serbien veröffentlicht haben, bedürfen keines Kommentars mehr. Ihre Aufnahme erfolgte zu Lodz, nachdem der Feind zum Rückzug genötigt war. Man wird auf der zweiten Photographie nicht übersehen, daß die Zuschauer der gräßlichen Szene sich unwillkürlich die Hände gereicht haben, um ruhig Blut zu bewahren und nicht davonzulaufen.“

the war effort to be a defence of the country's culture. But the French caption and appropriated image suggest that a barbarous reality lay underneath these assertions. In his pamphlet where this comparison appeared, *Propaganda und Wahrheit* (Propaganda and Truth), Avenarius tried to forge a corrective to these uses of photography by introducing a range of further examples. Here and elsewhere he appealed to his readers to become vigilant before what they see. In other words, he hoped to popularize a critical reception of photography that would dismantle 'the lie as a means of war' and disallow 'the cultivation of hatred between peoples'. He had anticipated the battles of mass-reproduced photography that would animate the subsequent Weimar era.[4]

After the war, this critique that Avenarius helped cultivate became a broader climate of cynicism as Germans learned of how their own government and military had long deceived them about the course of the conflict. For many citizens, fed on a diet of photographically illustrated magazines and postcards celebrating the latest German military successes, the country's defeat came as a total surprise. Once the revolution toppled Wilhelmine authority, new publications detailed this deception. They bore titles such as *Wie wir belogen wurden* (How We Were Lied To, 1918) by Munich-based writer and political revolutionary Kurt Mühsam, and *Die grosse Zeit der Lüge* (The Grand Epoch of Lies, 1921) by politician and journalist Hellmut von Gerlach. These accounts stressed themes of deception, mistrust and credulity, and they frequently employed the word 'lie'. The Weimar era's extraordinary developments in photography arose – in part – from a growing enthusiasm for this mechanical means of making pictures. But these conditions also emerged when an environment of deep suspicion about public information and modernity met the medium most often associated with evidence and dispassionate objectivity: photography.[5] The period's great advances with the camera were in part a product of this deep ambivalence.

The illustrated press offered one of the more conspicuous public forums for airing the tensions between enthusiasm for modern technologies and suspicion about the veracity of evidence in an era of uncertainty. Weekly news magazines enthusiastically availed themselves of post-war press freedoms, larding their pages with *Bildreportagen* (pictorial reports, to cite one typical neologism) on events and people who, only weeks earlier during the war, had been utterly banished from the press. The widely circulating *Berliner Illustrirte*

43 Halftone image juxtaposition in Ferdinand Avenarius, 'Propaganda and Truth, vol. I: The Photographic Documents', from the series *The Powers in Global Madness: Writings for Genuine Freedom*, originally printed in a 1915 wartime pamphlet.

Zeitung / BIZ (Berlin Illustrated Magazine), for example, reported excitedly on the agents of the revolution in the first two months after the armistice, scarcely captioning their quickly gathered pictures of agitators and rebellious soldiers. It was as if the speed of rapidly unfolding events made such framing impossible, leaving events seemingly to transcribe themselves. As right-wing paramilitary troops employed by the government violently suppressed the uprising, the same magazine increasingly reported from the urban battlefield with spectacular relish. In these subsequent arrays of photo-saturated reporting, each picture helps build a scene of the chaos supposedly generated by left-wing radicals, while the troops appear to restore order. Utterly new for Germany's mass periodicals, such layouts effectively made the *BIZ* and its competitors national photo albums of the revolution. For the great majority of stunned readers who had not witnessed the isolated fighting at first hand, the revolution was its photographic representation.[6] Yet, because this flood of emulsion crested during a moment of deep suspicion and cynicism, disseminators and consumers of the medium often found themselves torn by mixed feelings about photography's value. It could persuade with the captivating power of spectacle, void of political relevance. But it could also appeal with a specific and rather naked agenda. That motive could be one you shared, but the next day it could be one you opposed.

This photographic conundrum of the early Weimar period found one of its best critical expressions in another illustrated periodical established as an alternative to the mainstream commercial press. Titled *Die freie Welt* (Free World), it was published by the Independent Social Democratic Party (the Unabhängige Sozialdemokratische Partei Deutschlands, USPD) as a weekly supplement to its daily paper, *Die Freiheit* (Freedom). It thereby built on the tradition of party papers that dominated Germany's nineteenth-century press. But its critical use of photography was new. The magazine's editor was the Prague-born journalist Felix Stössinger, who had served in the German military news service during the war drafting propaganda reports. He later wrote about this experience in an article for his magazine suitably titled 'How the German People Were Lied To'.[7] His mission with this radical-left periodical was to address similar deceptions now being foisted on the public – particularly the working class – by the mainstream illustrated press. As an unsigned editorial in the magazine's first issue of 1 May 1919 formulated it:

> While the bourgeoisie possesses the means for widely distributed propaganda, patriotic brainwashing and intellectual enslavement in its numerous illustrated magazines, German workers have still not been able to create any corresponding organ. Thus the many hundreds of thousands who grab an illustrated paper for relaxation and stimulation are forced to buy papers, which are alien to them and only serve capitalist speculation and enrichment . . . *Die freie Welt* will be the illustrated paper of the proletariat.[8]

With these terms, *Die freie Welt* credited the mainstream illustrated press with a perception-shaping capacity so powerful as to constitute an enslavement of its working-class audience. This was the force increasingly attributed to photography in the subsequent years, whether for bad or good.

One of Stössinger's editorial strategies was to turn the purpose of a photograph on its head so as to instruct readers in the critical reception of images. For example, one cover page reproduces the celebrated picture of a worker hanging thirty floors above New York City's harbour, but not as a further tribute to the man's heroism and America's breakneck modernization. Instead its efficient caption frames the photo as a condemnation of contemporary working conditions. 'The life of a worker is full of hardship and danger,' the text intones. Another visual strategy was to juxtapose two photographs so as to contrast the familiar with the overlooked. In one feature, a picture showing the burial of a general stands next to the horrific collecting of soldier corpses (illus. 44). 'How a General from the Command is Buried', runs the caption showing the grand pomp of his entombment, followed by 'and how those massacred on the front are consigned to a mass grave'. The second caption describes a shocking photo of corpses being piled sky-high onto a wagon. The first shot was the sort regularly available to the press during the war, whereas the second was absolutely banned from publication, making the mass casualties of common soldiers on the front effectively invisible. The magazine employed this juxtaposition to reveal the class-based injustice exercised by the Wilhelmine military, the public use of photography to hide – rather than expose – that inequity, and the grotesque corporeal consequences of invisible military bias.

Even more piquant were the photo-caricatures by satirist Karl Holtz that poked sardonic fun at what the magazine perceived to be the misuse of the

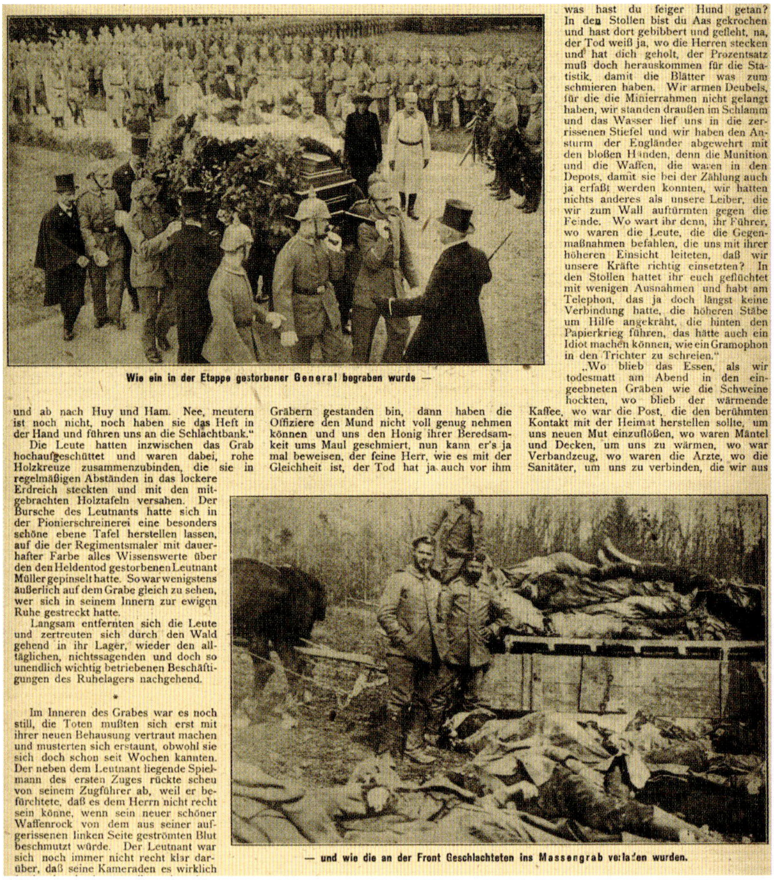

Wie ein in der Etappe gestorbener General begraben wurde —

und ab nach Huy und Ham. Nee, meutern ist noch nicht, noch haben sie das Heft in der Hand und führen uns an die Schlachtbank.“

Die Leute hatten inzwischen das Grab hochaufgeschüttet und waren dabei, rohe Holzkreuze zusammenzubinden, die sie in regelmäßigen Abständen in das lockere Erdreich steckten und mit den mitgebrachten Holztafeln versahen. Der Bursche des Leutnants hatte sich in der Pionierschreinerei eine besonders schöne ebene Tafel herstellen lassen, auf die der Regimentsmaler mit dauerhafter Farbe alles Wissenswerte über den den Heldentod gestorbenen Leutnant Müller gepinselt hatte. So war wenigstens äußerlich auf dem Grabe gleich zu sehen, wer sich in seinem Innern zur ewigen Ruhe gestreckt hatte.

Langsam entfernten sich die Leute und zertreuten sich durch den Wald gehend in ihr Lager, wieder den alltäglichen, nichtssagenden und doch so unendlich wichtig betriebenen Beschäftigungen des Ruhelagers nachgehend.

*

Im Inneren des Grabes war es noch still, die Toten mußten sich erst mit ihrer neuen Behausung vertraut machen und musterten sich erstaunt, obwohl sie sich doch schon seit Wochen kannten. Der neben dem Leutnant liegende Spielmann des ersten Zuges rückte scheu von seinem Zugführer ab, weil er befürchtete, daß es dem Herrn nicht recht sein könne, wenn sein neuer schöner Waffenrock von dem aus seiner aufgerissenen linken Seite geströmten Blut beschmutzt würde. Der Leutnant war sich noch immer nicht recht klar darüber, daß seine Kameraden es wirklich

Gräbern gestanden bin, dann haben die Offiziere den Mund nicht voll genug nehmen können und uns den Honig ihrer Beredsamkeit ums Maul geschmiert, nun kann er's ja mal beweisen, der feine Herr, wie es mit der Gleichheit ist, der Tod hat ja auch vor ihm

was hast du feiger Hund getan? In den Stollen bist du Aas gekrochen und hast dort gebibbert und gefleht, na, der Tod weiß ja, wo die Herren stecken und hat dich geholt, der Prozentsatz muß doch herauskommen für die Statistik, damit die Blätter was zum schmieren haben. Wir armen Deubels, für die die Minierrahmen nicht gelangt haben, wir standen draußen im Schlamm und das Wasser lief uns in die zerrissenen Stiefel und wir haben den Ansturm der Engländer abgewehrt mit den bloßen Händen, denn die Munition und die Waffen, die waren in den Depots, damit sie bei der Zählung auch ja erfaßt werden konnten, wir hatten nichts anderes als unsere Leiber, die wir zum Wall auftürmten gegen die Feinde. Wo wart ihr denn, ihr Führer, wo waren die Leute, die die Gegenmaßnahmen befahlen, die uns mit ihrer höheren Einsicht leiteten, daß wir unsere Kräfte richtig einsetzten? In den Stollen hattet ihr euch geflüchtet mit wenigen Ausnahmen und habt am Telephon, das ja doch längst keine Verbindung hatte, die höheren Stäbe um Hilfe angekräht, die hinten den Papierkrieg führen, das hätte auch ein Idiot machen können, wie ein Gramophon in den Trichter zu schreien.“

„Wo blieb das Essen, als wir todesmatt am Abend in den eingeebneten Gräben wie die Schweine hockten, wo blieb der wärmende Kaffee, wo war die Post, die den berühmten Kontakt mit der Heimat herstellen sollte, um uns neuen Mut einzuflößen, wo waren Mäntel und Decken, um uns zu wärmen, wo war Verbandzeug, wo waren die Ärzte, wo die Sanitäter, um uns zu verbinden, die wir aus

— und wie die an der Front Geschlachteten ins Massengrab verladen wurden.

44 Halftone print illustration, ‘How a General from the Command is Buried – and How Those Massacred on the Front are Consigned to a Mass Grave’, in an August 1920 issue of *Die freie Welt*.

medium in the mainstream press, that sworn enemy of *Die freie Welt*. In one 1920 contribution to *Die freie Welt* titled ‘The Council Dictatorship in Berlin: A German Nationalist Election Tale’ (illus. 44), Holtz altered photographs with traditional touching-up techniques. Through such doctoring, he narrated the fevered dream of a right-wing nationalist in which the radical left topples the national government, communist goons are released from city prisons to run riot, the doomed President Ebert is guillotined and his head sold on the black market, and the city’s radical working women detonate the mayor of Berlin into a curious cloud of body parts and newspaper headlines. As the feature suggested with photos, captions and extraordinary varieties of montage, these were the sort of imaginings spurred on by anti-left propaganda and the photojournalism of magazines like the *BIZ*. Yet despite its critical and inventive use of the medium, the magazine also employed photography in uncritical ways to enthusiastically laud its party's leaders and deliver overwrought evidence of living and working conditions among the country's working poor. Stössinger and his contributors, in other words, approached photography with strongly mixed feelings.

Die freie Welt ran for only one and a half years before the USPD dissolved as a party and closed its press. Yet the magazine's pages, rich in pictures and pictorial criticism, fully registered the photographic conditions of early Weimar. In the period's general climate of conflicting hope and despair, *Die freie Welt* could lean heavily on photographic messaging even as its editor, contributors and others worried that the technology was overwhelming

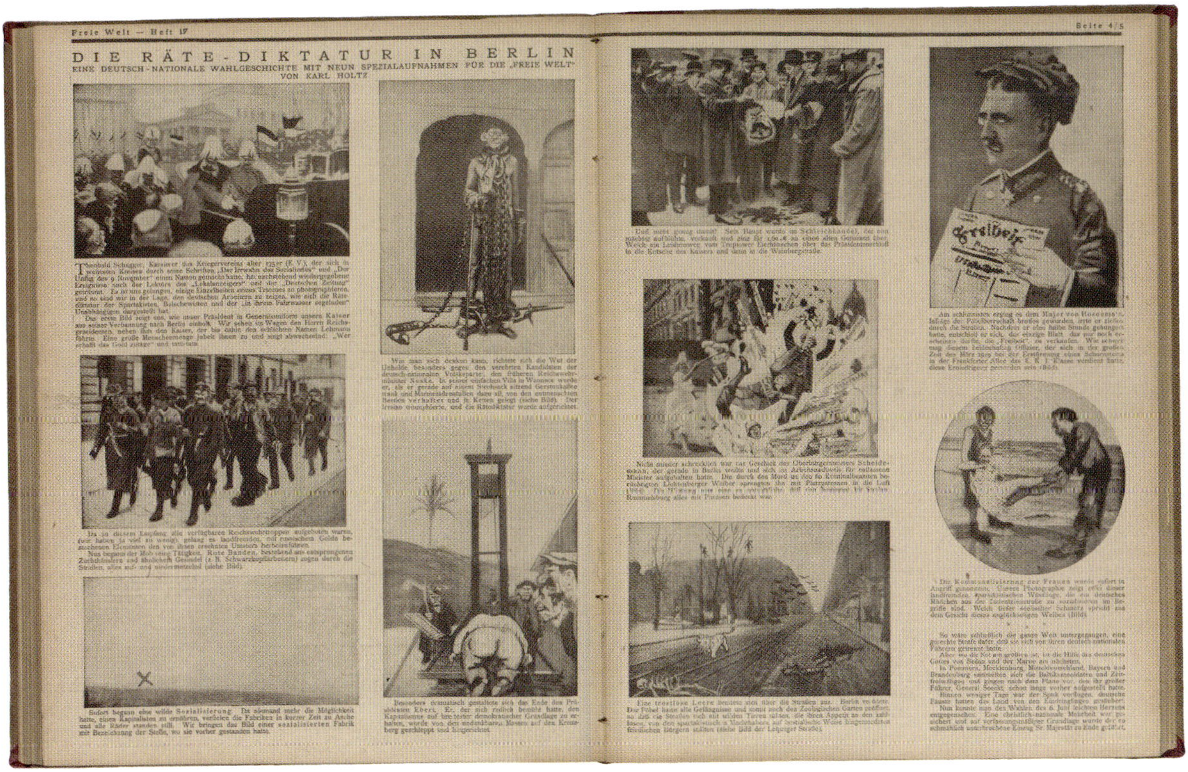
Freie Welt — Heft 17

DIE RÄTE-DIKTATUR IN BERLIN

EINE DEUTSCH-NATIONALE WAHLGESCHICHTE MIT NEUN SPEZIALAUFNAHMEN FÜR DIE „FREIE WELT" VON KARL HOLTZ

45 Karl Holtz, halftone print illustration, 'The Council Dictatorship in Berlin: A German Nationalist Election Tale', in a May 1920 issue of *Die freie Welt*.

human perception, rendering the eye a passive threshold of persuasion. The product of this ambivalence was a reinvention of the picture press as both a deluge of photographs and – as in *Die freie Welt* – a lesson in navigating that flood.

Photography and the Avant-garde

Illustrated papers may have been carefully watching each others' use of photography, as did broad audiences of readers. But avant-garde artists were also looking at these pages, often with the same ambivalence. Berlin's Club Dada, for example, found itself nearly obsessed with deceptive uses of photography in the press during the war and the subsequent revolution. But the members of this rambunctiously countercultural group nonetheless embraced the technology as a modern and objective form of image making that could re-engage a frequently isolated modern art with the tumultuous times. For instance, the Dada member John Heartfield (born Helmut Herzfeld) had learned from the war 'that you can lie to people with photos, really lie to them'.[9] Yet his brother Wieland Herzfelde (born Herzfeld) lauded the medium in a Dada exhibition catalogue text, explaining that it, along with film, 'provided people with a view of things . . . incomparably better and more completely than painters of any era'.[10] This apparent contradiction mirrored the sentiments of *Die freie Welt* and established the complex understanding with which other Weimar-era artists approached photography in the years to come.

Born in 1916 in a low-rent cabaret in Zurich, Dada largely drew from a community of exiled artists and writers of various countries who had fled to neutral Switzerland to escape the war, which they saw as senseless slaughter and an indictment of Western civilization. Dada's great contribution came in its use of popular culture to reinvigorate fine art, to make art fresher, more accessible, more fully expressive of 'this unutterable age', as Hugo Ball, one of Dada's founding members, explained.[11] One year after its Swiss birth, Dada landed in wartime Berlin transplanted by one of its co-founders, Richard Huelsenbeck. Always politically motivated at some level, the movement developed an expressly politicized character in the starved and depressed

German capital. 'Instead of continuing to produce art,' as Huelsenbeck declared in 1920, 'Dada . . . went out and found an adversary.'[12] It was this political attack, largely targeting dominant cultural values, that brought Berlin's Club Dada to what many artists viewed as the quotidian, non-aesthetic but highly communicative medium of photography.

Three of the group's members in particular focused squarely on photography in mass print during the revolution: Heartfield, his brother Herzfelde and their close friend, the painter George Grosz. All three despaired that the new German Communist Party, which they supported, seemed unable to defend itself against a barrage of propaganda. In response, they decided to wage a counter-campaign by founding an illustrated periodical. Titled *Jedermann sein eigner Fussball* (Everyone His Own Football), the first and only issue punned on how the everyday man and woman were being kicked about by reactionary forces, as the title figure sporting the body of a ball suggests (illus. 46). Below that, the cover offered a satirical montage that spread photographed portraits of the country's Social Democratic leadership and of the reactionary wartime General Ludendorff (among two other important men) across a folding fan. These proud political important visages, shown in photographs published in other illustrated papers, become the stuff of a beauty pageant. 'Contest. Who is the most beautiful?' asks the feature's title, while the words below style the array as 'German masculine beauty, part 1'. Working squarely in the realm of publicity rather than fine art, Heartfield, Herzfelde and Grosz satirized their political opponents as attention-hungry and vain. But they also drew attention to the role photography played in – as they saw it – falsely gussying up this leadership as strong and even imperial in the Wilhelmine pictorial vein. The artists were essentially underscoring

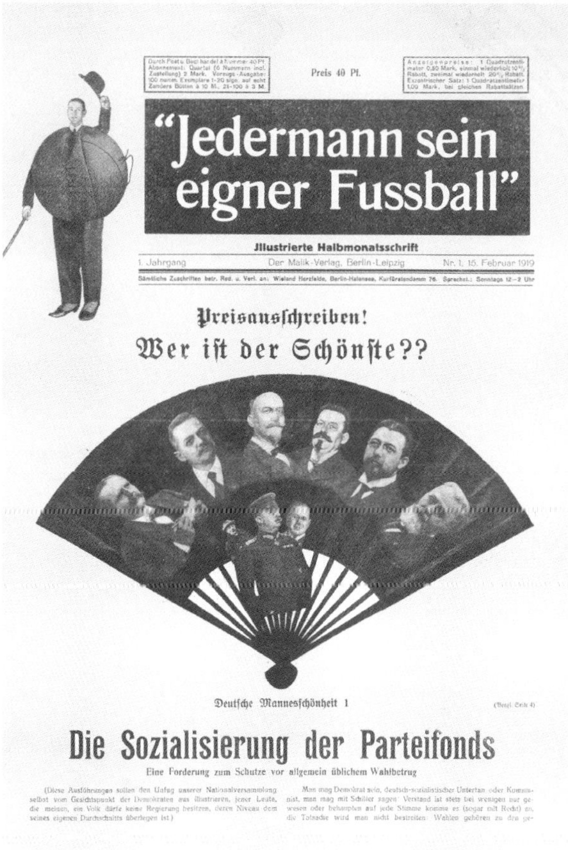

Preis 40 Pf.

"Jedermann sein eigner Fussball"

Jllustrierte Halbmonatsschrift

1. Jahrgang — Der Malik-Verlag, Berlin-Leipzig — Nr. 1; 15. Februar 1919

Preisausschreiben!
Wer ist der Schönste??

Deutsche Mannesschönheit 1

Die Sozialisierung der Parteifonds

Eine Forderung zum Schutze vor allgemein üblichem Wahlbetrug

46 John Heartfield (typography, graphic design and photomontage) and George Grosz (photomontage), 'Contest! Who is the Most Beautiful? German Masculine Beauty 1', on the cover of *Jedermann sein eigner Fussball*, no. 1 (15 February 1920), halftone print.

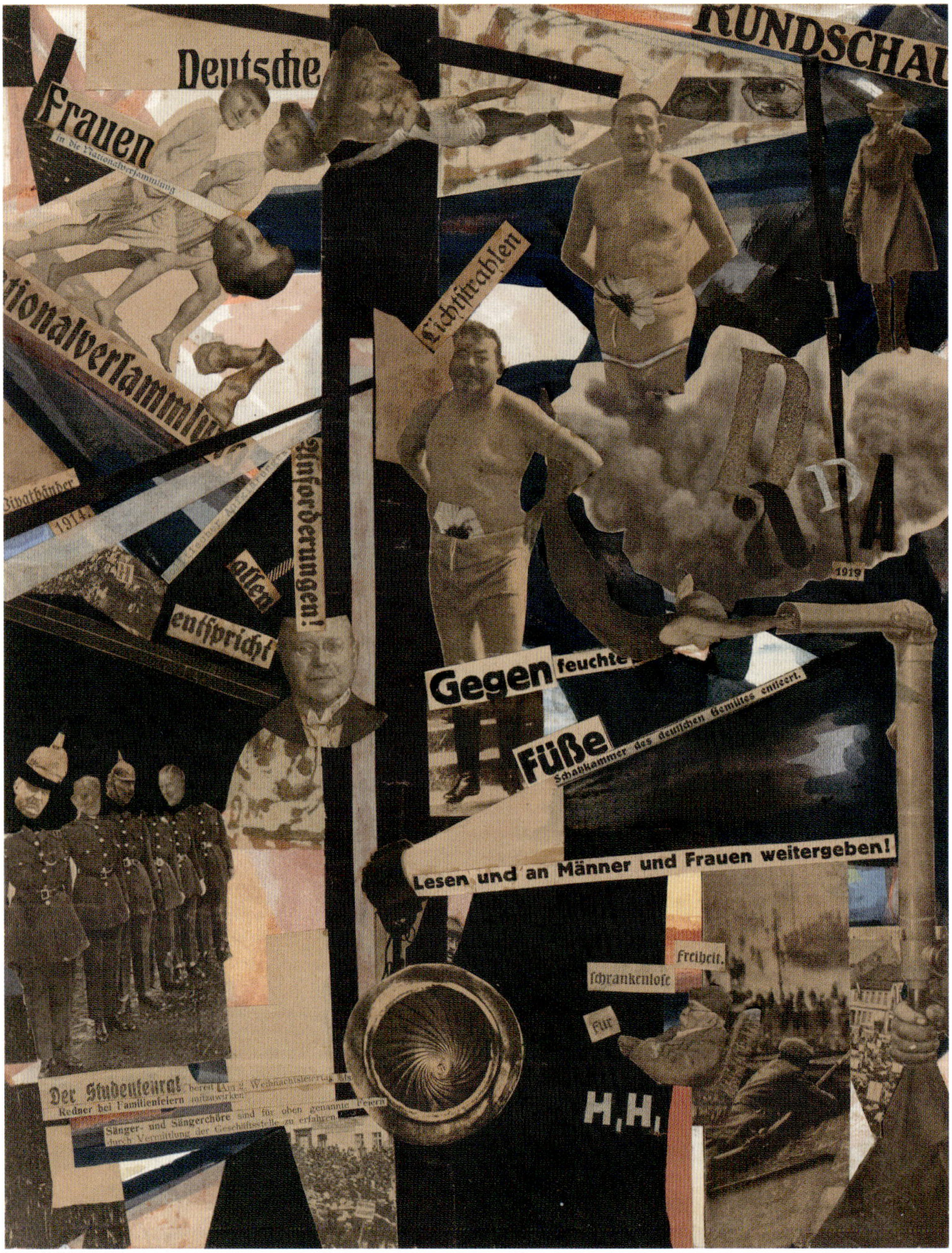
Deutsche
RUNDSCHAU
Frauen
Lichtstrahlen
Anforderungen!
allen
entspricht
1914.
1919
Gegen
feuchte
Füße
Lesen und an Männer und Frauen weitergeben!
Freiheit.
schrankenlose
für
H.H.
Der Studentenrat

photography's unstable meaning, the capacity of any one print to become a football kicked back and forth by competing parties in the sort of image campaign that had become modernity's new form of warfare. They had critically transformed earlier montage practices of advertising and soldier portraits into deeply cutting satire.

A year later, after the revolution had been soundly squelched, these men, along with Berlin Dada's other members, began making sharply disjointed photomontages that proffered the very impossibility of coherent meaning in a time of political and cultural reaction. These pictures constituted a strike against the growing acceptance of the new Weimar status quo, and an attack on narratives of peace, prosperity and stability that enabled this state of affairs. Hannah Höch's *Dada Rundschau* (Dada Review, illus. 47) explodes the sense of a consolidating post-war social order by taking mass-reproduced photographs, snipped from the popular press, and arranging them according to a logic of satire and disruption. The same pictures that increasingly made sense of current events for millions of readers in illustrated magazines here become the scarcely digested informational nourishment of the moment, cut loose from the stomach of the body politic and rendered unproductive of clear, pre-digested meaning. Höch's montage not only pokes fun at the country's new leaders by scrambling and even feminizing their images as mediated in the picture press, but she also attacks standard photography itself as an agent of disseminating reactionary belief systems. Höch and Dada's other members felt that these ruptured montages actually reinvented the medium's realism, making photography more representative of the troubled times by subjecting its surface to the physical battering and jumbling that citizens experienced on the tumultuous urban street. Critics were shocked by these montages and complained bitterly about what such compositions said of the era's cultural decline, essentially proving Dada's point. The group's photomontages pummelled human perception of the world by employing photography and scissors in tandem. This new way of thinking of the medium, as an unusually powerful way of shaping perception, became photography's call in the years to come.

47 Hannah Höch, *Dada Review*, 1919, photomontage with gouache and watercolour on cardboard. The depiction in the *Berliner Illustrirte Zeitung* of two politicians, Friedrich Ebert and Karl Noske, in swimsuits caused a scandal, which Höch revisits.

Die Neue Sachlichkeit – A New Realism

The crises of the early Weimar years reached their climax with the great hyperinflation of 1923, which resulted – in part – from the over-printing of money to pay the indemnities demanded by the Versailles Treaty. Life savings disappeared and salaries quickly meant nothing as the cost of everyday commodities exploded, such that a loaf of bread cost trillions of marks. Starting in October 1923, the Weimar government introduced a currency reform to stabilize the economy and the country entered a period of relative prosperity. The alternating hope, disillusionment and disorientation that Dada's photomontage expressed now seemed to subside in favour of a cool and sober disposition that came to be known as *die neue Sachlichkeit*, roughly translated as the New Objectivity.[13] Gustav Hartlaub, the museum curator widely credited with this coinage, explained in 1925 that the 'unbridled intensity' commonly associated with Expressionism and Dada in art had given way to a 'new will to objectivity', to dispassionate forms of observation that were expressed in a realist or harshly veristic mode of representation. Hartlaub had painting in mind when he wrote of contemporary artists who were now 'disillusioned, sobered, often resigned to the point of cynicism'.[14] In essence, the Neue Sachlichkeit may have come to reflect a more level-headed approach toward images. But his stress on disillusion and cynicism betrays an underlying equivocation about the value of such images that would also come to characterize the reception of straight photography at the era's twilight.

His description of this larger national disposition toward cool objectivity came to be closely associated with photography, the medium that appeared to be this mood's closest visual analogue.[15] So thoroughly was the camera perceived as the new aesthetic model that by 1926, design professor Heinrich Wieynck could suggest that, 'photography, generally speaking, no longer imitates art, rather art imitates photography.'[16] Behind this conviction lay the burgeoning and hopeful belief that the medium reported on the world in all its detail far better than any other form of representation, and it did so with dispassionate neutrality. As photographer Albert Renger-Patzsch wrote in 1929: 'photography works faster, and with greater precision and greater objectivity than the hand of the artist.'[17] Among other things, such words

48 Albert Renger-Patzsch, *Kenper Blast Furnace Plant, Herrenwyk*, 1927, gelatin silver print.

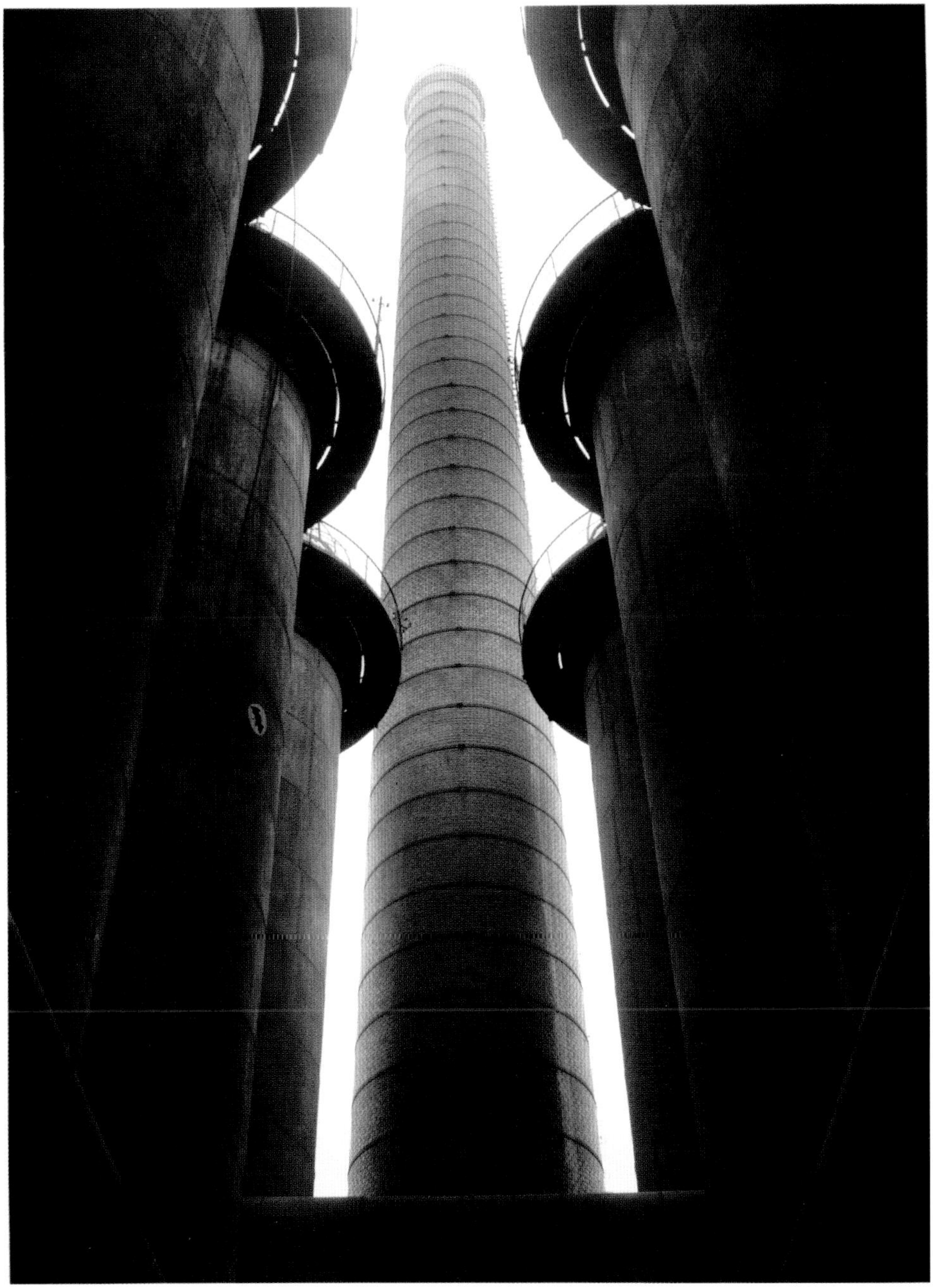

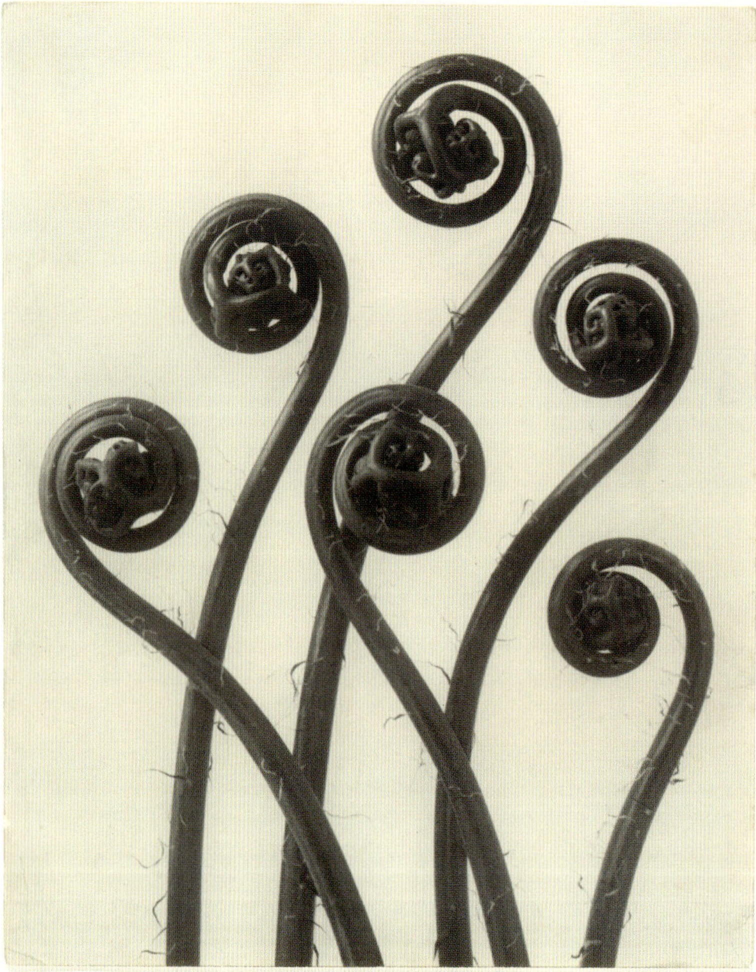

49 Karl Blossfeldt, *Adiantum pedatum* ('American Maidenhair Fern. Young Rolled-up Fronds Enlarged 8 Times'), before 1928, gelatin silver print.

formed a rebuke to the soft-focused and hazy Pictorialism of photographers such as Heinrich Kühn. Pictorialist images seemed to ape painting and deny the mechanically and chemically based precision of contemporary photographic technologies. Their subject matter also seemed drawn from an earlier epoch of tradition-bound society. By contrast, the sharply focused shots of faces, architecture, plants and machine-made objects typical of Neue Sachlichkeit photography, often taken with dramatic close-ups and unusual vantage points, came to characterize a suitably modernist imagery for a technologically advancing and prosperous Germany.

Even at the time, Renger-Patzsch's pictures were understood as the most representative of this aesthetic tendency in photography. His *Kenper Blast Furnace Plant, Herrenwyk* from 1927 concentrates its sharp focus appropriately enough on modern industry, the symmetrical vents and colossal chimney of the stoves suggesting mechanical prowess and efficiency (illus. 48). But his closely framed and scaly picture of an *Adder's Head* from 1925 proposes a similar deftness of nature to assemble detail-resplendent creatures, a proposition also made of his precise photographs of plants. Renger-Patzsch employed the camera's reproductive dexterity to foreground surface texture, to play with light and shadow, and, in turn, to stress his object's materiality nearly to the point of abstraction. In so doing, he exploited the precision of photographic technology to highlight an object's defining formal features and thereby reveal things about the manmade and natural worlds that otherwise escaped the unaided eye. His clear and objective manner of achieving this distillation was understood as modern. The critic Wilhelm Lotz observed that Renger-Patzsch's 'photographs teach us an entirely new way to see' such that 'we learn to see the thing, so to speak, as it corresponds to our times.'[18] What these *sachlich* or objective pictures suggested with modern tools, and that otherwise went unnoticed, was an underlying order that united man-made and natural creations.[19] Such visions of order could help salve the actual political and cultural fragmentation of the times, a therapy made possible by the conscious employment of photography's power over perception.

The idea that detail-rich photographs of objects could reveal an intangible regularity united much Neue Sachlichkeit photography. Karl Blossfeldt's famous microscopic photographs of plants, such as his *Adiantum pedatum*, similarly confused the distinction between the natural and artificial, and proposed an underlying accord between both (illus. 49). The plant's swirling tendons recall the wrought iron decoration of Art Nouveau design (Jugendstil in Germany), while the central portion of each twist seems to be a small hand clutching a bud. Despite looking as appropriately modern as Renger-Patzsch's work, Blossfeldt's photographs largely date to the turn of the last century, when he produced them as visual aids for his students in the

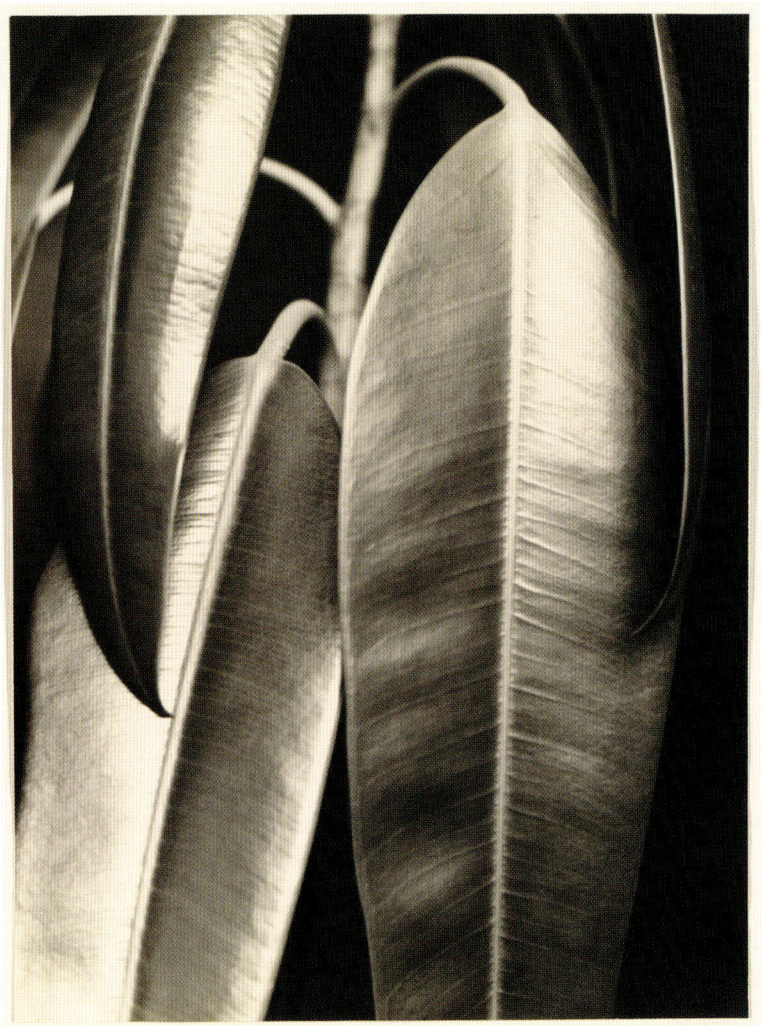

50 Aenne Biermann, *Ficus elastica*, 1926, gelatin silver print.

art academy where he was a professor. When he later reprinted the negatives during the Weimar period under the sign of objectivity, he often retouched his prints by emphasizing lines or highlighting light and shadow, altering what were otherwise supposed to be straight, unmanipulated photographs.[20] In a sweet irony, he made his photographs from the Pictorialist era *sachlich* by employing interventions typical of the Pictorialist hand. Perhaps better representative of the mode were Aenne Biermann's exceedingly close-framed photographs of plants, such as her *Ficus elastica* of 1926, which effectively transforms a potted plant into a shimmering architecture of shiny surfaces and stems (illus. 50). Biermann was a major proponent of this new objective style and was exhibited widely at the time.

Portrait studio photographer August Sander also hoped to convey an intangible order in his mode of objective work that he called 'exact photography'. In a project that he began before the war and came to title *Citizens of the 20th Century*, he orchestrated carefully posed portraits of people from various social and professional strata, such as his *Bricklayer* (illus. 51) and *Secretary at Westdeutschen Rundfunk* (illus. 52). Sander held that modernity produced its social breakdown along an arc running from the land-bound farmer, up to the artist and intellectual, and down again to the urban unemployed. His portraits, for which he worked collaboratively with his subjects, visualize that arc by offering the typical look of each of that bow's corporeal segments. Wearing clothes that identify him as working class, the bricklayer conveys masculine confidence as he stares intently from a brow tilted toward the viewer. He carries his heavy load with scarcely any visible strain. By contrast, the secretary withdraws into her chair and behind her cigarette as she sports an androgynous gender identity signalled by her smoking habit, her short-cut hair, her non-form-fitting dress and the advanced radio technology of her work. She was the famous 'New Woman' who had entered the workplace as a salaried employee and helped define Weimar society's social modernity. Each of these photographs of a human typology served to make the underlying social structure of the country visible, allowing physiognomy to serve as a form of cultural self-diagnosis.[21] As the period wore on, commentators such as Walter Benjamin and Bertolt Brecht worried that the close formal stress of photographers like Renger-Patzsch removed factories, for example, from their complex social context and made everything look vacuously beautiful. But Benjamin praised the social significance of Sander's project, proclaiming it an Übungsatlas or 'training manual' that would grant its audience critical eyes to see the world socially.[22] It would be a different group of photographers who pushed this photographic extension of human perception to an aesthetic and conceptual extreme.

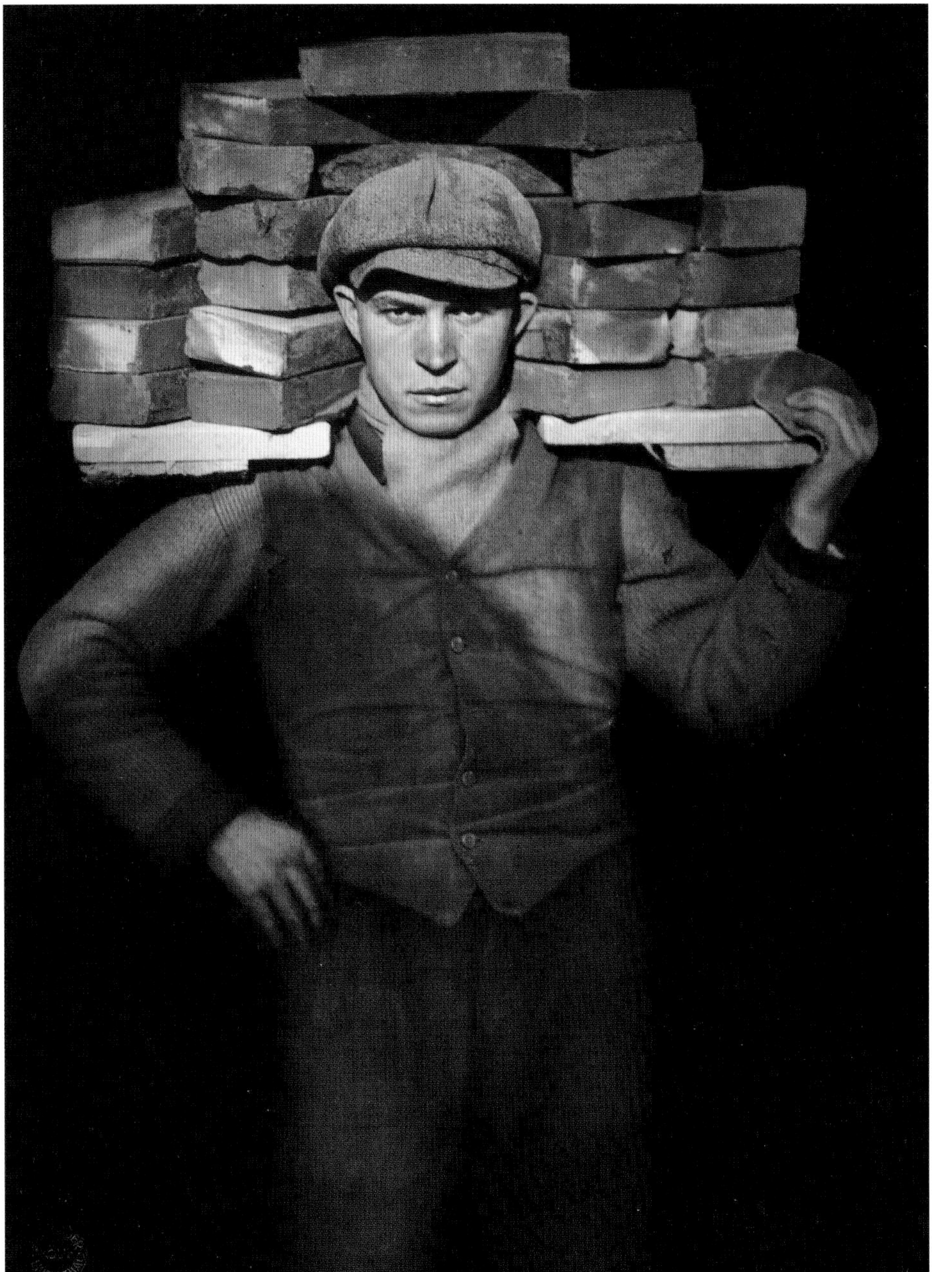

51 August Sander, *Bricklayer*, 1928, gelatin silver print.

52 August Sander, *Secretary at West German Radio, Cologne*, 1931, gelatin silver print.

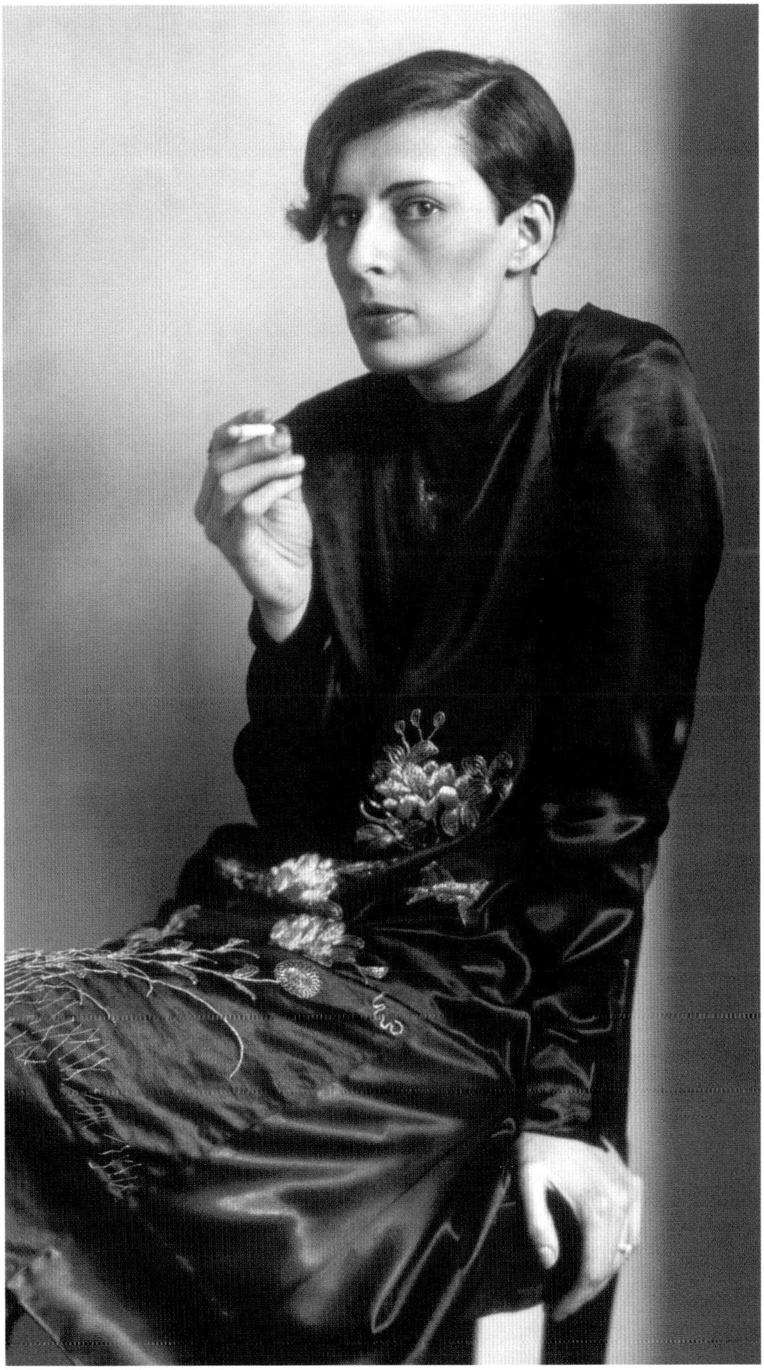

New Visions

Running parallel to developments in Neue Sachlichkeit photography was an avant-garde strand even more conscious of what photography did to shape perception, and with an even stronger rhetoric of enthusiasm. The person most famous for promoting this cutting-edge imagery as an enhancement of vision was the Hungarian artist and Bauhaus professor László Moholy-Nagy. Before being appointed to the famous art school in 1923, he published the first of a series of statements on photography that defined an approach to the medium that came to be known as *Das neue Sehen* (the New Vision). This initial essay, titled 'Produktion-Reproduktion' (Production-Reproduction, 1922), argued that modern technologies such as the gramophone, film and photography should no longer be made to reproduce the recognizable world of sounds and visions. Instead, they should offer new and radically unfamiliar experiences to perception aided by other modern technologies such as blimps, aeroplanes and microscopes. Aerial photography, for example, constituted a new ideal. He explained that this approach could result in photographs that do not merely *reproduce* existing relationships found in the lived world but *produce* entirely new ones independent of that reality. These would be associations that stimulate and develop the human sensorium for an ever-transforming modernity.[23] Whereas Benjamin saw Sander's work as a training atlas for contemporary social vision, Moholy-Nagy and popularizers of his ideas, notably the polymath artist Werner Graeff, proposed a photography that would instruct its audiences in modern perception far more broadly.

At first, he and his photographer wife Lucia Schulz strove to generate unfamiliar relationships with cameraless pictures. They made these photograms by placing objects on sensitized paper or celluloid and exposing each assembly to light. Their *Untitled* from 1923–4 correspondingly offers an array of inverse silhouettes and white shadows, the latter created when the area covered by objects remained unexposed and, thus, undarkened by exposure to light (illus. 53).[24] One could guess at what these light areas represented, be they razor blades, spheres and wire, or other three-dimensional objects that left unrecognizable two-dimensional traces. But Moholy-Nagy hoped one might see that these light effects, what he called 'moments in the play of light', called on nothing in the material world. These abstracted compositions should strike the eye as wholly new. Just as importantly, he and Schulz had realized these images by reducing photography to 'the essence of its function': to capture light on a sensitized surface. By 1927, in the second edition of his famous Bauhaus book *Painting, Photography, Film*, Moholy-Nagy began referring publicly to this avant-garde take on reduced photography as 'The New Vision'.

In these same years, he and Schulz turned to camera – in addition to cameraless – photography. But Moholy-Nagy in particular leaned heavily on strategies of disorientation to stress the form over the content of his pictures. One of his famous views from the Berlin Radio Tower, which had been

53 László Moholy-Nagy and Lucia Schulz, *Untitled*, 1923–4, gelatin silver print.

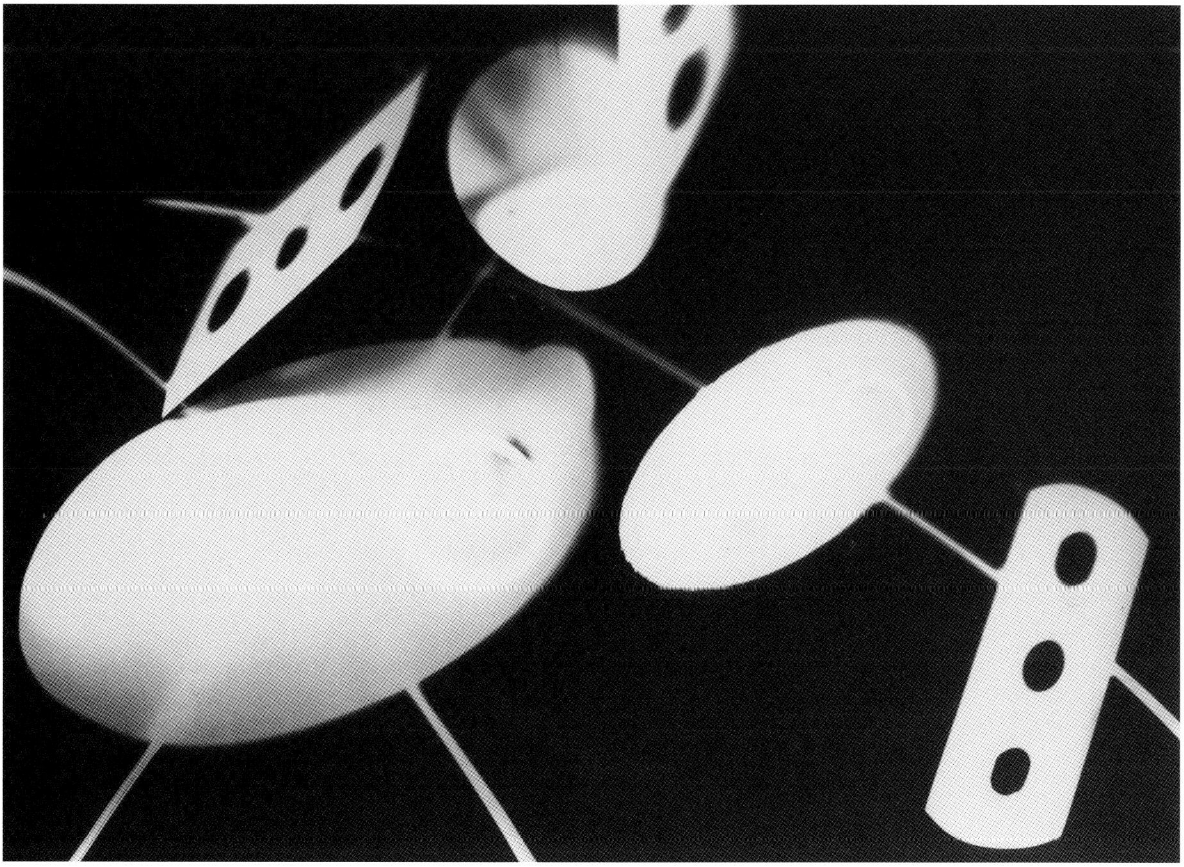

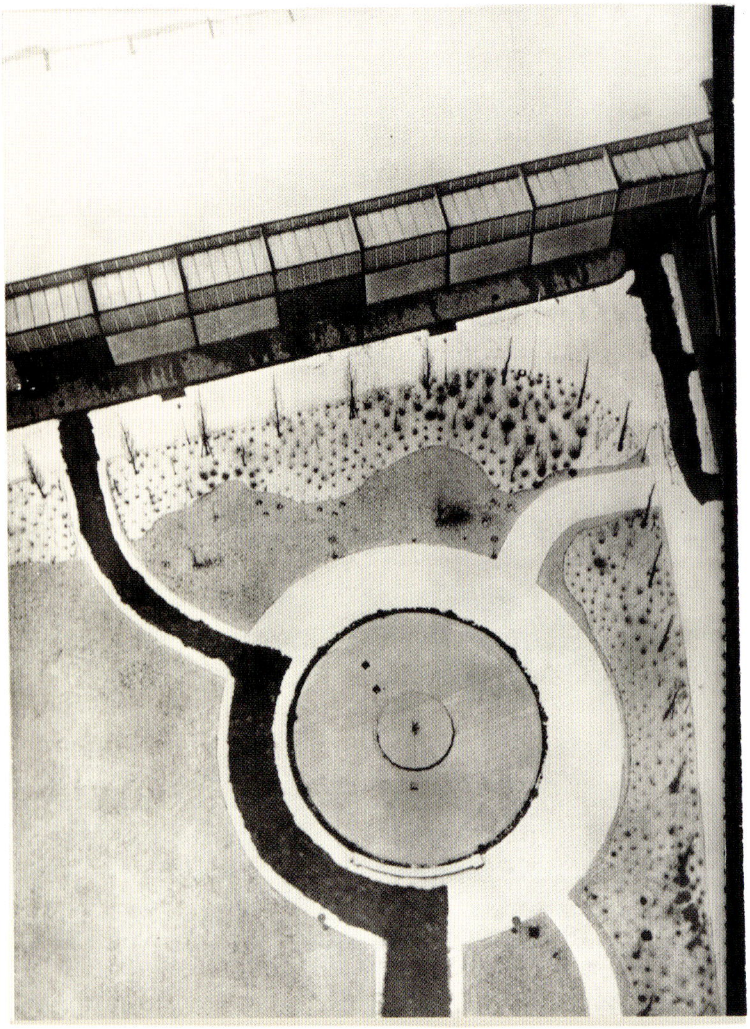

54 László Moholy-Nagy, *Radio Tower, Berlin*, 1928, gelatin silver print.

completed in 1926, offers a range of forms and light contrasts not unlike the photograms (illus. 54). Closer inspection reveals snow-covered ground with a path ploughed through it, an enclosed building from which the path leads, and small trees near a circular construction (probably a dormant fountain). To take this picture, Moholy-Nagy ascended the tower and pointed his camera directly downward, essentially aping aerial photography. This vantage point eliminated a horizon line and compressed any measure of depth legible in the building or on the ground. Instead, the viewer is encouraged to gather the perceptual experience of flattened forms and alternating shades.

Other photographers and a good number of amateurs found themselves deeply inspired by Moholy-Nagy's New Vision and pursued similar strategies in their own pictures. Bauhaus students such as the polymath Marianne Brandt took photographs of reflective convex or concave surfaces to distort a picture's contents and disorient viewers (illus. 42). In a self-portrait she snapped at the school's Dessau campus, volume and surface, interior and exterior spaces, line and circle all become a play of effects at the side of which Brandt's face and camera peer upwards. She and other students saw these works as the pictorial expression of the school's modernist architecture, which famously sported extensive glazed surfaces and interpenetrating interior and exterior spaces. Photographs such as hers also conveyed the institution's broader and near-utopian goal of transforming the experience of everyday life through a marriage of avant-garde aesthetics and modern manufacturing.

The Domestication of Modernist Photography

Both *neusachlich* and *neues Sehen* photography significantly expanded the consciousness of photography's perceptual power beyond small groups of artists. Many advertising and fashion professionals enthusiastically adopted the new approaches and, in so doing, domesticated these styles for the broader public. The advertising studio of ringl + pit, for example, was particularly successful at employing techniques of the Neue Sachlichkeit. Its two principals, Ellen Auerbach and Grete Stern, had been private students of the commercial photographer Walter Peterhans before taking over his Berlin studio in 1929. He had left for the city of Dessau to serve as the first Bauhaus photography course leader. The women gave the studio their childhood nicknames Ringl and Pit, but their work for general audiences was distinctly grown-up and sophisticated. Their 1931 advertisement for Komol hair lotion provides a good example (illus. 55). Using sharp photographic fidelity, they set the wavy texture of dyed and undyed hair samples against the rigid,

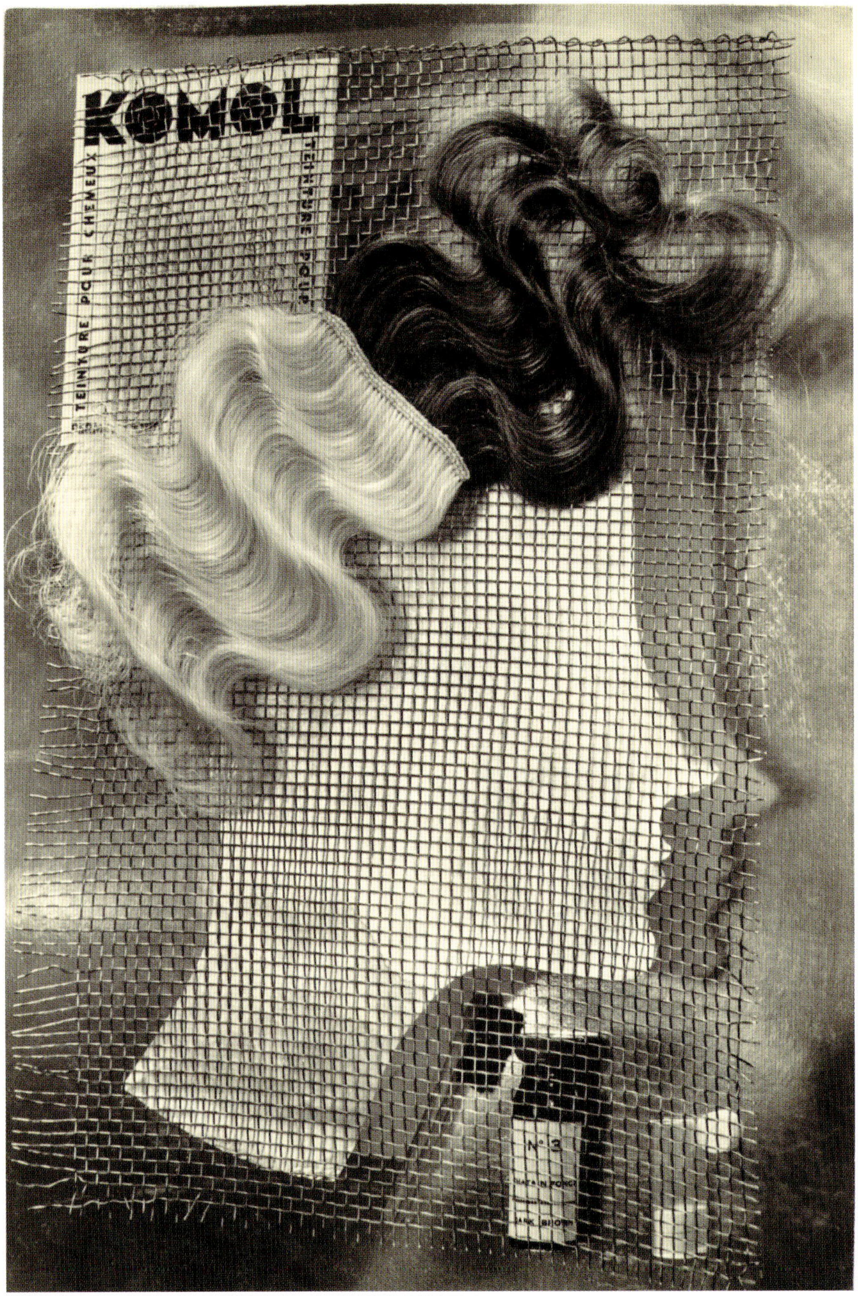

56 Hans Finsler, *Incandescent Bulb*, 1928, gelatin silver print.

55 ringl + pit (Ellen Auerbach and Grete Stern), *Komol*, 1931, gelatin silver print.

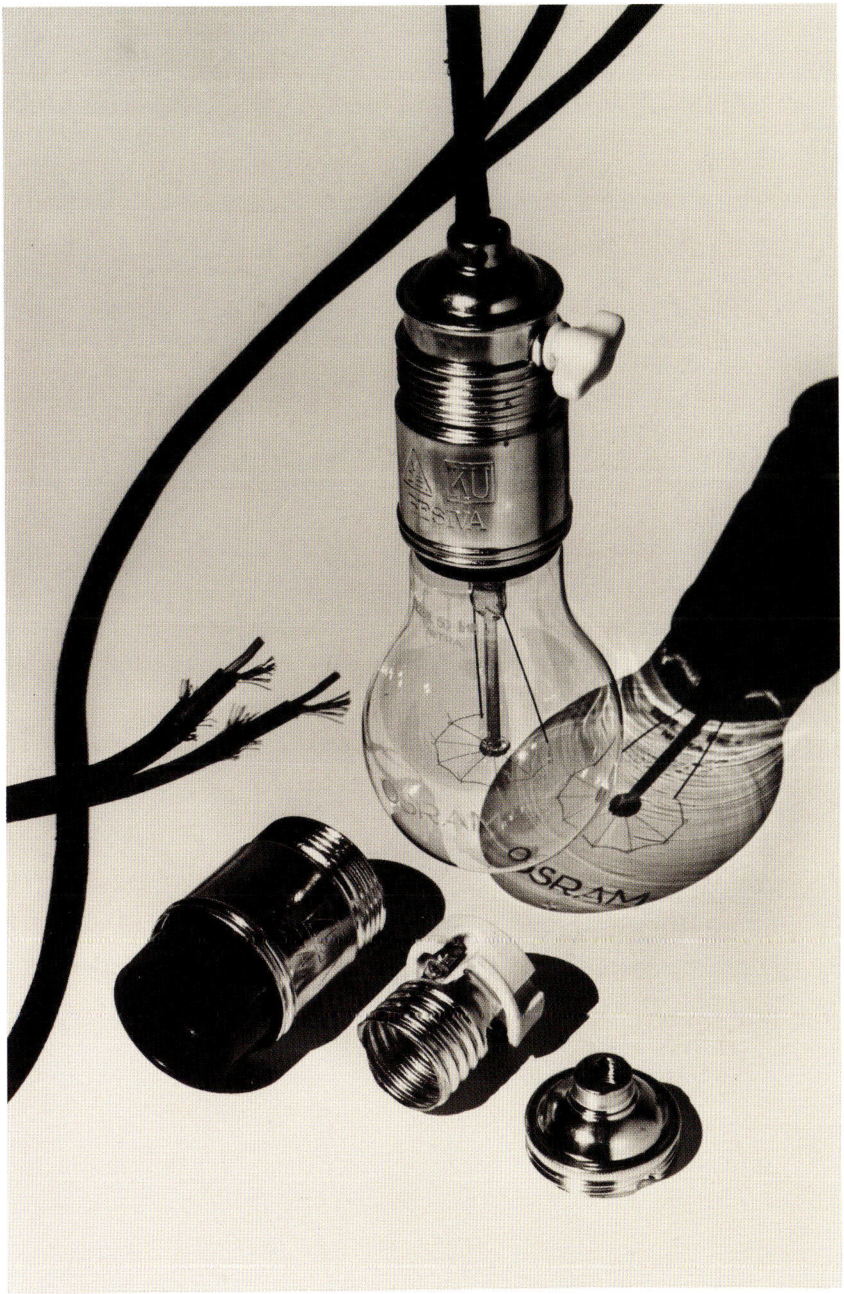
OSRAM

rectilinear pattern of wire mesh. Underneath this grid lies the partially obscured silhouette of a female profile, the lotion, a brush applicator and – surprisingly – the product's near illegible name and slogan. This work used a play of formal tensions, as much as content, to promote the product's appeal. And it did so while specifically drawing attention to its unique pictorial approach.

58 Yva (Else Simon-Neuländer), *Hands Study* (also known as *Jewellery*), *c.* late 1920s–early '30s, gelatin silver print.

The Swiss-born and German-trained photographer Hans Finsler achieved a similar *sachlich* control over the objects in his *Incandescent Bulb* advertisement of 1929 (illus. 56). Against a seemingly immaterial ground, he arranged the bulb, its socket, an electrical wire and various fixtures in such a way that the primary object being advertised, the bulb, nearly disappears in strong, raking light. Correspondingly, the shadow cast by the bulb reveals its distinct form and brand name. Inspired just as much by *Das neue Sehen* as *Die neue Sachlichkeit*, the Berlin fashion

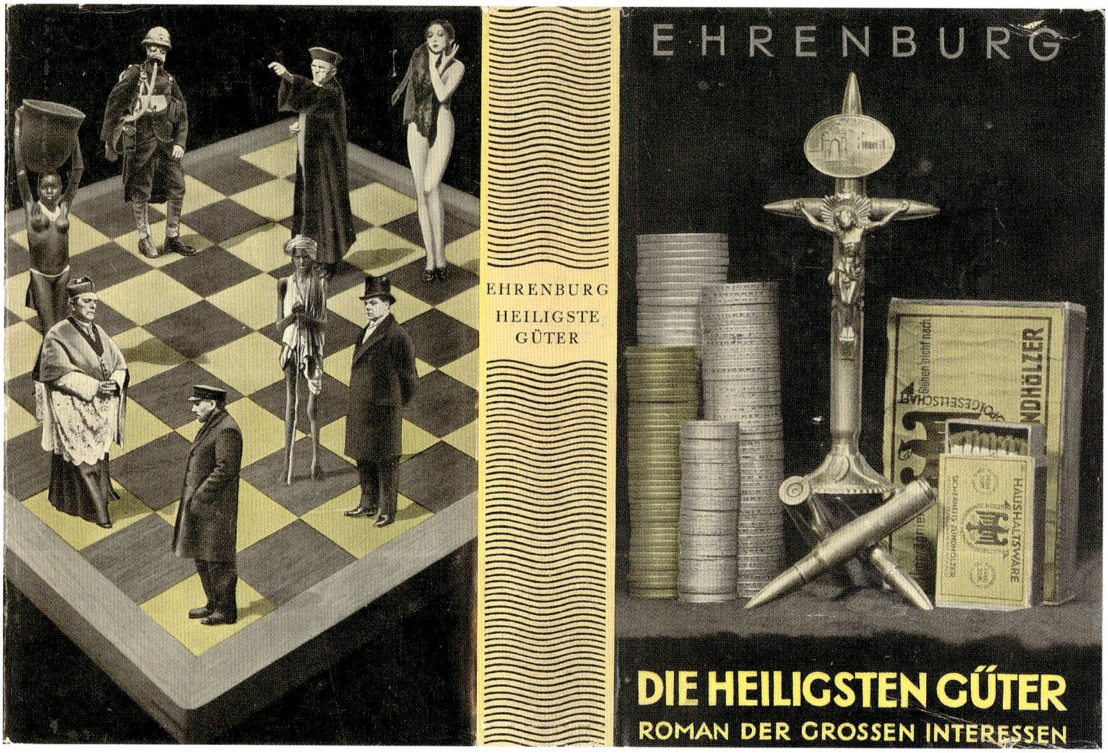

57 John Heartfield, book cover for Ilya Ehrenburg's *The Holiest Goods: A Novel about the Big Interests*, a 1931 German translation of his 1930 Russian-language novel on the Soviet-promoted 'United Front' against incipient fascism.

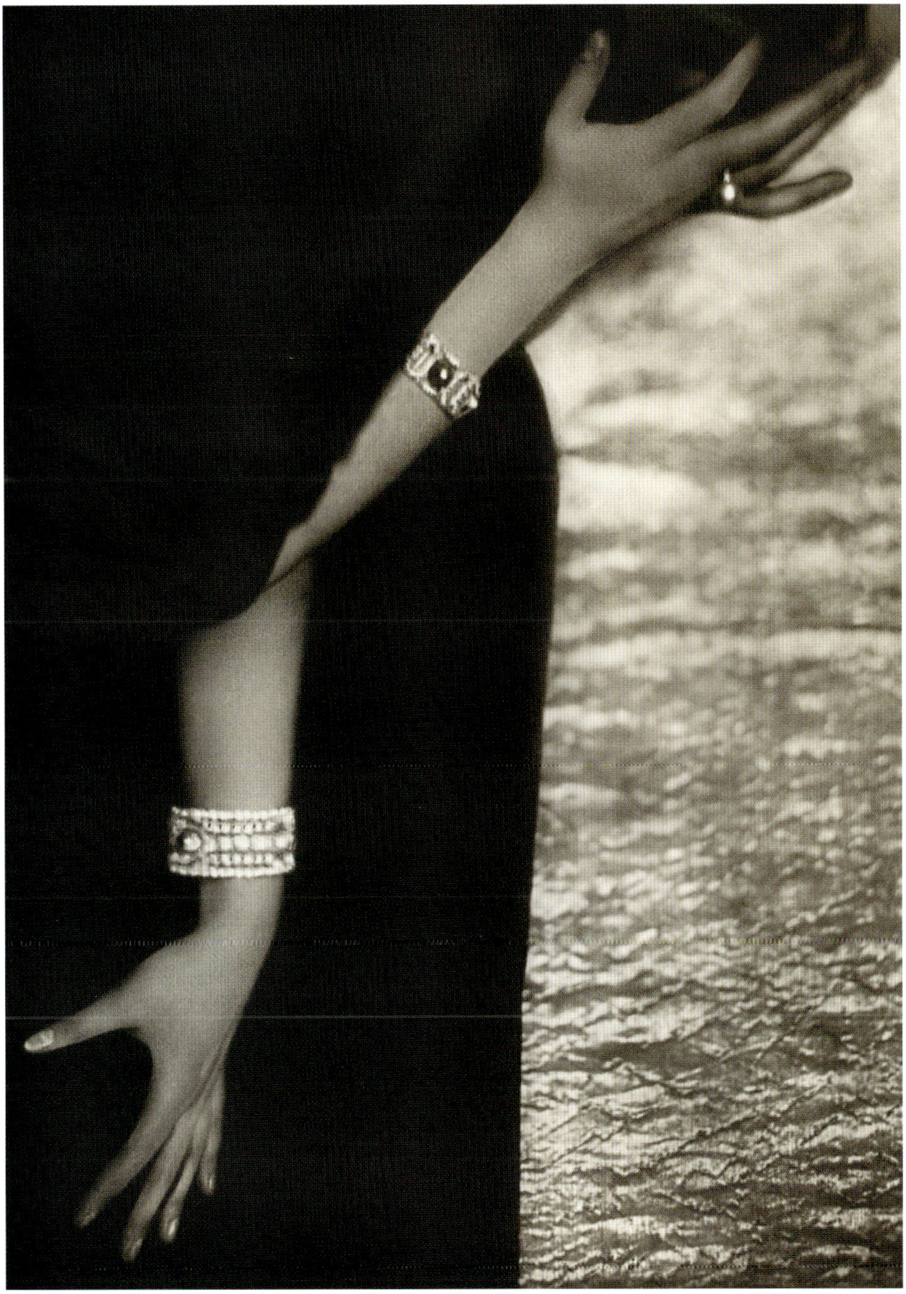

photographer Yva (a pseudonym for Else Simon-Neuländer) could play with apparent inversions of negative and positive exposure, and the representation of space, even as she focused on the various textures of her advertised jewellery (illus. 58). Commercial images such as these popularized the experiments of avant-garde artists such as Moholy-Nagy and Brandt, and further spread the realist strategies of photographers like Renger-Patzsch. In fact, all three of these photographers also produced commercial photographs for mass publication in magazines and on posters, thereby joining these women and men in teaching broad audiences how to see – and shop – with new eyes. The photographs also drew attention to themselves as engaging in just these lessons, making this awareness of the medium's power part of its modern aesthetic. Notably, it was Jewish photographers who played an outside role in pioneering the deployment of cutting-edge photography into the broader public sphere.[25]

The increasingly important practice of political persuasion in Weimar-era Germany also played a role in popularizing avant-garde approaches, particularly photomontage. John Heartfield, for example, transformed the sort of imagery he had earlier developed as a Dadaist into a satirical practice realized on posters, book covers and in magazines. In many of his pictures, he sought to extend the lessons in critical photographic reception that Stössinger had pursued in *Die freie Welt*, as on his cover for the 1931 novel *Die heiligsten Güter. Roman der grossen Interessen* (The Holiest Goods: A Novel about the Big Interests) by the Russian author Ilya Ehrenburg (illus. 57). The back shows a political chessboard on which various character types, from the prostitute to the cleric, figure as power brokers and pawns. Cut out of their original photographic context and pasted smoothly onto this new surface, the snippets appear more clearly to be the polished products of social construction put to the service of established powers, rather than documents generated from objective photographic observation.

Heartfield became famous for the photomontages he contributed to the widely circulated, radical left-wing *Arbeiter-Illustrierte Zeitung* (or *A-I-Z*, Worker's Illustrated Magazine), beginning with May 1930. But this sort of photographic strategy and political critique had long formed the magazine's focus since it first began publishing under its *A-I-Z* title in 1925.[26] The complaint by its editor Willi Münzenberg that a photograph's meaning could be reversed

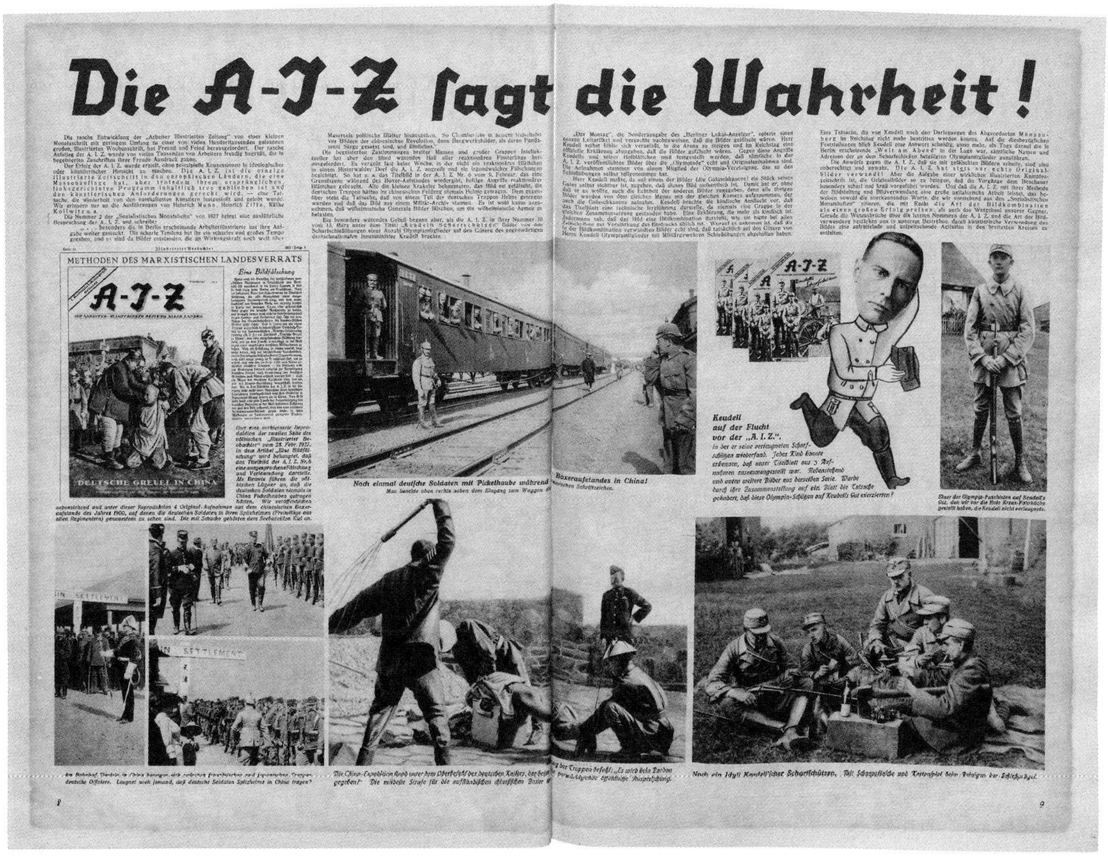

Die A-I-Z sagt die Wahrheit!

59 'The A-I-Z Tells the Truth!', rotogravure illustration in a 1927 issue of the 'Worker's Illustrated Magazine' A-I-Z.

by a caption (quoted at this chapter's beginning) became one of the primary lessons he hoped to teach his pupils. But he was also subject to the same protest. In 1927, the A-I-Z published a two-page spread titled 'The A-I-Z tells the truth!' (illus. 59). At issue was a cover photo it had issued a few weeks earlier showing fascist militia men scandalously posing on the country estate of German Interior Minister Walter von Keudell. Competing periodicals and the minister himself had called out this picture as a fraud, and now the A-I-Z confessed that, although its cover was in fact a montage, it nonetheless told the truth about the government's coddling of fascists. This exchange between mass periodicals and even a politician over the veracity of a picture typified the charged photographic conditions of Weimar-era Germany and the need to teach the broader public how to read pictures critically, to call out deceptions in emulsion. But as the *A-I-Z*'s invocation of 'truth' suggests, this veracity in the eyes of political extremists had less to do with the physical world standing before the camera's lens than with a sense of authenticity wilfully intuited by a photograph's targeted constituency. The imagining of facts through photography would become a customary practice in the era of one-party rule to follow.

A Growing Consciousness of Photography

Underlying all these deployments of modernist photography in the public sphere was not just the desire to instruct beholders in the critical perception of the medium, but also the very idea that one should be conscious of what photographs do. Even at the dawn of the Weimar era, audiences found themselves inundated by a flood of photographic images *and* an equally cresting wave of critical attention paid to these prints. This period of awareness about photography arose when the medium seemed to epitomize modern technologically driven progress. Renger-Patzsch's praise for the efficiency of photography over the hand expressed this equation, just as it suggested a new Germany bounding forward into modernity rather than stuck in the tradition-bound past. But the era's consciousness of photography also betrayed an anxiety about modernity's actual impact on the country, as Münzenberg's complaint regarding the medium's capacity to deceive might suggest. That this broader ambivalence with modernity struck on photography as one of its principal foils meant that a great deal appeared to be a stake with photography's growing dominance of the public sphere.

In fact, the rising swell of photographs led to a flourishing critical literature on the medium. Great thinkers like playwright Bertolt Brecht, the commentators Siegfried Kracauer and Walter Benjamin, the radical critics Lou Märtens and Gertrud Alexander, the art historian Franz Roh and the artist Werner Graeff produced a vast body of literature on photography that has now become a standard point of reference in the medium's history. One could justifiably claim that Benjamin's writings on photography inaugurated the field of media studies, which continues to advance in leaps and bounds today, particularly as applied to our culture of digital imaging.[27] In addition to these great thinkers, many of the country's most famous photographers engaged and significantly enhanced this discourse by publishing their pictures in books. These volumes generally feature an introduction and scarcely any more text, save the captions, which often appeared at a book's conclusion. The volumes effectively realized photography's growing dominance by making nuanced arguments with pictures alone. This was the new genre of the modern photo book in which the images often appeared one to a page or one for a two-page spread. The most noteworthy of these were *Die Welt ist schön* (The World Is Beautiful, 1928) by Renger-Patzsch, *Urformen der Kunst* (Art Forms in Nature, literally Archetypes of Art, 1928) by Karl Blossfeldt, *Antlitz der Zeit* (Face of Our Time, 1929) by August Sander and *Berlin in Bildern* (Berlin in Pictures, 1929) by the German resident Russian photographer Sasha Stone.

The extended photo essays that these publications offered found innumerable equivalents in illustrated magazines and journals that also put photography to story telling, with very little text. The *Münchner Illustrierte Presse* (Munich Illustrated Press), edited by the famous Hungarian film and photography enthusiast Stefan Lorant, made its fame from these essays, such as its 'Bruno Walter Dirigiert' (Bruno Walter Conducts, illus. 60) of 13 March 1932. These four photographs, taken by the celebrated photographer Erich Salomon, show the conductor's facial expression and gestures as they correspond to the different tempos of music he conducts (largo, pastorale and so on). Each snap offers a pictorial and physiognomic expression of the symphony's audio production. This feature, typical of Lorant's 'variations on a theme' layouts, suggests that photography can open the world of sensation to the eyes alone, if only one can learn how to look.[28] The photographer Salomon famously gave his audience regular revelations by bringing his camera into not just the concert hall but the courtroom and diplomatic conferences, where affairs of the day were otherwise conducted behind closed doors. As the title of his 1931 photo book suggests, Salomon gave his readers pictures of *Berühmte Zeitgenossen in unbewachten Augenblicken* (Famous Contemporaries in Unguarded Moments). These disclosures were made possible by Salomon's handheld camera. New to the market in the 1920s, these Hasselblad, Ermanox and Leica devices could take high-quality snapshots on roll film in low light. German manufacturers invented and

BRUNO WALTER DIRIGIERT

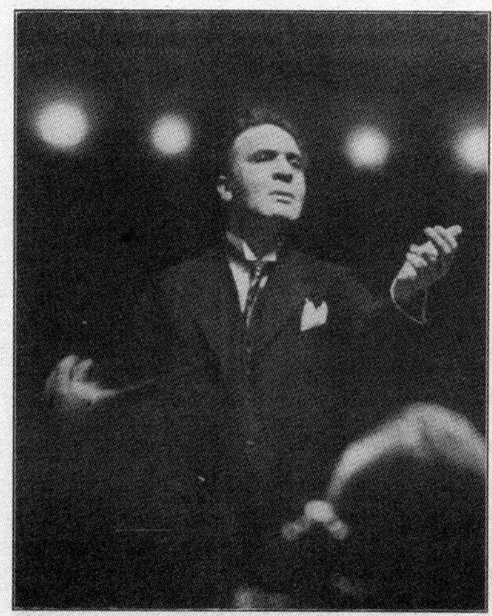

LARGO

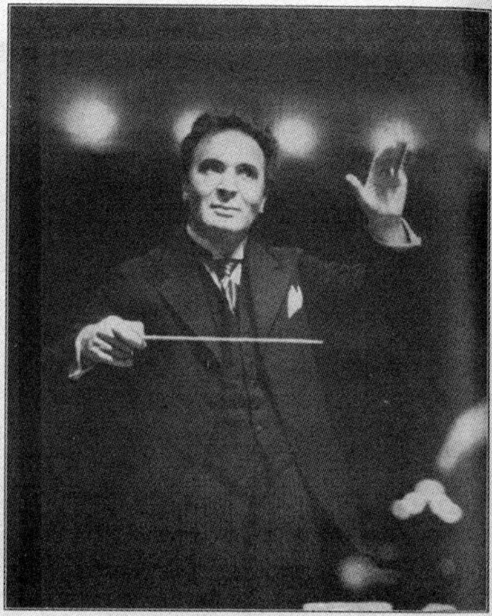

PASTORALE

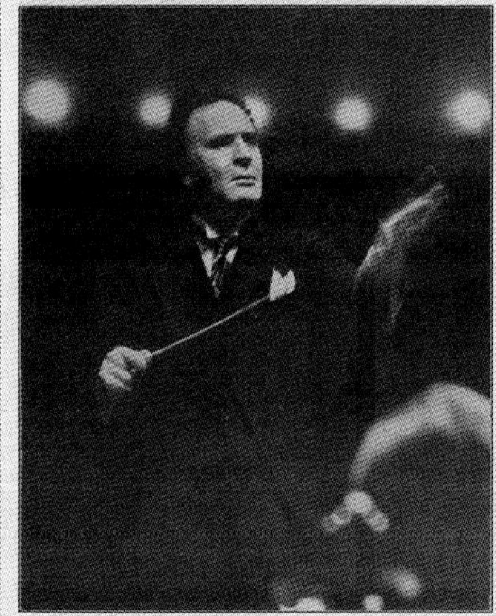

ANDANTE

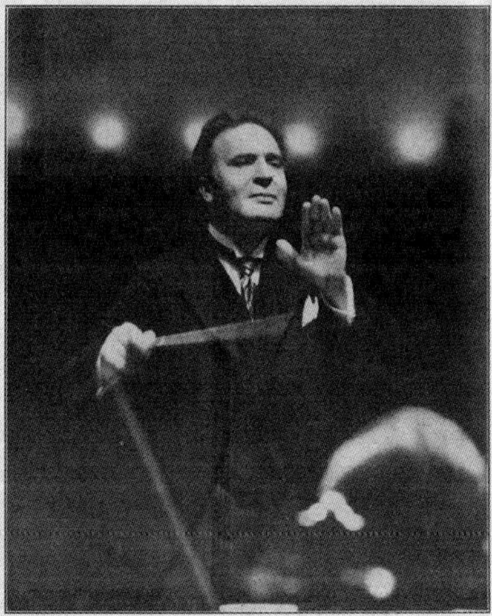

ALLEGRO

AUFNAHMEN: Dr. E. SALOMON

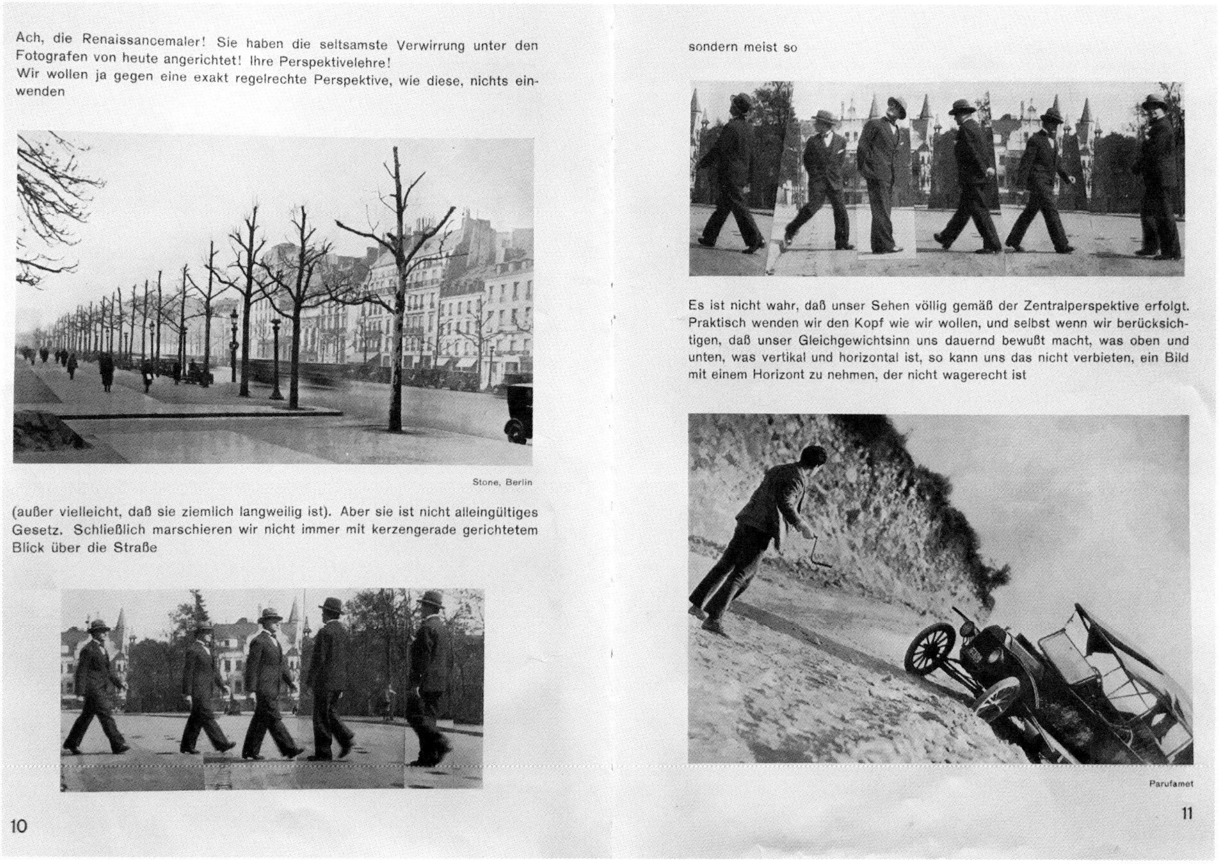
Ach, die Renaissancemaler! Sie haben die seltsamste Verwirrung unter den Fotografen von heute angerichtet! Ihre Perspektivelehre!
Wir wollen ja gegen eine exakt regelrechte Perspektive, wie diese, nichts einwenden

Stone, Berlin

(außer vielleicht, daß sie ziemlich langweilig ist). Aber sie ist nicht alleingültiges Gesetz. Schließlich marschieren wir nicht immer mit kerzengerade gerichtetem Blick über die Straße

10

sondern meist so

Es ist nicht wahr, daß unser Sehen völlig gemäß der Zentralperspektive erfolgt. Praktisch wenden wir den Kopf wie wir wollen, und selbst wenn wir berücksichtigen, daß unser Gleichgewichtsinn uns dauernd bewußt macht, was oben und unten, was vertikal und horizontal ist, so kann uns das nicht verbieten, ein Bild mit einem Horizont zu nehmen, der nicht wagerecht ist

Parufamet

11

61 Werner Graeff, halftone illustrations from his 1929 book *Here Comes the New Photographer!*

60 'Bruno Walter Conducts', halftone photographs by Erich Salomon in a 1932 issue of *Münchner Illustrierte Presse*.

championed this market in cameras, as well as the photographic aesthetic it promoted, all under the sign of modern progress.

The photo essays arising from these shoots on the fly might best be deciphered through another sort of photo book that specifically taught readers how modern photography accommodated the hectic pace of contemporary life and how it might be consumed. These include *Es kommt der neue Fotograf!* (Here Comes the New Photographer!, 1929) by Graeff, and *foto-auge* (Photo Eye, 1929) by Roh and Jan Tschichold, both published in conjunction with the landmark *Internationale Ausstellung des Deutschen Werkbunds Film und Foto* (International Exhibition of the German Werkbund Film and Photography, or *FIFO*), which first opened in Stuttgart in 1929 before travelling widely. Graeff's book included a spread that riffed on the boring nature of Renaissance one-point perspective, as embodied by a view plunging down an avenue toward a vanishing point (illus. 61). By contrast, as he shows in two montages of his own making, photography can offer far more exciting snippets of a man walking in many different directions at once, with no vanishing point necessary. Photography, he suggests, can employ modernist aesthetics to express most appropriately the industrialization and rationalization of everyday urban life, as so many Germans now experienced it. The giant *FIFO* exhibition did just the same with its many rooms of modernist prints and photo-covered objects – such as book jackets – and most especially with an introductory display that combined contemporary modernist prints and utilitarian pictures such as x-rays. Assembled by Moholy-Nagy, this first room demonstrated to its many visitors that modernist photography both arose from and reflected the practices of everyday modernity.

By 1929, when the *FIFO* opened, the country had become so photo-mad that some commentators worried that this 'photo boom' had devolved into 'photo inflation'. According to this reckoning, there were simply too many pictures, and they were overwhelming human perception. Paul Westheim, editor of the art magazine *Das Kunstblatt* (The Art Paper) referred to the consequences of this phenomenon in 1932 as *Bildermüde* or 'image fatigue', while historian Wilhelm Hausenstein complained that too many experimental photographs repeating the same vertiginous or closely framed views had become formulaic and visually numbing.[29] As the photo historian Olivier Lugon has explained, an ascendant photo-inflation had led to a collapse in the photograph's value. Pictures had been over-printed, like paper money, and the presses now refused to stop spinning, much as in the 1923 currency inflation. Even vision itself increasingly seemed a devalued resource, susceptible to weakening or loss through overuse.[30] These concerns reflected the broader ambivalence with modernity that so many Germans projected onto photography, and they even resemble our sense of an Internet-fuelled image profusion today. But by the period's political end in early 1933, these mixed feelings had generated one of the most inventive and productive moments in photography's history. The photo self-consciousness of the Weimar era reverberated with great impact through the West as modernist photography both on gallery walls and in mass print flooded the public sphere from the United States to Soviet Russia and migrated into subsequent decades. Germany today continues to be a photo-mad country, albeit with far less ambivalence about the medium and modernity more broadly.

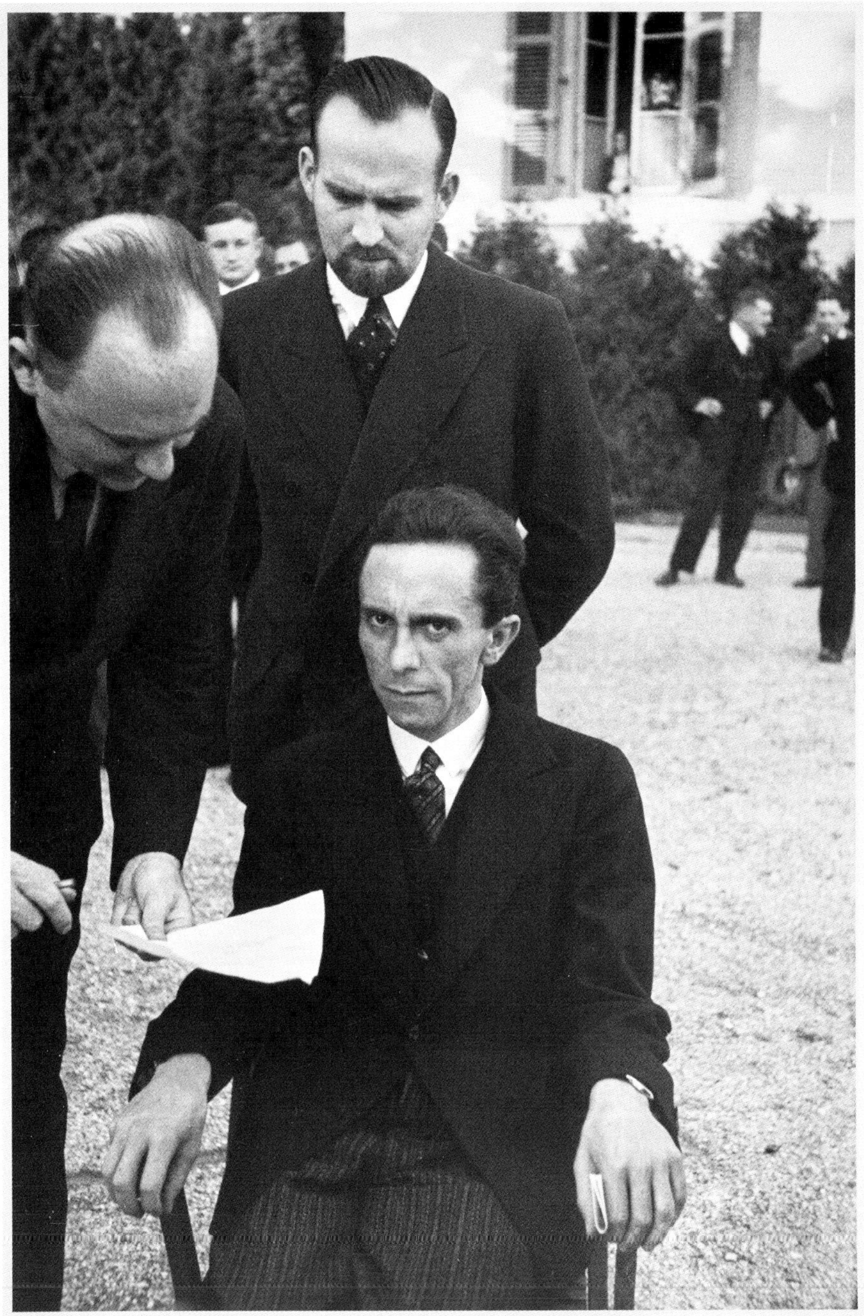

four

The Alluring Surface, 1933–1945

We can scarcely think of German National Socialism without recalling photographs of its Austrian leader, Adolf Hitler. But aside from his stern visage, one of the most heavily photographed subjects during his rule was the New Reich Chancellery (Neue Reichskanzlei, illus. 63). This seat of dictatorial power, designed and built by architect Albert Speer in 1938, quickly came to represent not just Germany's National Socialist governance, but the Third Reich's administrative efficiency and aesthetic style. Widely circulated photographs of the austere exterior and ornate interior also reveal that much like the alluring surface of Nazi Germany more broadly, the building was primarily a slick facade. For instance, it may have appeared a dominant presence in photographs, but it actually occupied a lot so narrow that it offered little more than oversized halls to serve as stage sets for ceremonial pomp.[1] On a similar but grim allegorical level, the regime claimed that its chancellery was completed in just under a year, but this pace was only made possible by brutally exploited slave labour that few people saw.

The attention showered on this building's alluring surface by architects and photographers typifies the stress on appearance over reality found in much photography of the Nazi era. Between 1933 and 1945, politics became a seductive performance in emulsion that lured domestic audiences to envision a seamlessly unified German polity and culture, and to overlook the brutality visited on those who did not fit this superficial image. In essence, the sophisticated but ambivalent approaches to photography developed in the Weimar era had given way to a cynical employment of the medium by the regime that followed.

62 Alfred Eisenstaedt, *The Propaganda Minister Joseph Goebbels with his Personal Secretary and Hitler's Interpreter at the 15th General Assembly of the League of Nations in Geneva, September 1933*, 1933, gelatin silver print.

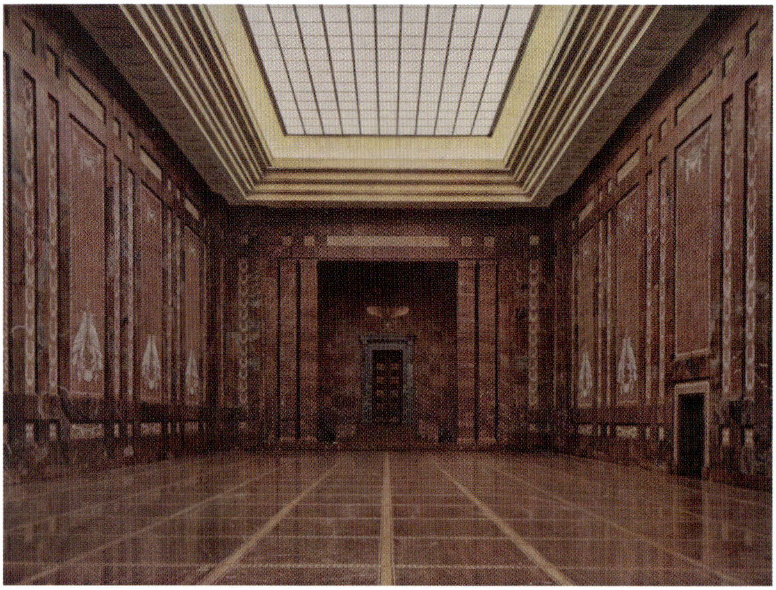

63 'Mosaic Hall Viewed from the East Portal, New Reich Chancellery' in *The New Reich Chancellery: Architect Albert Speer*, published by the National Socialist Central Press c. 1940, photo by Müller & Sohn. Format unknown.

But great fissures ran through this vision. Some appeared in pictures snapped by photographers consciously opposed to German fascism's various public messages. Others arose from internal party and governmental struggles over what those messages would actually be, or they appeared as oversights that strike us today as clear contradictions or even expressions of resistance. Hitler, in fact, purposefully sowed discord amongst his subordinates as a governing style, a strategy that generated numerous inconsistencies and lapses.[2] There also existed a great mass of banal amateur and commercial photographs made and consumed by the country's citizens over these years, images that are difficult to read as openly fascist. According to the era's more agitating photographs of party rallies and anti-Jewish tirades, Germany now defined itself by swift cultural upheaval and radical racial thinking. But the majority of pictures in magazines and public spaces showed a country that had returned to reassuring regularity after the perceived chaos of Weimar. In the subsequent war, these photographic illusions of peace and prosperity became chimerical images of victory and pride that permitted little by way of defeats and atrocities to intervene. The Nazi era may have seen the cynical use of self-consciously modernist photography and, in others cases, this mode's rejection. But the variety found in the vast count of pictures made in the era reveals a culture no less engaged with the medium. In spite of posterity's tendency to lump all photographs from this era together as 'Nazi photography', the medium was deployed in many conflicting ways. Whatever remained of the fissured but alluring surface toward the war's end finally came crashing down with defeat when Allied forces and photojournalists such as Margaret Bourke-White documented the evidence of staggering war crimes. These photographs and films were used not just as documentation, but to justify Allied sacrifices and to shame German citizens who had otherwise nourished themselves on the seductive surface of fascism. This unveiling constituted a final twist in the self-conscious use of photography, this time by the country's conquerors.

National Socialism and Its Evolving Image

When exactly the Weimar period ended is just as difficult to define as its tumultuous beginnings in defeat and revolution. Many of the authoritarian tendencies that came to a head with Hitler's ascension to the chancellery were already in motion. Following an inconclusive national election in September 1930, the government began bypassing the Reichstag and ruling by emergency decree. A similarly inconclusive vote on 6 November 1932 led to Adolf Hitler's appointment as Chancellor on 30 January 1933. But the final axe to the republic and its dissipating rule of law came with the burning of the Reichstag building in Berlin on the evening of 27 February 1933. Though probably ignited by a Dutch anarchist, Hitler's government jumped at the opportunity to solidify its hold on power under the pretext of a national emergency.[3] As a magazine cover by the former Dadaist and now pugnacious photomontage artist John Heartfield declared, Germany had gone 'through light to night', from the literal light of the Reichstag fire and subsequent book burnings, to the night of political oppression (illus. 64). Heartfield suggested in this photomontage that National Socialism had forged political consensus not from transparent public deliberation but instead from spectacular displays of power, particularly violent ones taken under the cloak of night. But in fact, most of these exhibitions of force were tailored for the camera in the bright light of day.

Since its early days in the Weimar Republic, the National Socialist German Workers' Party (Nationalsozialistische Deutsche Arbeiterpartei) powered its movement with mass rallies at which leaders churned their audience with fiery nationalist and anti-Semitic rhetoric. The powerful alchemy of hard-right oratory and the camera flourished in particular at the 1924 Hitler-Ludendorff trial, where the charismatic party leader who was being prosecuted for treason effectively became the prosecutor instead. Press photographers snapped pictures of this previously invisible man and filled the pages of illustrated periodicals, thereby helping to establish his public image as a gifted orator and electric presence. Hitler lauded the 'magical power of the spoken word' in his infamous Weimar-era book *Mein Kampf* (My Struggle), which he wrote during his subsequent prison term. But he also explained that mass rallies specifically offered an 'image . . . of the greater community' that served party messages well.[4] This slick and consciously cultivated picture of ideological solidarity required a parallel image of the orator who called the *Volksgemeinschaft* (people's/racial community) into being. Correspondingly, after his release from imprisonment, Hitler arranged with his personal photographer Heinrich Hoffmann to produce carefully crafted publicity pictures. The alluring public surface of National Socialist self-presentation essentially began at this point.[5]

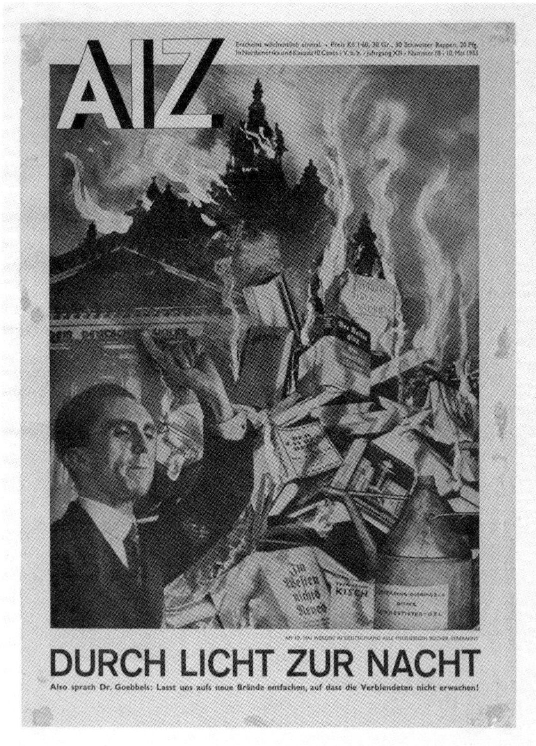

64 John Heartfield, 'Through Light to Night', rotogravure cover illustration for a 1933 issue of the 'Worker's Illustrated Magazine' *A-I-Z*.

Hoffmann snapped a particularly important series of these photographs in 1926 as Hitler practised oratory before a mirror (illus. 66). According to Hoffmann, this was done in the photographer's Munich studio with dramatic stage lighting and equally excited music playing for accompaniment.[6] The aggressively gesticulating hands, rolling eyes and gaping mouth show the extent to which Hitler now made his political persuasion a visual affair, one tailored to attentive eyes and ready cameras. This strategy worked, particularly as the party leader reduced his repertoire to five or six gestures that he repeated endlessly for his audiences.[7] Hitler's optically enriched

65 Erwin Blumenfeld, *The Dictator*, 1936, gelatin silver print.

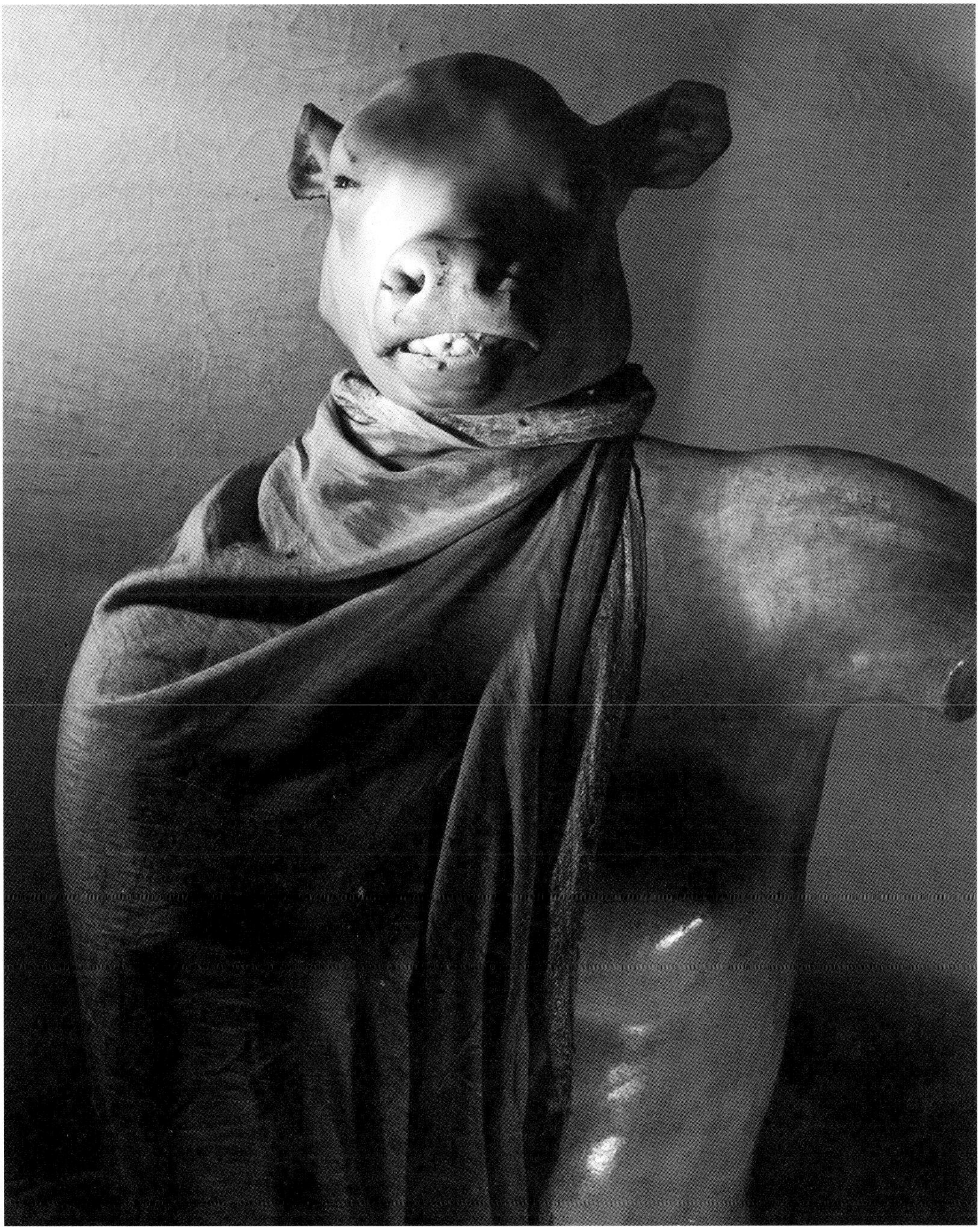

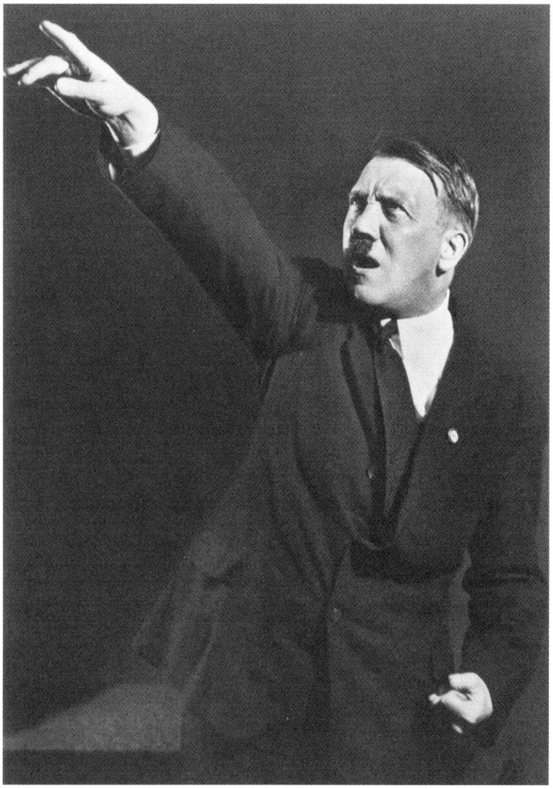

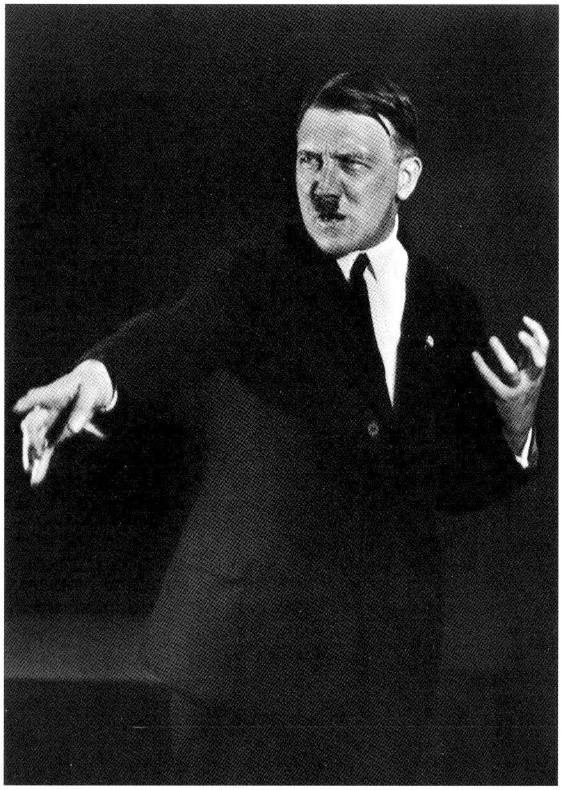

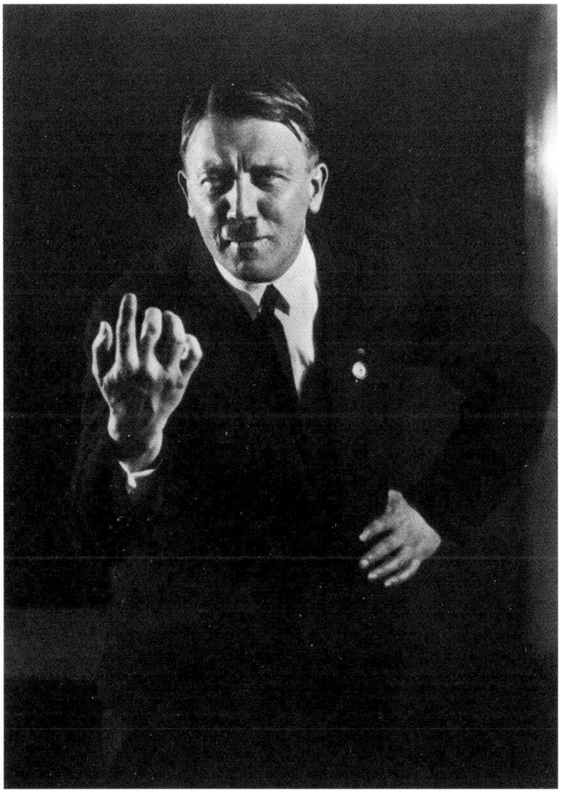

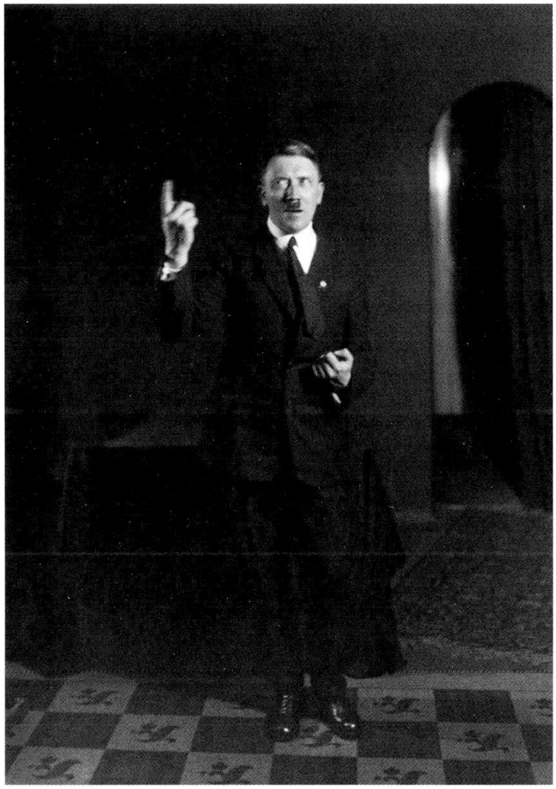

oratory ultimately made Nazi Party rallies a sensation for photojournalists wielding their own cameras, particularly those contributing to the party's illustrated paper, *Der Illustrierte Beobachter* (The Illustrated Observer).

previous:
66 Heinrich Hoffmann, *Practising Poses for Orating in the Atelier of Heinrich Hoffmann*, 1926, gelatin silver prints.

Heartfield the political photomontage artist remained ever-attentive still to the pictorial grammar of Hitler's public image and famously mocked it in numerous compositions for the *A-I-Z* both before the Nazi seizure of power and thereafter, from exile in Prague. Such open dissent within the country's borders became rare by that point in the winter of 1933.[8] But like Heartfield and the *A-I-Z* magazine in Prague, image makers in neighbouring countries exercised their disgust. The Berlin-born fashion photographer Erwin Blumenfeld, for example, staged a ghastly image in 1936 by setting a pig's head atop a classical female statue partially wrapped in a shawl. Titled *The Dictator* (illus. 65), the pig gazes forward with dead eyes while its open snout suggests an ominous oration, particularly as enhanced by the raking light. Blumenfeld forged this grisly satire from the safety of Amsterdam. More subtly critical was a press photo that Alfred Eisenstaedt took of government minister Joseph Goebbels in Switzerland in 1933 (illus. 62). Goebbels had travelled south to prepare Germany's aggressive withdrawal from the League of Nations. Though initially friendly with the photographer, the minister scowled when Eisenstaedt continued to snap the pictures, leaving the impression of a menacing authority. Two years later, the German-Jewish photographer, still based in Berlin, fled with his family to the United States.

Meanwhile, the regime established institutions that relied heavily on photography to persuade citizens of all the good that flowed from the 'new epoch' being established. The most important of these organizations was the Reich Ministry of Public Enlightenment and Propaganda, set up and led by Goebbels in March 1933. Underneath its roof, the Photography Department officially oversaw matters concerning the medium. But it largely charged itself with recruiting skilled photojournalists and talented amateurs to contribute material to the larger propaganda effort.[9] The ranks of such image makers were growing steadily slimmer. Many of Germany's greatest talents, such as Eisenstaedt, were fleeing the country or finding themselves forcibly removed from their practices for being Jewish or associated with the political Left, a process the new government termed *Gleichschaltung* (bringing into line or coordination). But the ministry's efforts remained an ad hoc affair that lacked a central organization for photographic propaganda and built no solid theory for the medium's persuasive use.

The New Epoch on Display

A handful of public exhibitions on which the ministry heavily collaborated or that it directly staged demonstrate at least what a handful of high-ranking officials had in mind for photography under National Socialist rule. The earliest was *Die Kamera*, a photo industry trade fair that the organizers of the 1929 *Film und Foto* and the 1928 *Die Presse* (The Press) exhibitions originally planned as a follow-up to those successful events. The show opened in

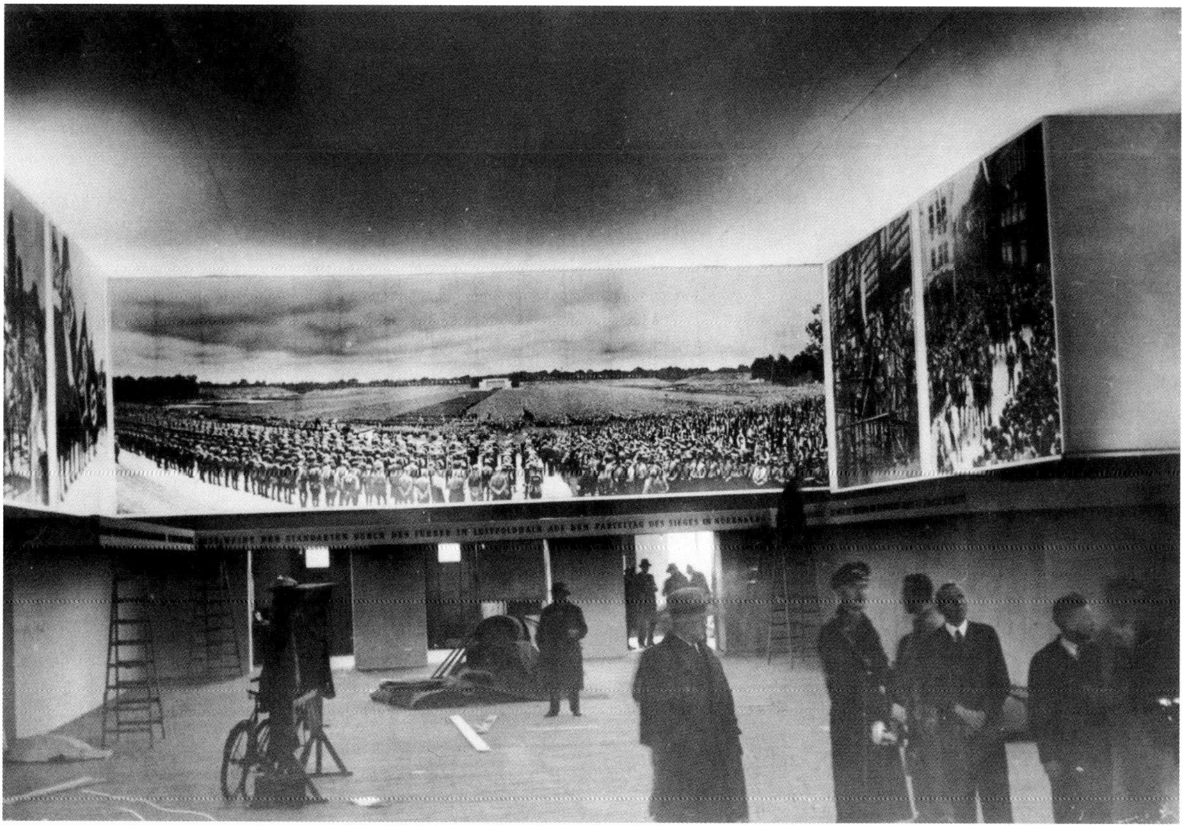

67 An installation view of the lobby of *The Camera*, a photography industry exhibition held in Berlin, November 1933, gelatin silver print.

November 1933 in Berlin, by which time the new regime had solidified its hold on power. *Die Kamera* brought together a collection of photography industry leaders, amateur associations, press and book printing companies, professional photographers and exhibition architects to advocate one of the ministry's still undefined goals: to push modern photography off the mass-printed page and into something resembling film, working in three dimensions.[10] The preceding exhibitions, along with others famously designed by Bauhaus professor Herbert Bayer, had been working in just this direction. They had bracingly advocated for such things as commodities, housing and modernist photography.[11] But here, the goal was to fashion a space of immersive political propaganda.

Visitors could see this effort most clearly in the first two exhibition halls, through which one entered the fair. These introductory rooms were devoted specifically to the National Socialist Party. The large reception lobby offered a history of the 'movement' in sixteen massively enlarged photographs by Heinrich Hoffmann, each showing a key rally or mass gathering (illus. 67). Together, the prints formed a monumental photo-frieze around the upper portion of the room at cinema-screen height. Each featured a caption naming a pivotal event of party myth. A visitor would have to view this cycle of photographs by looking up as in a movie house, and then rotating in a style of awe-filled reverence generally reserved for a cathedral.[12] The flat printed page simply could not provide this sort of immersive experience with photographic propaganda.

The largest panorama occupying a full wall exemplifies this approach (illus. 68). The vast picture shows a marching field where seemingly endless cadres of Brown Shirt Nazis were being consecrated into the new SS

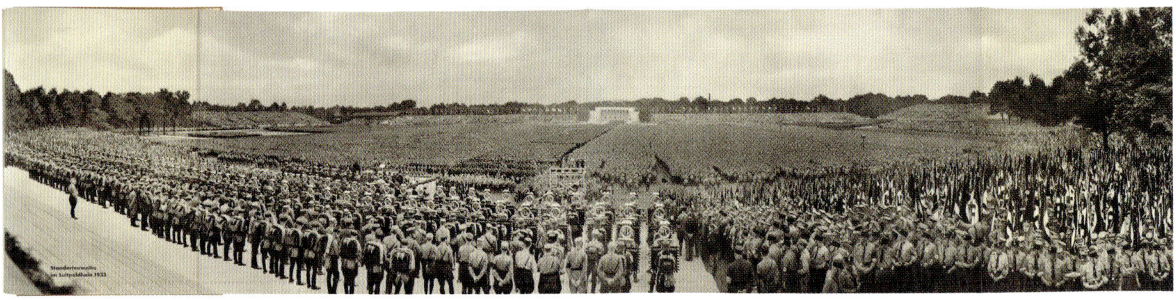

68 Heinrich Hoffmann, panoramic foldout in Winfried Bade, *Germany Awake: The Emergence, Struggle and Victory of the NSDAP* (1933), format unknown.

paramilitary that same year, 1933. From the left and towards the centre of the vista, the swell of men nears the viewer while on the right they seemingly tumble off the picture's edge and into the pavilion space. In turn, the other photographs on the neighbouring wall at the left provide closer views of the flags, marching men and Hitler himself, foregrounding details that partially disappear in the vast panorama. The total effect was cinematic, resembling the shot-reverse-shot of film editing that sutured viewers into a *mise en scène*. But this took place across a three-dimensional exhibition space rather than on a two-dimensional screen, making for a uniquely intensive sort of immersion, a saturation of space with fascist ideology. The identical panorama appeared that same year as a foldout in a book titled *Deutschland erwacht* (Germany Awakes). Once extended, the printed composition became three times larger than the book, showing how the volume's designers eagerly wanted to have this picture surpass its physical limitations and approach the experience of the exhibition space. The designer of *Die Kamera* achieved an enhanced experience by following on from an important avant-garde precedent: the vast picture covering the entrance to the ground-breaking *Fotomontage* exhibition, held in Berlin in 1931. Titled *The Museums of Berlin*, this introductory photomontage, by Berlin-based Dutch artist Cesar Domela-Nieuwenhuis, merged highlights of the city's treasures over an entire wall, plunging visitors into a kaleidoscope of heritage that Hoffmann's large panorama presented instead as an infinite vista. *Die Kamera* learned from such precedents to expand the photograph into three dimensions.

At least as stated in public, the idea motivating this approach to photography was the medium's privileged relationship to reality and, in turn, its truthfulness over other means of communication. Propaganda minister Goebbels declared in a speech at the opening of *Die Kamera* that, 'We believe in the objectivity of the camera and are sceptical of anything mediated aurally or in type.' The previous fourteen years of deception in the Weimar Republic had made the average German so distrustful that he now 'wants to see for himself'. The photograph proved in black and white that 'a new epoch is born that has truly won all hearts.' In what must have been an unintentional salute to Moholy-Nagy's New Vision, he declared that 'Our modern artificial eye, the camera, has become a means of testimony for the new time.' By providing such objective yet emotional evidence, particularly after jumping from two to three dimensions, photography could now fulfil its 'great political mission'.[13] But that goal was exceedingly tendentious and it was the product of little more than nationalism and anti-Semitism tied into a crude and ugly ideological knot. This rhetoric of testimonial objectivity cloaked the awareness that Goebbels and others had developed about photography. They understood that the medium could be made to communicate just about anything, given the proper caption, context and – at *Die Kamera* – expansion of magnitude. Goebbels was, in other words, employing the Weimar era's modernist consciousness of photography to construct a compelling, even overwhelming, vision of 'the new epoch' that passed itself off as transparent, as self-evident. In addition to the ostensible look of modernist photography on display, this less attractive aspect of the modern aesthetic was smuggled into showcase exhibitions such as *Die Kamera* that were sponsored directly or indirectly by the Propaganda Ministry.

Another of these shows, *Gebt mir vier Jahre Zeit* (Give Me Four Years, 1937), was almost purely a ministry product that propagandized for a new four-year plan, doing so in even more boisterous formal terms than had *Die Kamera*. The show's grand entrance featured colossal 'photo books' of German industry that stood upright against walls and literally flipped their

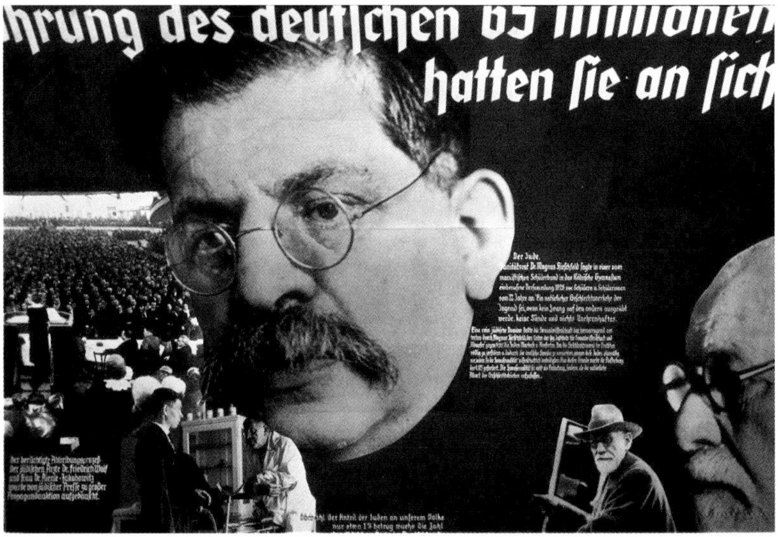

69 Panel in *The Eternal Jew*, a travelling exhibition vilifying Jews first held in Munich, 1937–8, format unknown.

pages to reveal further pictures. The third room billed itself as a hall of industry with mammoth photomontages showing people and machines at work, including actual machines stamping out products. It even featured model freeways. The pictures formed a photomontage realized across this hectic space, its image fragments being placed in many different locations and at various angles. This strategy allowed them to mark distinct thematic areas and experiences.

This more openly modernist mode of public photographic exhibition space found its most odious employment in the exhibition *Der ewige Jude* (The Eternal Jew) of 1937–8. Among other things, this show featured large concave display boards laid out like magazine spreads with 'evidence' of Jews' machinations and corrosive influence. One featured the oversized heads of German and Austrian men of medical science, such as the famous Berlin sexologist Magnus Hirschfeld and the Viennese psychology pioneer Sigmund Freud (illus. 69). Oversized reproductions of their heads abut photographs and documents attesting to their work's pernicious 'destruction of the family', as asserted in one of the captions. Here the remotivation of each photograph's meaning entered into high gear, to the point of being obviously over-determined by size, juxtaposition and captioning text. The boards on which these compositions appeared bowed forward as they climbed above the visitor's head, thereby enveloping her or him and transforming the supposed social threat of Jewish Germans into a physical one. This was the ugly face of the vision officially constructed for the new epoch, the 'them' against 'us' of the German *Volksgemeinschaft* that made a harsh break in an otherwise alluring picture being stitched together. The enrolling of modernist strategies and highly attuned photo self-consciousness necessary for these exhibitions worked at the meeting point of printed matter and cinema. Ultimately the seductive photographic surface and its troubling counterpart, as seen in this last exhibition, found their greatest dissemination in magazines, books, stereo cards and other mass-printed products that indoctrinated, officially or not, on an even greater mass level.

The bulk of photographs produced in these years poured from innumerable outlets often associated with the government and its many institutions. But this printed matter was just as often the product of private companies run by people who may have been hardened fascists, or merely conscious of market demands and government censorship. The pictures they printed appeared in books and magazines, on postcards and posters, or even in luxury portfolios that, as a whole, fed the broad fascination with photography definitively stimulated in the Weimar era. Their largely positive depiction of national community and international relations built a pleasant vision of National Socialist Germany that otherwise seemed the product of central planning. However, it was largely a consequence of coercion and complicity.

The mass-circulation *BIZ* (Berlin Illustrated Magazine), for example, was probably a product of direct ministry control. But it was typical of the general-audience magazines published in the years before the fascist seizure of power. The Ullstein corporation that owned it had been 'Aryanized' in the mid-1930s, a process that usually involved stealing assets from Jewish owners or forcing them to sell at ludicrously low prices to investors willing or even eager to do the government's bidding. An issue from January 1935, published under the magazine's new direction, sports a cover image that might seem predictable: a 1931 Heinrich Hoffmann shot of Hitler with Josef Bürckel. The latter was the fascist Saarland advocate who served as the Nazi government's commissioner for the autonomous region, up to this same month of January a League of Nations protectorate. The Saar had just voted in a plebiscite to rejoin Germany. As demonstrated here, current events made sense only in their relation to the *Führer* (leader).

The magazine's interior featured photo-reporting on the week, complete with pictures of Hermann Goering speaking to an attentive audience, Saarland citizens caressing a painting of Hitler and others voting in the plebiscite. But further pages beyond these features printed more mundane material, such as stories on the fastest international airmail routes, a town in northern Norway where the sun slips away for two months and a movie under production about Frederick the Great (illus. 70). In this last piece, the central photograph of the young 'Fritz' playing

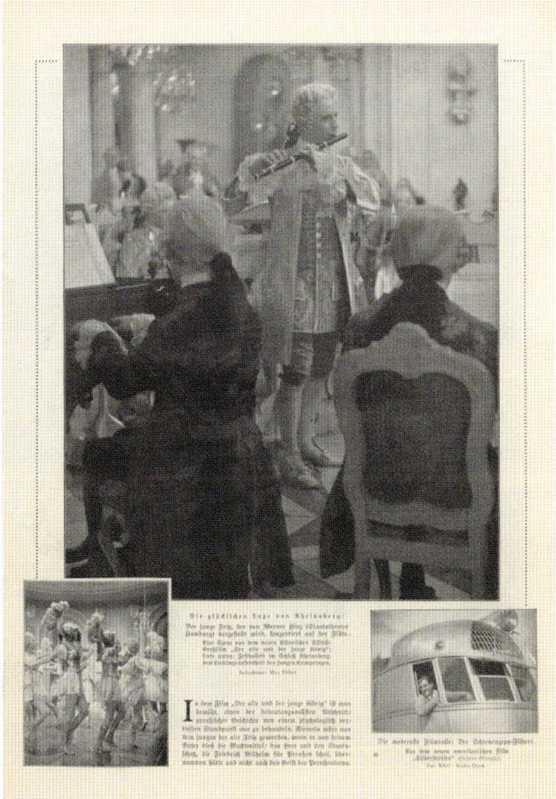

70 Max Ehlert, 'The Halcyon Days of Rheinsberg', halftone photo spread about the filming of *Der junge Fritz*, in a 1935 issue of the *Berliner Illustrirte Zeitung*, page 73.

flute in period costume was taken by Max Ehlert, a press photographer who had matured in the Weimar-era movie industry and later joined the Nazi party just after the fascist takeover. He went on to photograph many party events *à la* Hoffmann. But here he exercised his well-honed talent as a cinema and fashion photographer. Like the magazine itself, he was capable of producing hard party propaganda and the soft lowbrow kitsch that provided a pleasant distraction from the period's tumultuous events and increasing repression. Beyond the general-interest magazines in which this mixture of pictures appeared, the government and its party published an endless stream of magazines for restless partisans. Titles included *Volk und Rasse* (People and Race), *Signal* (Signal) and *Das deutsche Mädel* (The German Girl). These featured examples of the pure 'race', adoring photographs of party leaders or soldiers, and particularly crude anti-Semitic pictorial rants.

Given the better-quality paper and frequent use of colour, photo books proved particularly fertile ground for both the appealing and troubling visions of National Socialist Germany. In many cases, presses that published seemingly neutral books in the Weimar era continued releasing books along similar lines. Some of this material could be easily plugged for its pro nationalist potential. Before 1933, for example, the Universum-Verlagsanstalt (Universe Publishing House) began planning an extensive series of picture books to survey the country's districts. It ultimately realized 300 volumes by 1940. Each number attended to a city's or region's most notable landmarks or works of art, such as in the Frankfurt am Main volume from 1933. With greater frequency, fascist rhetoric and symbols appeared in these books, showing how easily such visual clues colonized everyday culture. Further numbers in the series covered places that were not within the political boundaries of Germany, such as Flanders, thus creating a not-so-subtle mandate for conquering them in wartime.

On the more neutral side of the ledger, picture books with the theme of young animals continued to be published, following on Weimar-era works such as the 1929 *Tierkinder* (Animal Babies) by famous animal book author Paul Eipper. The pictures for this book were taken by Hedda Walther, who was celebrated as a great photographer of animals and babies. Examples to follow were a popular 1934 Czech-authored book about a puppy's life and a 1940 volume featuring pictures of lambs, chicks and calves. These books were particularly banal and contained few explicit Nazi references. But quotidian commodity, fashion and cinema photography, even if it appeared as a mode of innocent distraction, inevitably found itself peppered with the symbols or people of the period, such as a routine dedication to Hitler. Even when not, such images often stood committed to the conservative values, the German heritage and the traditional gender roles advocated by National Socialism.

Openly propagandist picture books before the Second World War ranged in intensity and subject matter. Many of these were devoted to the country's building projects, infrastructure and armaments industry, all of which the government sought to expand. One particularly popular subject was the new Autobahn, which the government had inaugurated in 1933 to generate employment and awe. It ended up relying on slave labour, given the difficult working conditions that attracted fewer recruits than anticipated. Many books glorified it as a strip of German industrial prowess traversing the beautiful countryside, even if there were few cars to drive on it. A series of volumes released each year highlighted this mix of bucolic beauty and modern transport. In a similar mode, a book published on the New Reich Chancellery in 1940 emphasized its great spaces, severe Neoclassical facades and smaller art fixtures, such as mosaics and chandeliers (see illus. 62).[14] This tome was just a capstone in the larger edifice of books, postcards, collectors' albums, posters and more that papered the country with what was intended to be an inspiring vision of this seat of government, a building complex where only limited administration could actually be completed.

One of the publishers of Autobahn books, the Volk und Reich Verlag, was privately owned but received generous subsidies from various government ministries, including Goebbels's own. It could therefore lead the field in construction-fetish publications. Its *Deutschland zwischen Nacht und Tag* (Germany between Night and Day, 1934) juxtaposes photographs of misery

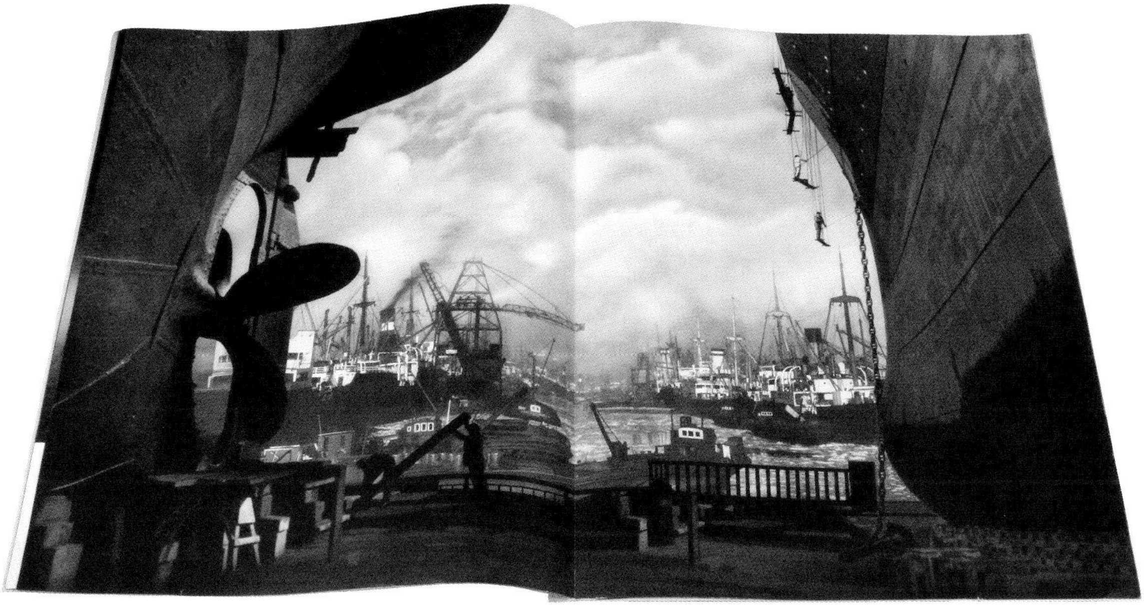

71 Pay Christian Carstensen, Hans Hitzer, Friedrich Richter, spread from their book *Deutschland* (1936), likely halftone print.

from the previous Weimar Republic with men and women at work under the new government. Among the contributors to the positive photographs of an advancing country was Albert Renger-Patzsch, who went on to publish many additional pictures in this publisher's books. The larger and carefully crafted vision of a harmonious country in construction reached its apex with Volk und Reich's 1936 book *Deutschland*, which also appeared in English and French for export. Much like the exhibitions, it featured dramatic modern photographs, such as one of a busy harbour framed by two titanic ships in dry dock (illus. 71), and images of building activity montaged over a light red horizon of happily rallying workers. This constituted the fulsome picture of happy prosperity that the publisher's editors and subsidizers wanted to present not just to their domestic market, but to foreigners as well.

Heinrich Hoffmann, who had a near monopoly on Hitler images, held the same international aspirations for his work. Within the country he used his exclusive access to great financial advantage, publishing a seemingly endless series of books that showered a confetti of führer pictures over Germany. The Hoffmann photographs filling the pages of *Jugend um Hitler* (Youth around Hitler), *Hitler in seinen Bergen* (Hilter in His Mountains) and *Hitler Baut*

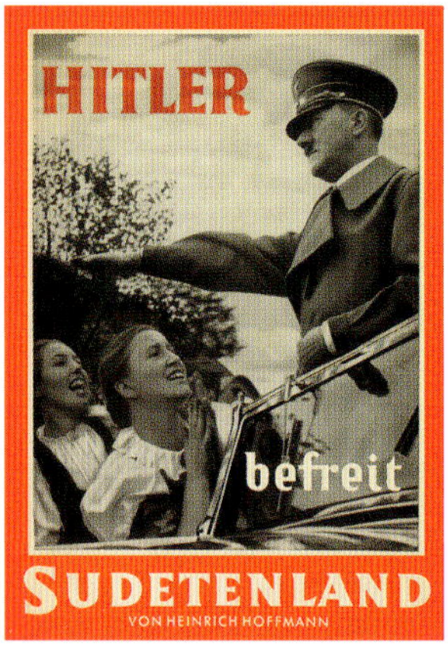
HITLER
befreit
SUDETENLAND
VON HEINRICH HOFFMANN

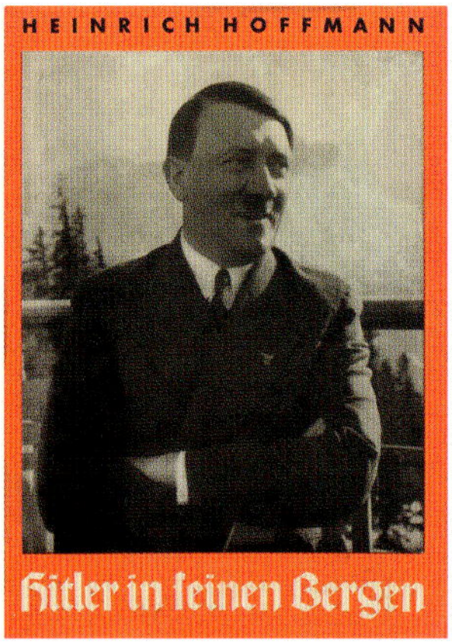
HEINRICH HOFFMANN
Hitler in ſeinen Bergen

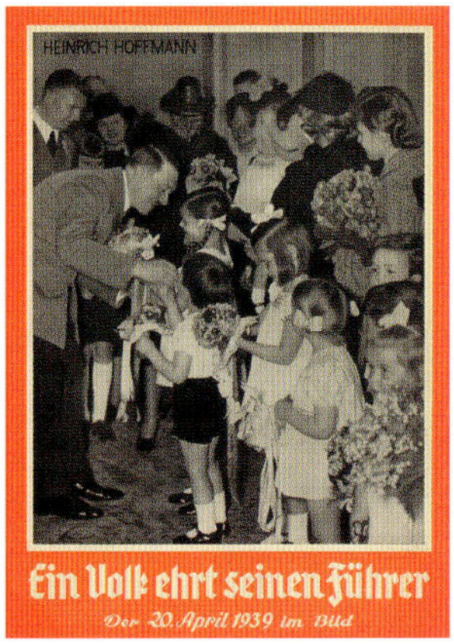
HEINRICH HOFFMANN
Ein Volk ehrt seinen Führer
Der 20. April 1939 im Bild

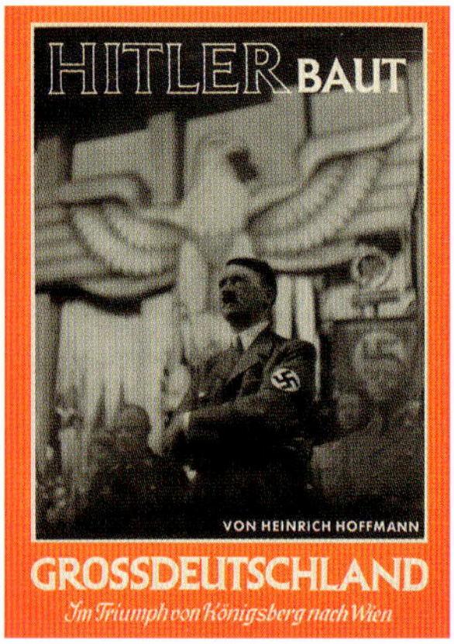
HITLER BAUT
VON HEINRICH HOFFMANN
GROSSDEUTSCHLAND
Im Triumph von Königsberg nach Wien

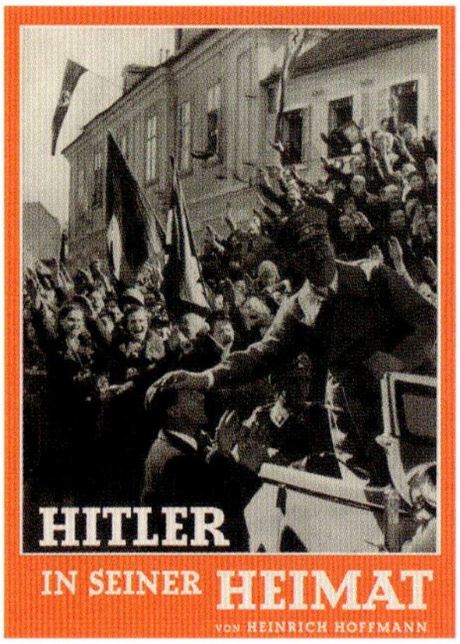
HITLER
IN SEINER HEIMAT
VON HEINRICH HOFFMANN

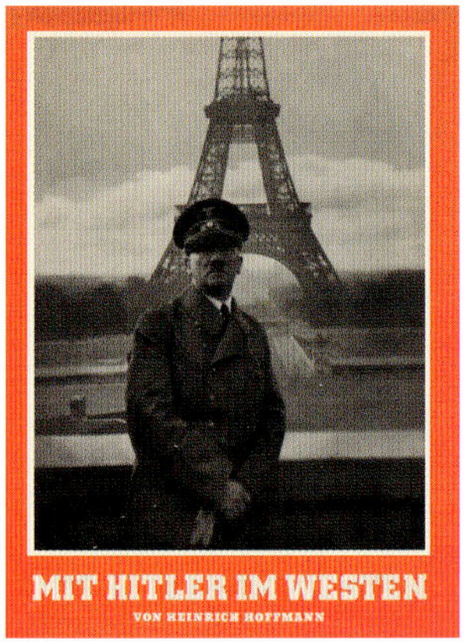
MIT HITLER IM WESTEN
VON HEINRICH HOFFMANN

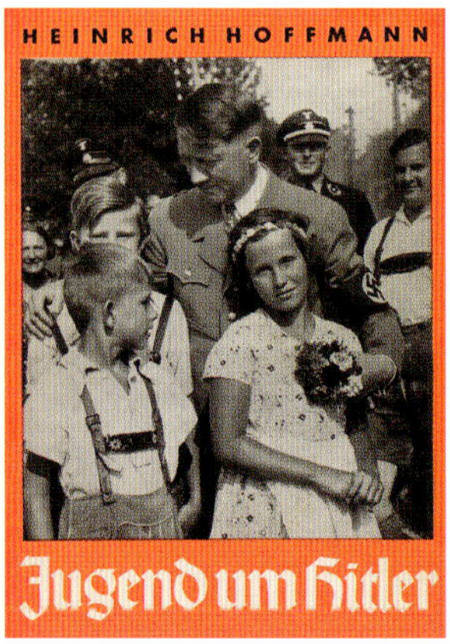
HEINRICH HOFFMANN
Jugend um Hitler

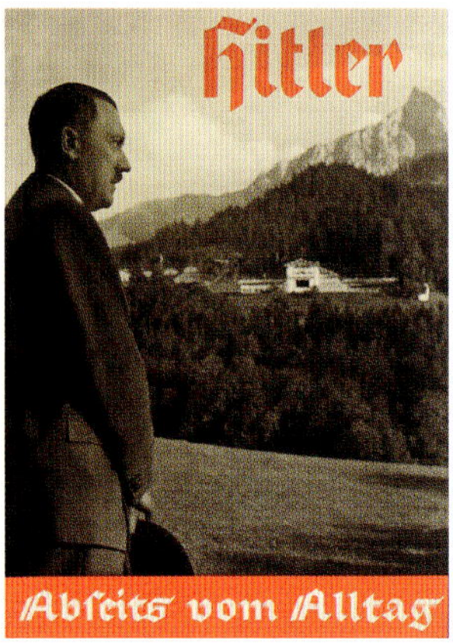
Hitler
Abſeits vom Alltag

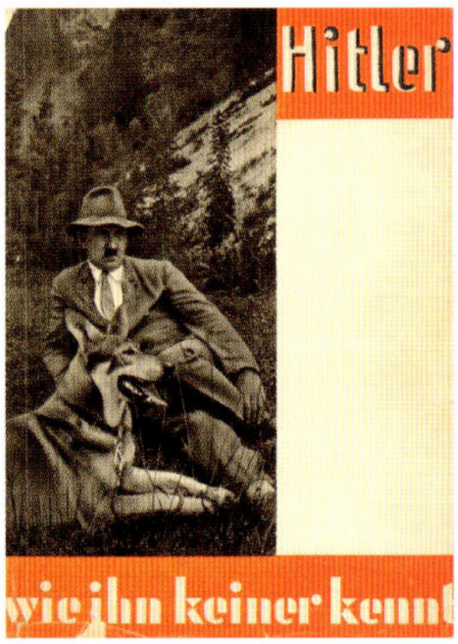
Hitler
wie ihn keiner kennt

Großdeutschland (Hitler Builds Greater Germany) (illus. 72) also appear in *Look to Germany, the Heart of Europe*, authored by an American and published by Hoffmann's firm in both German and English. The photographer's pictures also appear in a Japanese version of *Mein Kampf*. These pages present Hitler publicly as the charismatic leader of a harmonious country building a stable and peaceful future, and privately as an avuncular father figure, among other things.[15]

Other printed matter meant for domestic consumption realized more fully what much of the other material sought: the instrumentalizing of free time and recreation for ideological training. Cartophily, which was much like baseball-card collecting in the U.S., and stereoscopy enabled a heavy use of photography to this end. An album titled *Die Bunte Welt* (The Colourful World, 1934) encouraged its readers to collect cards that came with cigarette purchases. It offered pre-designated slots into which the owner could arrange these photographs as he or she collected them. The act of accumulating and pasting these pictures taught the engaged owner how to see the world through the terms of race so heavily pushed by this book and by fascist ideology. Stereo cards that created the illusion of three dimensions similarly transformed leisure into a propaganda opportunity.[16] Among many others, Heinrich Hoffmann worked in this field, publishing numerous collections that focused on party congresses or soldiers in the field. These series let consumers bring famous propaganda exhibitions into their homes, recreating both the Nazi party spectacle and its three-dimensional realization as display, here in a free-time activity, complete with a viewer and the cards he or she could touch and manipulate.

Bodies and Portraits

Despite the apparent continuity of this visual culture and its potential to saturate even one's leisure time, the image of the ideal human figure on which it relied proved difficult to forge. Today we look back to the fascist era and generally picture youthful, athletic bronzed bodies as the clear paragon. The dictator proclaimed just as much in his notorious speech at the opening of the 1937 *Grosse deutsche Kunstausstellung* (Great German Art Exhibition) in Munich, to which the *Entartete Kunstausstellung* (Degenerate Art Show, opening a day later) served as a grotesque counterpoint. 'Man has never been more similar

72 Heinrich Hoffmann, covers from a series of books focusing on Hitler in photographs, 1932–44, largely halftone.

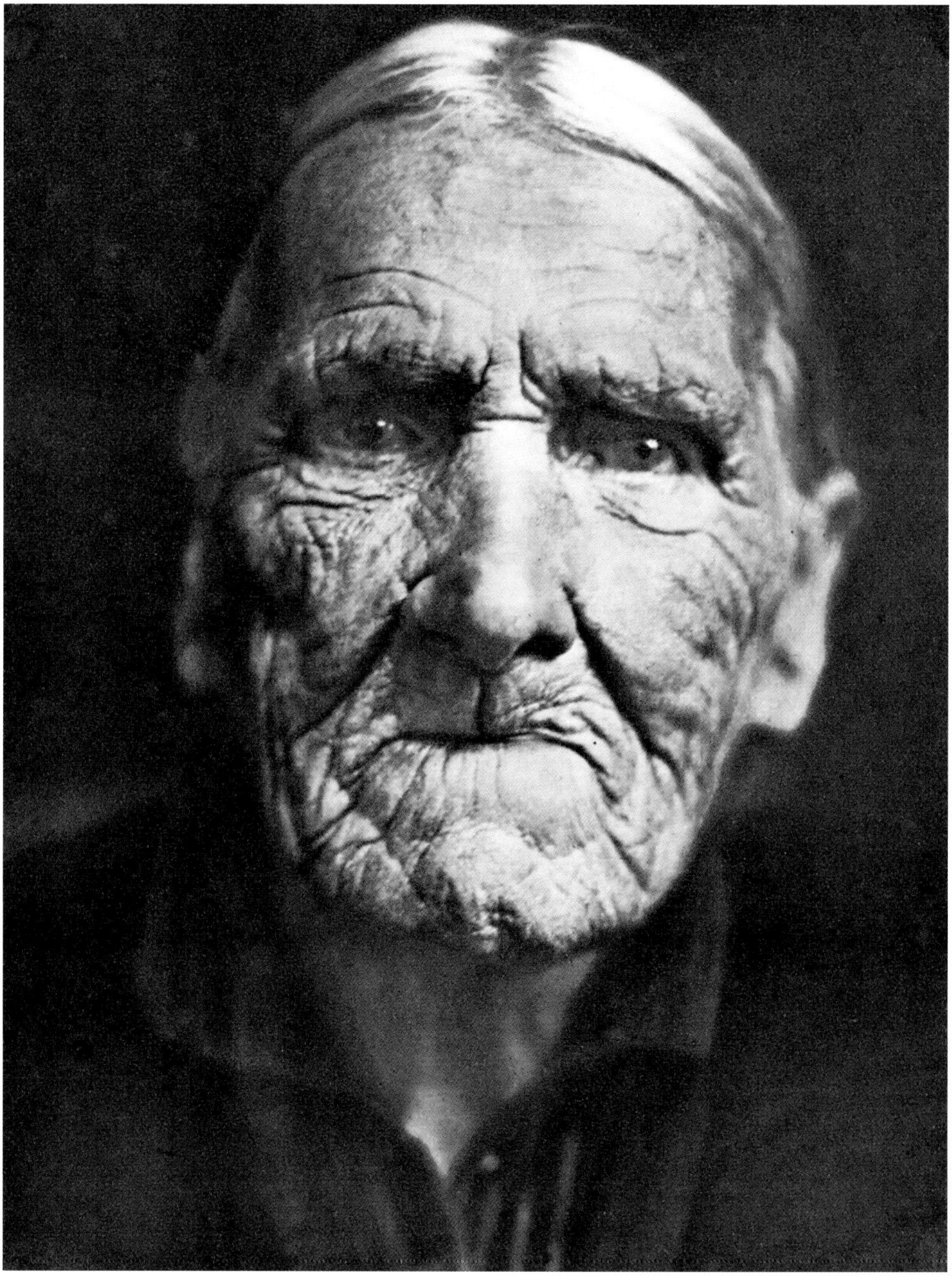

73 Erna Lendvai-Dircksen, 'Woman from Further Pomerania' in her 1932 book *Das deutsche Volksgesicht*, likely halftone print.

in appearance and in sensibilities to the men of antiquity than he is today,' declared Hitler. 'Millions of young people are steeling their bodies through participation in competitive sports, contests, and tournaments and, increasingly, are putting these bodies on display in a form that has not been seen, much less imagined, in perhaps a thousand years.'[17] Such model bodies, directly drawn from classical statuary, seemed best represented by the photographic film stills and frames that actress/director Leni Riefenstahl featured in the prelude to her *Olympia* film one year later.[18] Hitler contrasted this 'new type of man' to the 'deformed cripples and cretins' produced by the 'prehistoric artistic stammering' of the Weimar era.[19]

Yet, one of the photographers who published the greatest number of the era's portrait books began her multi-volume series *Das deutsche Volksgesicht*

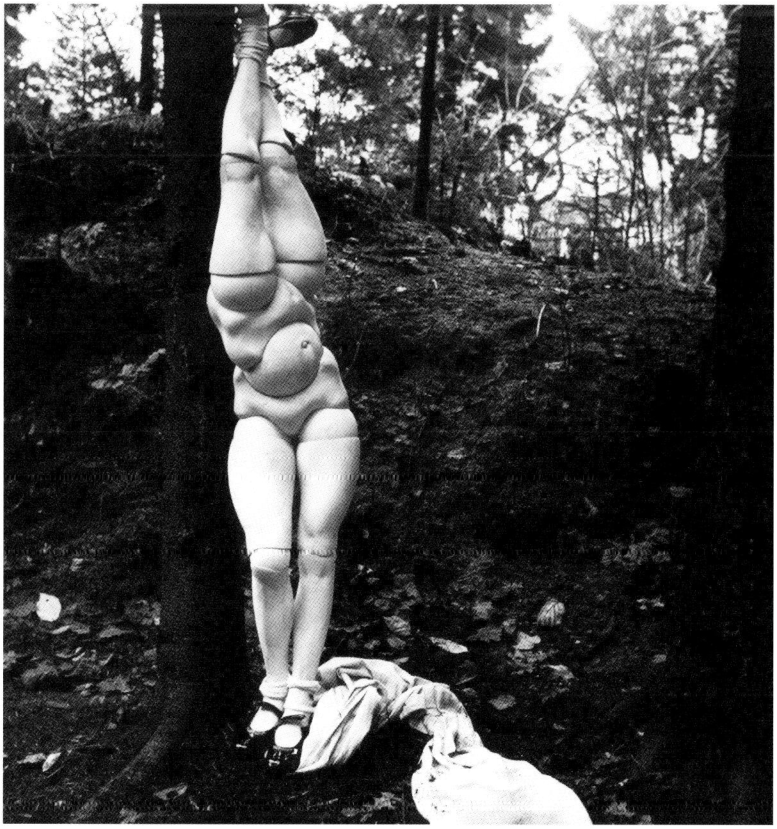

74 Hans Bellmer, *The Doll*, 1935, gelatin silver print.

(Face of the German People/Race) with a heavy stress on what could have been deemed 'deformed' people. Erna Lendvai-Dircksen had made her living in Berlin as a studio photographer and began taking portraits of farming peasants in the mid-1920s. She assembled these pictures into a fine-quality photo book in around 1931, complete with Romantic-era poetry and racial tracts.[20] The great majority of her subjects, whom she categorized by region rather than profession, as August Sander had done, were exceedingly old. Lendvai-Dircksen even played up their advanced age with dramatic studio lighting and uncomfortably close framing (illus. 73). She believed that the true German arose from the native soil, and her pictures stressed the degree to which life on the land impressed itself in the heavy wrinkles and other physical impressions of that contact. Though she also turned her lens to younger peasants in subsequent books, she continued to pay special attention to visual expressions of the *Blut und Boden* (blood and soil) ideology that she found in her older and sometimes visibly infirmed subjects. Her work was one part of a larger pictorial laboratory in which various visions of the authentic German type were being cooked up. Here lay another fissure in the alluring image of the fascist era, a wrinkle in its consistency.

In an environment where powerful ideologues presented German identity as fixed, the actual pictorial realization of that character could vary by the modern conditions generating it and a photographer's individual belief system. The artist Hans Bellmer fell on the latter side of this ledger, having turned sharply away from the heroic and attractive ideal to pursue a personal obsession with women's bodies, as expressed through two life-sized dolls that he created in the mid-1930s. He continually dismantled and reassembled these oddly realist objects, photographing corporeal arrangements that might feature a disembodied head or, in other cases, two pairs of legs with an abdomen as a central joint and no head at all (illus. 74). He photographed the second of these carefully situated against a tree in a Berlin park, as if she were out to enjoy the fresh air in the nude and coyly appeal to a passer-by. Her fleshy legs and cute shoes, two of which face the sky, signal a corporeal verisimilitude that the arrangement of her parts grotesquely denies. Bellmer later explained that these dolls sprang from a childhood obsession with a cousin, and his fascination with author E.T.A. Hoffmann's Romantic-era short story *Der Sandmann*, in which a man falls love with a woman, unaware that she is a doll. Though the second was a classic German literary influence, Bellmer pursued a vision starkly at odds with the 'steeled body' praised by Hitler as ideally German. After publishing two books of his doll photographs, Bellmer saw the writing on the wall and left for France, where he was welcomed by the Surrealists, who had already reviewed his books enthusiastically.[21] Here again ran some of the inconsistencies and outright clefts in the period's alluring image.

Behind the Surface

Fissured as it was by inconsistencies, variations from the gentle to the aggressive and the outright vapid, this period's enticing vision largely hid what were becoming daily horrors from citizens of Germany and the world, particularly if people wished not to see. In the early months of the regime, some press photographers managed to snap pictures of the swift repression that National Socialist paramilitary members exacted on their opponents. A picture attributed to Georg Pahl shows what was probably a group of communists restrained with straps as they raise their hands at the gunpoint

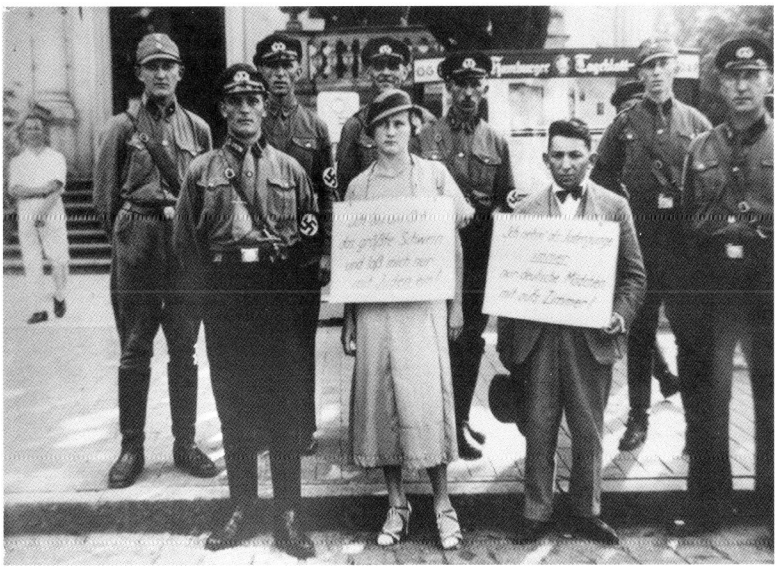

75 SA and SS members in Cuxhaven have themselves photographed with Jewish businessman Oskar Danker and his alleged Christian girlfriend, Adele, who were driven through the streets as 'discouraging examples'. The couple were forced to wear signs bearing rhymes discouraging Jewish-German integration. The young woman's sign reads 'I am fit for the greatest swine and only get involved with Jews' and the young man's 'As a Jew, I only take German girls to my room'. Dankner owned a cinema in Cuxhaven. 27 July 1933, gelatin silver print.

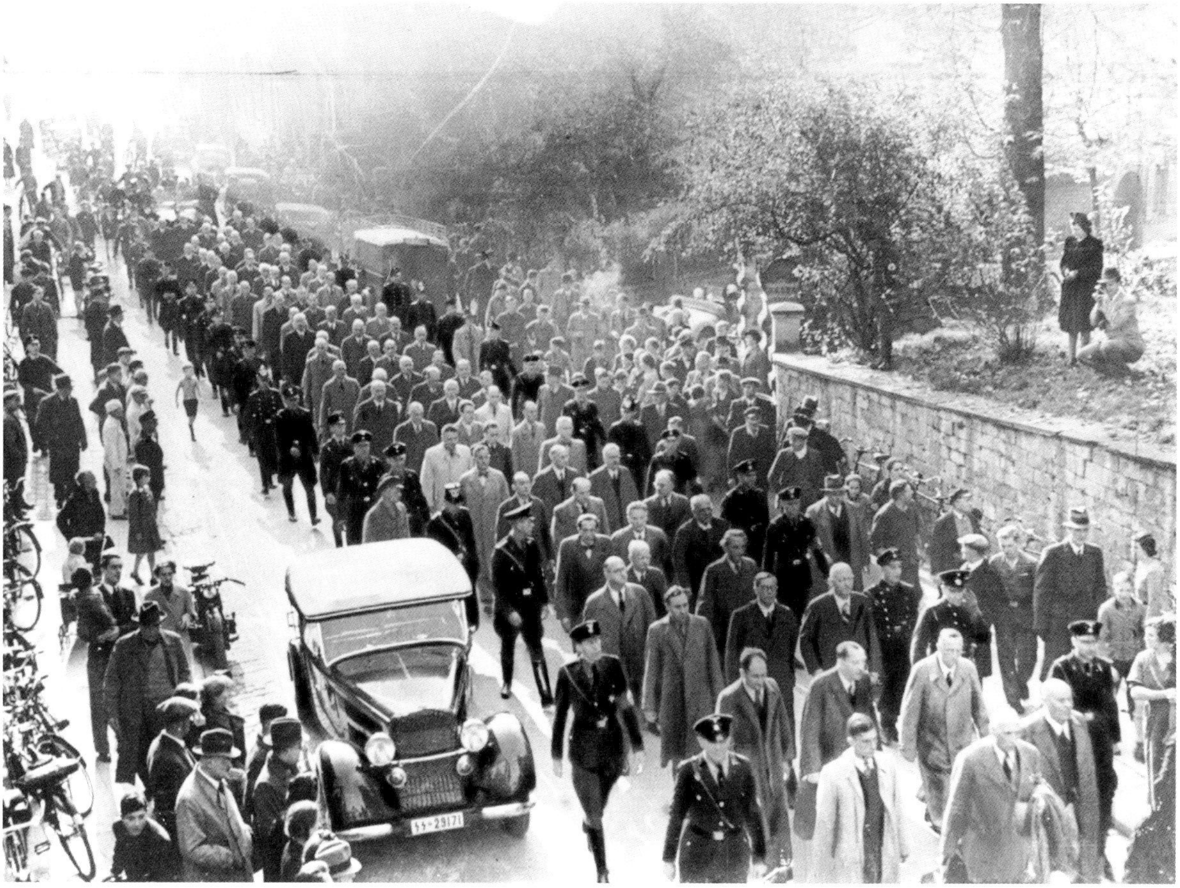

of SA men (Sturm Abteilung, the Nazi paramilitary force) in Berlin. Many of these men were sent to the first concentration camps, such as Dachau near Munich. Another shot, probably by an unidentified perpetrator, shows a woman and a Jewish man posing with signs mocking their supposed romantic relationship (illus. 75). The SA men stand rigid with their hands behind their back, taking the position of big-game hunters proudly before the camera.[22] Such pictures by press photographers and perpetrators of such crimes demonstrate how the medium could serve revelation, ghoulish boastfulness and surveillance all at once. As the government amassed greater power, these sorts of pictures became harder to disseminate. The government

76 Abraham Pisarek (attrib.), 'Detention of Jewish men in Baden-Baden in November 1938. After the fascist anti-Semitic pogrom of 9–10 November 1938, approximately 30,000 Jews were detained and deported to concentration camps' (9 and 10 November 1938), gelatin silver print.

and its collaborators actually answered the charges of abuse that these photos and other forms of evidence seemed to document by mounting counter-publicity campaigns. A 16 July 1933 feature in the *Münchner Illustrierte Presse* (or *MIP*; Munich Illustrated Press) claimed with ample photographs that Dachau was actually an enlightened site for educating political criminals through productive labour.

In subsequent years, such abuses became increasingly hard to photograph even as the country became inured to an exceedingly high level of daily violence and threat. Yet these crimes were not invisible. One picture captures Jewish men being marched to incarceration or even deportation to camps in the days following the notorious *Kristallnacht* (Night of Broken Glass) pogrom against Germany's Jewish population on 9 November 1938 (illus. 76). Like the pictures in the *MIP* Dachau issue, photographs such as these suggest that, rather than this being a cloaked atrocity, mass movements of people deemed criminal for their ethnicity took place in broad daylight with crowds of onlookers. Such openness contradicts post-war protests that 'they didn't know'. A woman at the top left of the post-*Kristallnacht* photo even seems to be filming the event with a handheld movie camera. Exhibitions such as *Der ewige Jude* and articles in the illustrated press left little to the imagination when it came to the hatred being ginned up against Jewish citizens. One did not have to be too observant to see what the country's publicly approved self-representation hid.

The atrocities of the subsequent war, which broke out with the German occupation of Poland on 1 September 1939, ostensibly remained unknown to citizens not involved in combat, although Nazi rhetoric made the intentions clear. In any case, soldiers and others participating in the hostilities generally took photographs as they wished. The personal photo album of an anonymous German warrior in Eastern Europe features attractive shots of the Tatra Mountains in southern Poland and local Russian scenes, but also Polish prisoners and rounded-up Jewish residents. As for the latter, a caption mockingly identifies the first shot of the grouped residents as 'The Chosen People'. The following caption adds 'And they learn it' under a shot of men from the same or a similar group, forced to clear debris and rebuild a destroyed bridge.[23] Such pictorial and textual rhetoric closely mirrors what the *Der ewige Jude* exhibition and other heavy-handed propaganda dispensed, although here it was parroted in the criminal acts for which the propaganda campaigns effectively laid the groundwork.

Other albums assembled by soldiers and officers could be even more horrific, showing a gruesomely hanged man in the Ukraine among pages of landscapes and local sites. Such pictorial collections of horror, beauty and the quotidian, set against each other cheek by jowl, show the degree to which brutality became the banal stuff of Nazi occupation: all were equally valid subjects before the camera lens. Soldiers such as Heinrich Jöst, and bureaucrats such as Walter Genewein, photographed the Jewish ghettos of Nazi occupation as though these open-air prisons were tourist destinations rather than spaces of unspeakable horrors. Their images survive in albums that the men assembled as amateurs. All of these collections provided for a picture of shocking extremes that soldiers sometimes shared with their friends and relatives back home.

Albums such as these continue to surface even many decades after the war. One of them, the so-called Karl Höcker album, was picked up by an American soldier in Frankfurt just after the war and taken home to the U.S.[24] Forgotten after he put it away, it re-emerged in 2006. The photographs it contains shows male officers who commanded the vast death camp of Auschwitz, and their female clerical staff, relaxing in a nearby retreat named Solahütte. In complete contrast to the atrocities the men were committing against more than a million Jews and other 'enemies', these men and women sing, giggle, relax and eat blueberries. One picture shows a gaggle of these perpetrators laughing and darting toward the camera, seemingly because it had begun to rain (illus. 77).

A different set of photographs made by inmates of the camps offers an alternative picture. Four shots of this sort were furtively snapped at great danger by the *Sonderkommando* (special detachment), the mostly Jewish prisoners who were forced to work the gas chambers and crematoria of industrialized mass murder. One of the four photographs, hauntingly taken from within a gas chamber, looks out to the other members of the detachment throwing recently murdered corpses onto burning pyres, a task resorted to when the crematoria were overwhelmed (illus. 78). This darkly framed picture of indescribable crime was meant to document what the inmates feared no one would believe, showing the operation of

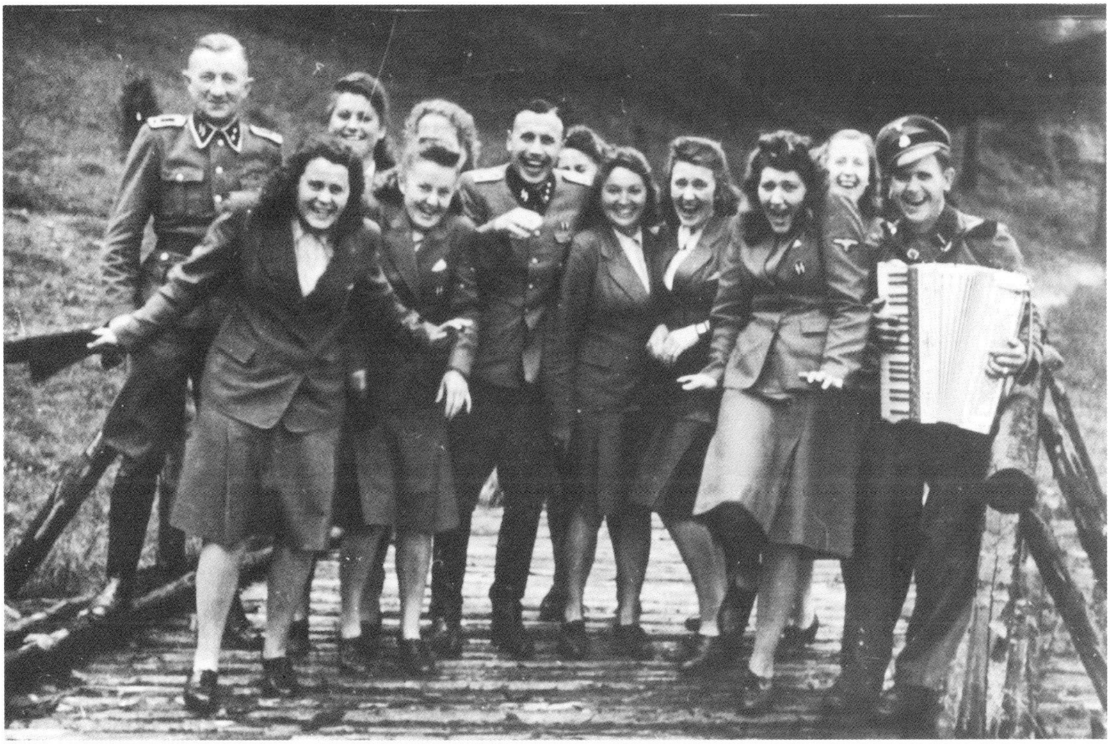

77 Karl Höcker, *Nazi Officers and Female Auxiliaries Run Down a Ramp in Solahütte. The Man on the Right Carries an Accordion. Karl Höcker is Pictured in the Centre*, July 1944, gelatin silver print.

genocide from the perspective of its cautious victims, who took great risk in snapping these pictures and smuggling them out of the camp. Photography at these sites was officially prohibited, given that the camps were declared a state secret. The images offer us an attempted mediation of a reality so unimaginable that no body of photographs could ever convey it. The furtiveness alone, visible in the blur and poor framing, pictorially conveys this impossibility.

For most Germans, the daily diet of photographs in wartime resembled what citizens had already digested in the years up to the conflict, but with a change of theme from peacetime. Endless series of magazines, posters, postcards and other printed matter now sported ever more soldiers in formation, diving aeroplanes and darting tanks. One magazine glorifying the armed forces and Germany's occupation of other countries, *Signal*, was intended for foreign distribution and published in multiple languages. Its

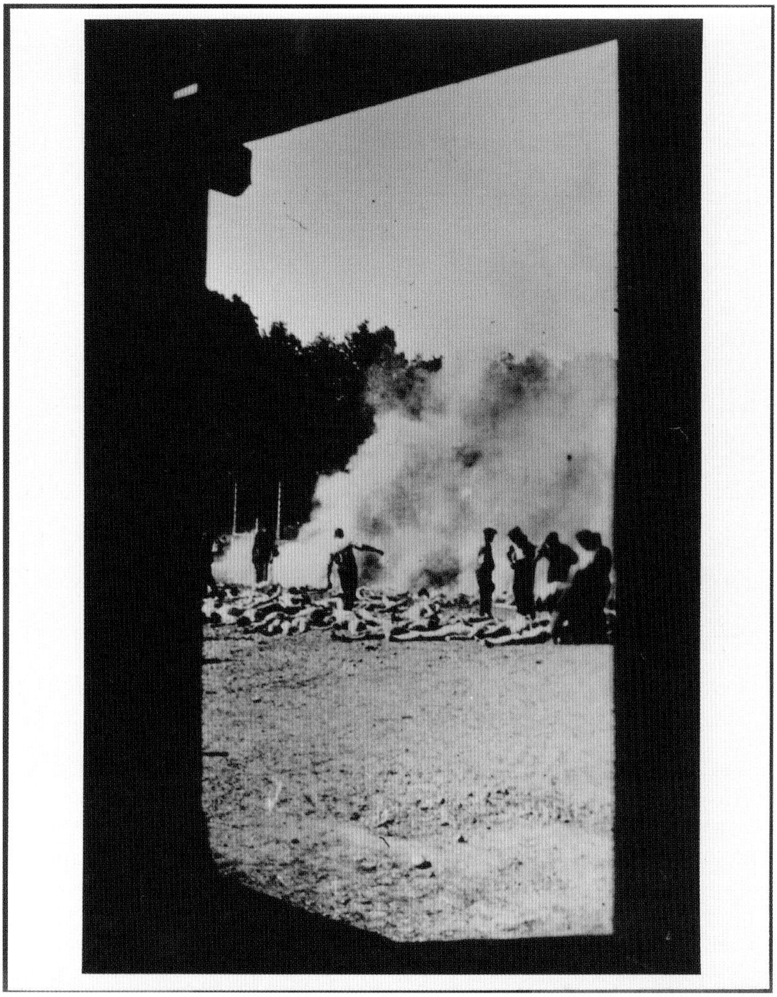

78 Alex, Aleko or Alekos, a member of the *Sonderkommando* from Greece; burning of corpses in the open air (neg. no. 280); picture taken secretly by members of the *Sonderkommando* in KL Auschwitz II-Birkenau in the summer of 1944, gelatin silver print.

designers based it on the American *Life* magazine, though they made their periodical even more attractive by including luxurious colour photographs. An issue from July 1941 shows fighter pilots relaxing in the North African desert underneath their plane. In widely circulated magazines such as this one, foreign audiences saw the mix of repose, adventure and heroism – rather than violence – that the German armed forces wanted potential sympathizers abroad to see. Another significant change in the war's pictorial course came in Hitler's disappearing image. As the Russian campaign in the East failed, the dictator withdrew from public view.

Meanwhile, German cities suffered relentless bombardment by American and British air squadrons, particularly after the Allies had destroyed German air defences in early 1944. The violence of the front returned as death dropped onto cities in a brutal air war. As Nazi authority weakened, citizens became braver in photographing the mounting destruction around them. Cologne resident Hermann Claasen took a particularly uncanny daytime picture of bombers above his city, leaving winding vapour trails as they flew in odd formation, dropping their exploding cargo over citizens below them. The resulting rubble became the subject of an important book that Claasen published after the war.

Defeat, Horror and Shame

Germany – or at least what remained of the Nazi regime – surrendered unconditionally to Allied forces on 7 May 1945. The death of its principal leaders in the conflict or by suicide reflected the country's broader physical and moral destruction, as was now visible in its bombed-out cities and the ragged refugees fleeing areas of eastern Germany that were taken by the Russians. As defeat neared, the Allied armies invading Central Europe and the photojournalists following them uncovered the horrific war crimes that have since been seared into the collective global memory via photography. The American photojournalist Margaret Bourke-White, who contributed important news pictures to *Life* magazine, found that her technique served as an ideal form of objective witness for the unimaginable scenes laid out before her. In her most famous photographs, she pointed her camera directly forwards at survivors and piles of corpses. But for a more haunting shot, she directed her lens downwards from slightly above, into one of the Buchenwald ovens, where a corpse remained only half-consumed by flames (illus. 79). Her images were not just about defeat and crime. In a picture highlighting survival, either she or the American forces gathered joyous inmates to celebrate their liberation before her camera. Another American photojournalist who followed the invading armies, Lee Miller, similarly

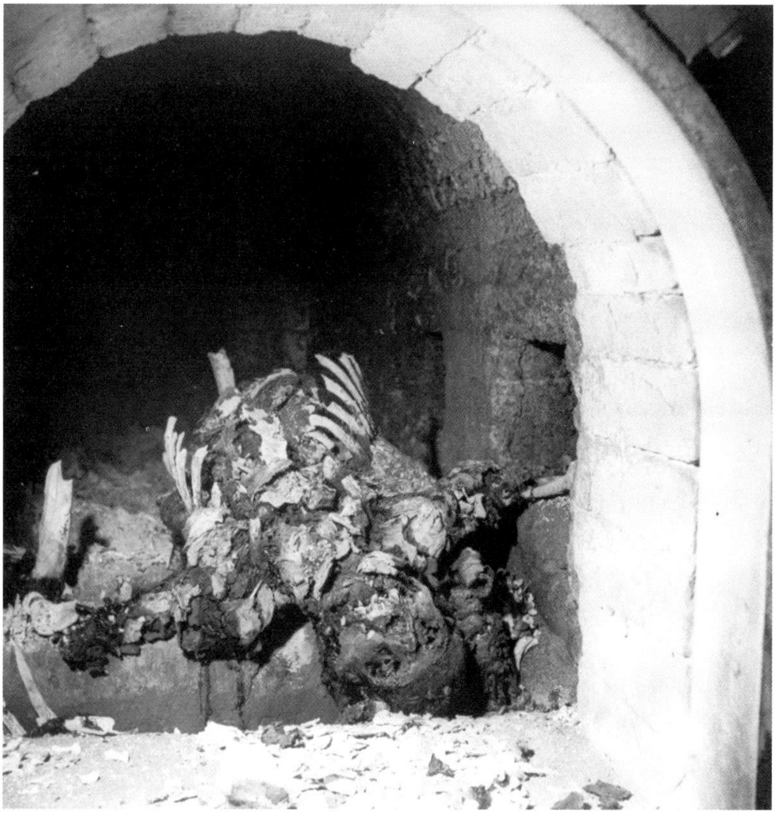

79 Margaret Bourke-White, *Ghastly View of the Charred, Boney Remains of a Prisoner Inside Buchenwald Cremation Oven, on Display for German Civilians Forced to View Nazi Atrocities Found by American Forces after they Liberated this Camp, April 28 1945*, gelatin silver print.

turned her camera on the victims and survivors of these atrocities. She also snapped the perpetrators. One of her pictures shows an ss prison guard who had tried to escape Buchenwald in civilian clothes but, after being recognized, was beaten by his former captives (illus. 80). Under the harsh light of Miller's flash, he stares with a bloody, broken face upwards in shock, wide-eyed before the potential of further retaliation. Miller spoke openly of her burning hatred of all Germans both in the final year of the war and thereafter. This nearly forensic shot glows with her flaming disgust, a sentiment she wished to convey visually to her larger magazine audience of *Vogue* readers. We have since come to see this sort of photographic mediation as the image of Nazi-era Germany, though they were taken after the regime's fall.

80 Lee Miller, ss *Prison Guard, Buchenwald, April 1945*, gelatin silver print.

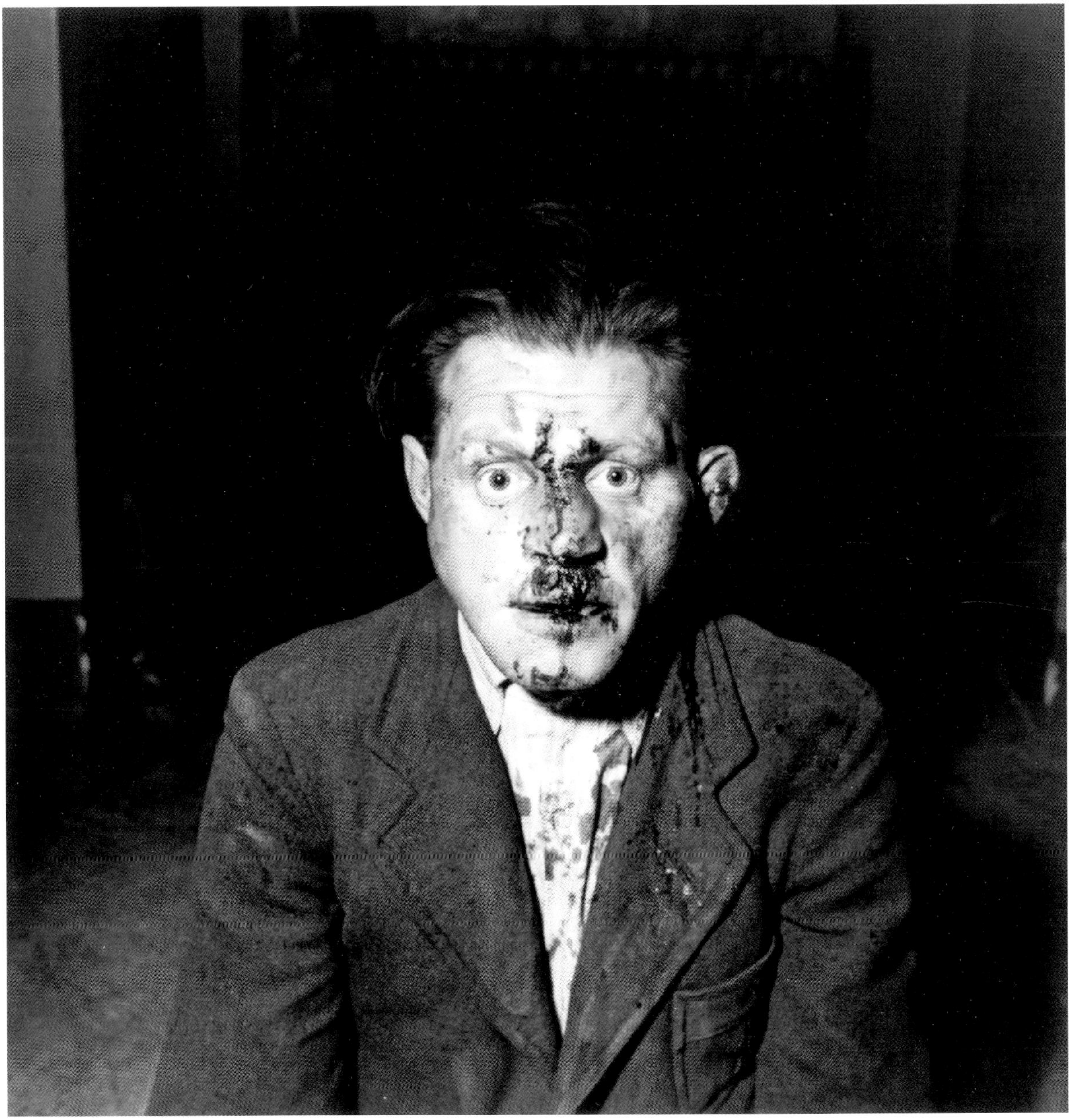

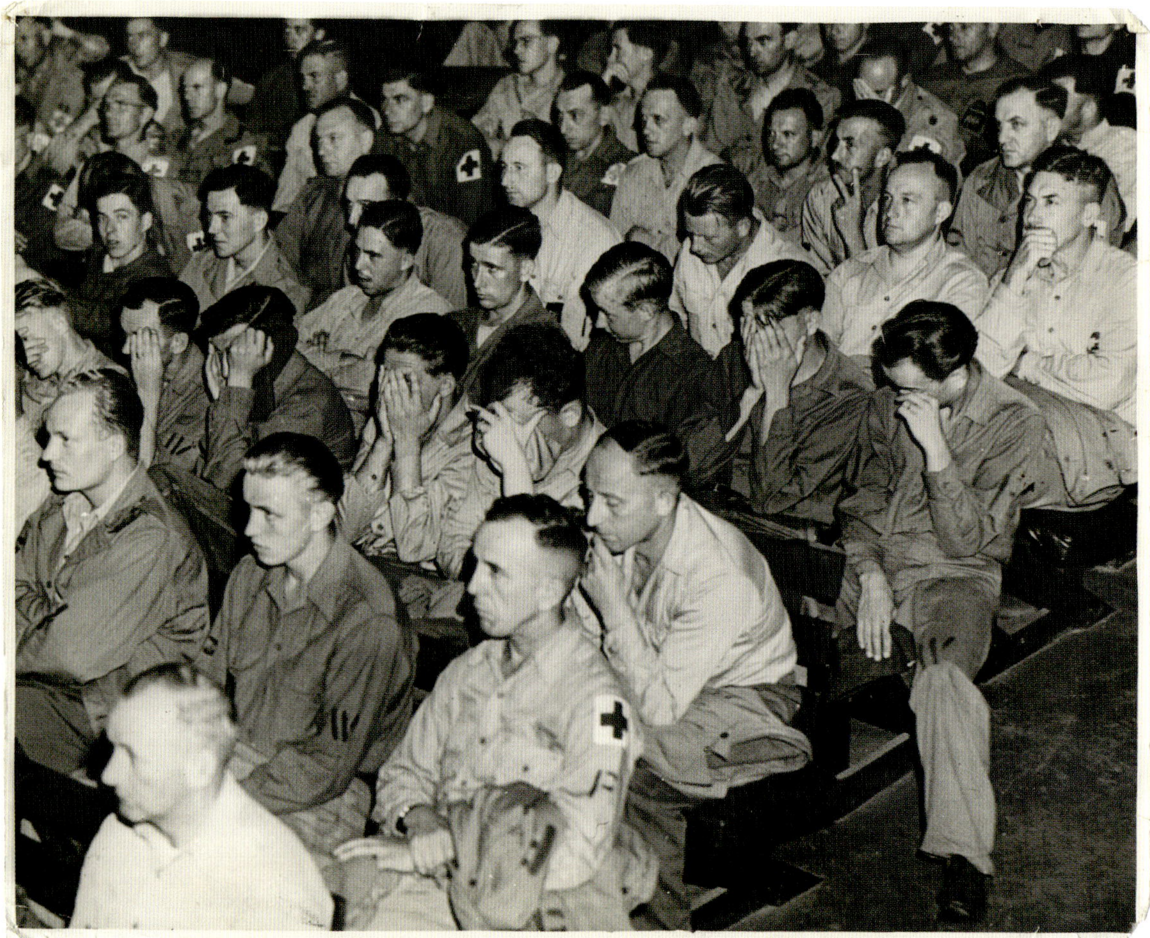

Deutsche Kriegsgefangene in amerikanischen Lagern sehen den Filmbericht über Deutsche Konzentrationslager

81 *German Prisoners of War Held in an American Camp Watch a Film about German Concentration Camps*, 1945, gelatin silver print.

Allied forces wanted to open the eyes of contemporary Germans as well, forcing them to see what their government had done in their name, and what had taken place on the other side of the seductive public image of fascism. Many were forced to tour the recently opened concentration camps in a process of de-Nazification and national shaming. Photographs of this process have also become iconic. But a lesser-known shot was snapped with a flash as American forces made German prisoners of war view footage of the camps in what became known as forced confrontation (illus. 81). Here one sees a range of responses, from a sober gaze forwards, to closed eyes, to hands covering the face. Whereas Germans who were forced to tour the camps often covered their eyes and nose before a flood of horrific sensations, here a reckoning with representation of war crimes had these men specifically reaching to occlude their vision. Such pictures of confrontation, purposefully amassed by the horrified and vengeful victors, forged an iconography of national shame with which the country, soon to be divided, would eventually have to reckon. But how would a rapprochement in photography take place in the context of the Cold War tensions that followed?

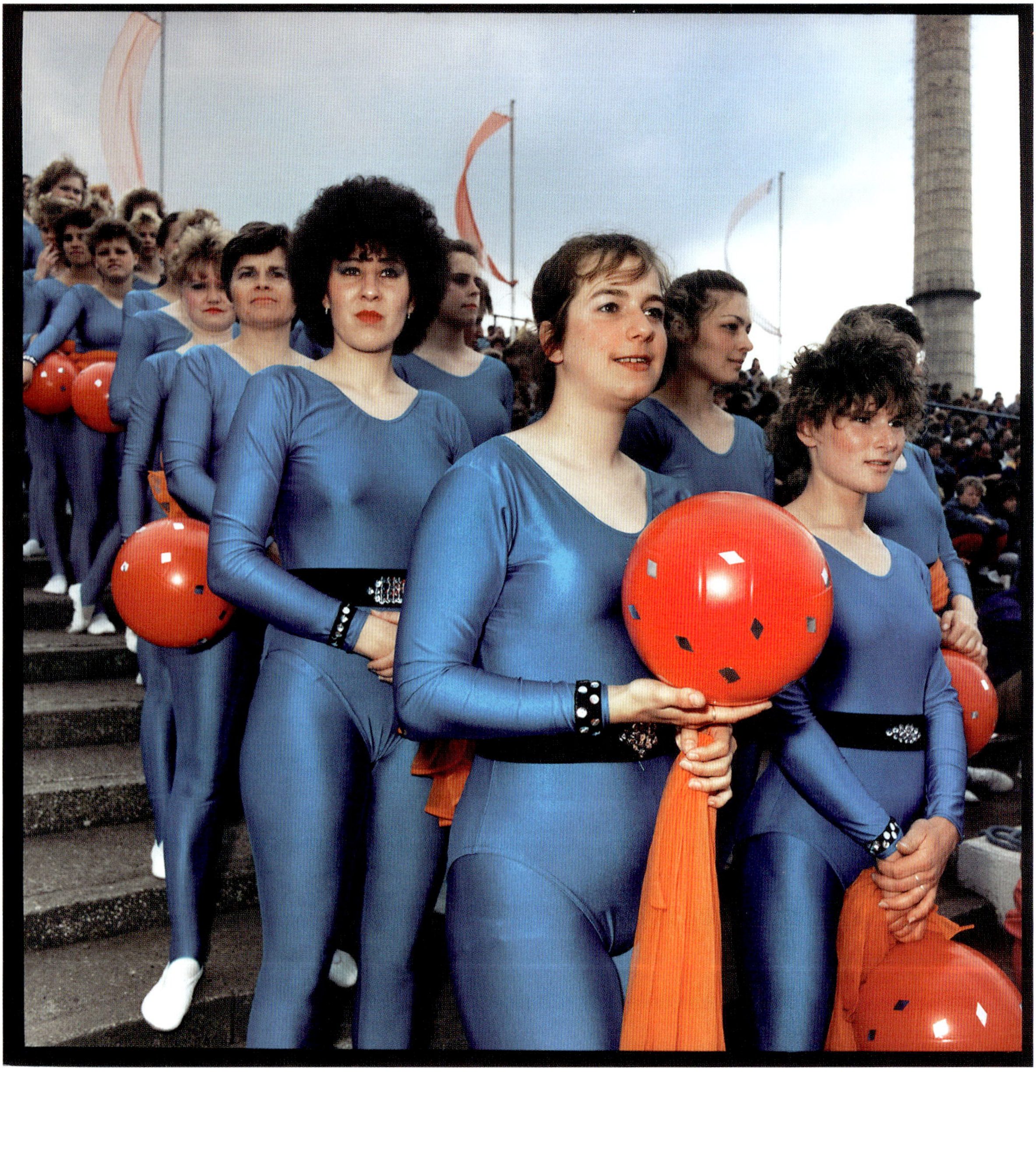

five

History, the Future and Photography, 1946–1989

'In the summer of 1943, during a long heat wave, the RAF (Royal Air Force), supported by the U.S. Eighth Army Air Force, flew a series of raids on Hamburg.' So begins German author W. G. Sebald's account of the firebombing of this northern German city in his book *Luftkrieg und Literatur* (1999). With a thoroughly straightforward – if sometimes fragmented – vocabulary, Sebald describes how the flames ignited by explosive and incendiary bombs merged into a firestorm that 'snatched oxygen to itself so violently' that burning hurricane-force winds rushed toward the city centre, lifting gables and roofs, flinging rafters, melting tram car windows, boiling stocks of sugar in bakers' cellars and driving human beings 'like living torches'. Just as terrifyingly, those who fled air raid shelters to escape their oxygen-deprived suffocation 'sank, with grotesque contortions, in the thick bubbles thrown up by melting asphalt' or simply experienced instant desiccation as the blast-furnace-like winds sucked away their hydration without mercy. The heat generated by these fires was so great that 'bomber pilots said they had felt [it] through the side of their planes.'[1]

Events such as these, experienced in numerous German cities – most infamously, Dresden – were unprecedented in their scale and horror. Moreover, they ran parallel to the indescribable atrocities of the Holocaust and other war crimes committed by National Socialism's armies and by fellow citizens. On top of all this lie the generalized density of totalitarian oppression that covered Germany through the 1930s and early '40s like a smothering blanket.

82 Jens Rötzsch, *Berlin (East), 1989 Pentecost Meeting of the FDJ (Free German Youth)*, c-print.

Given these deeply traumatizing conditions preceding the country's May 1945 defeat, post-war Germany faced a tremendous challenge in digesting and articulating its memory of the preceding twelve years of terror and complicity. This silence about Germans' own suffering, which would not be given a fuller voice until after reunification, became a problem of collective repression that photography, a medium associated with realism and evidence, had a particularly difficult time navigating.[2]

The task would become even harder by the decade's end. In the wake of the Second World War and the international public shaming to which Allied forces initially subjected Germans, an entirely new political dispensation settled over Central Europe. The Western powers and the Soviet Union came to view each other as mortal threats, and the vanquished Germany became the principal theatre for playing out these anxieties, particularly given its split into the Federal Republic of Germany and the German Democratic Republic in 1949. Under the frigid conditions of Cold War Europe, photography became a medium dedicated less to the memory of the recent past as found in the present than to a future defined by the competing systems of capitalism and socialism. For other Germans, photographic history lay not in the immediate past but in the Weimar era, when art and politics offered an acceptable range of images to emulate.[3] Meanwhile, officially sanctioned systems and a great deal of consensus led to waves of photographs dedicated to such things as renewal, rebuilding and commerce. Both states saw the medium used for suppressing memories of the Nazi era.

But despite this amnesia, significant recollections of the recent past nonetheless appeared in photography. Acts, artefacts and discoveries lunged before the lens and reintroduced unwelcomed historical topics to Germans who otherwise wanted to forget the Nazi era. By contrast, victims outside the country who desperately wanted to reflect on their experience of the country's previous regime often welcomed these images and the anger it reignited. This stirring of the traumatized imagination both domestically and abroad helped precipitate a new and exciting relationship between photography and Germany. A great flourishing of applied and art photography followed, making the Federal Republic in particular a photo-obsessed country by the 1980s. Photo-consciousness had definitely returned by that later decade.

Looking back, a number of signals delivered at the war's end suggested that national shaming and a confrontation with the recent past had stimulated new approaches to camera-based images. Wolfgang Staudte's 1945–6 film *Die Mörder sind unter uns* (The Murderers Are Among Us), for example, squarely focused on the unpunished war crimes of fellow citizens (illus. 83). In this famous *Trümmerfilm* (rubble film), the lingering trauma embodied by comfortably surviving persecutors, living in plain sight, is dramatically mirrored in towering slivers of ruined buildings that collapse into clouds of punishing dust between the movie's scenes. In another signal of aesthetic

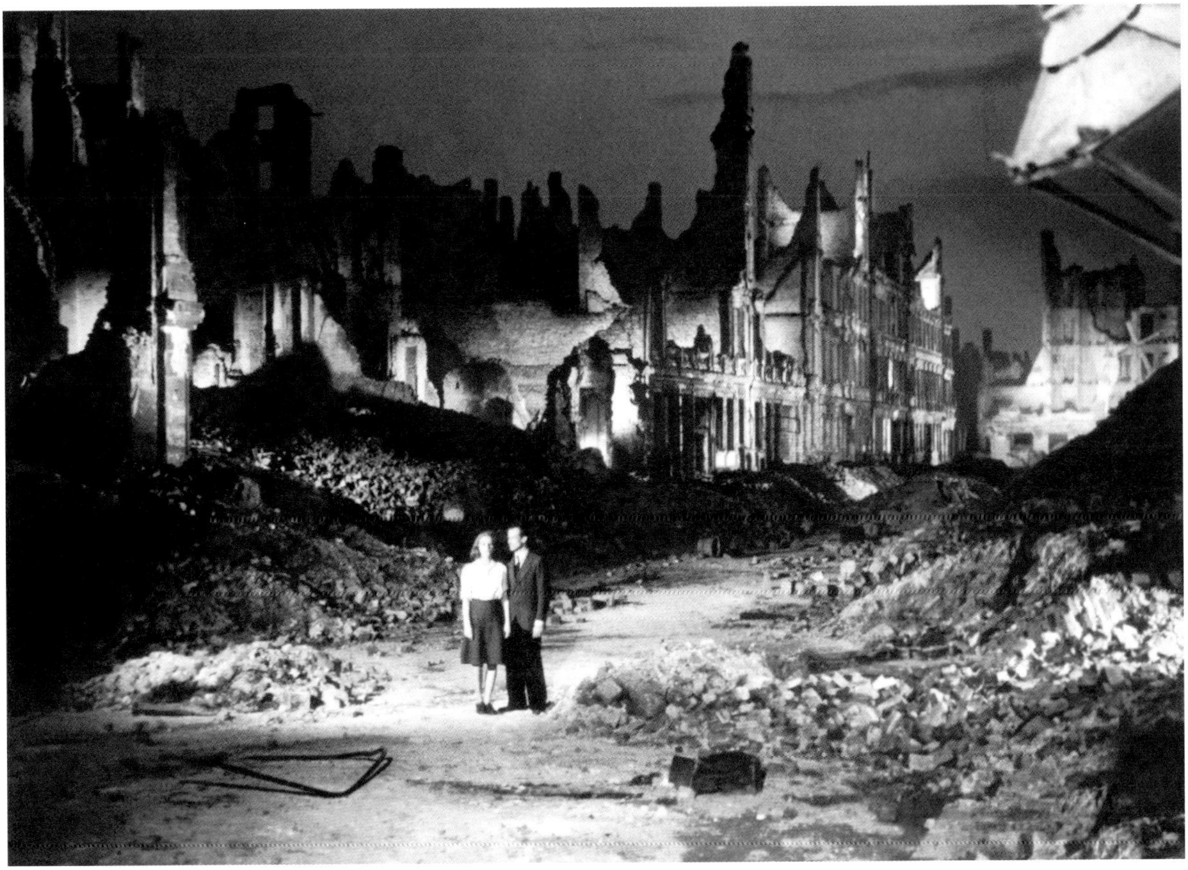

83 Photographic film still from Wolfgang Staudte's 1946 film *The Murderers Are Among Us*, gelatin silver print.

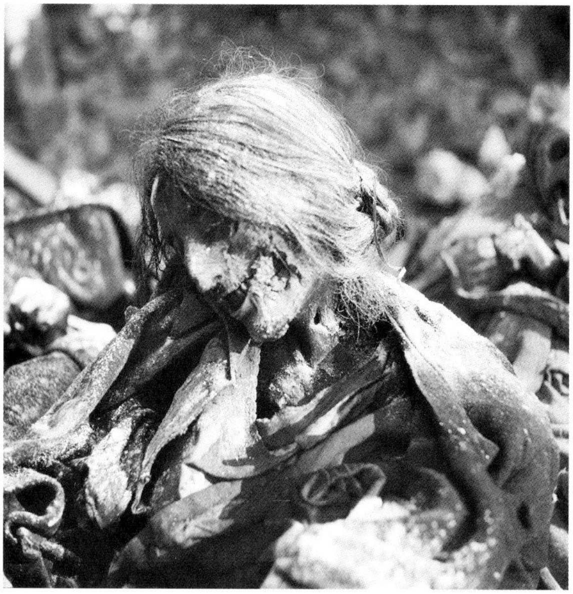 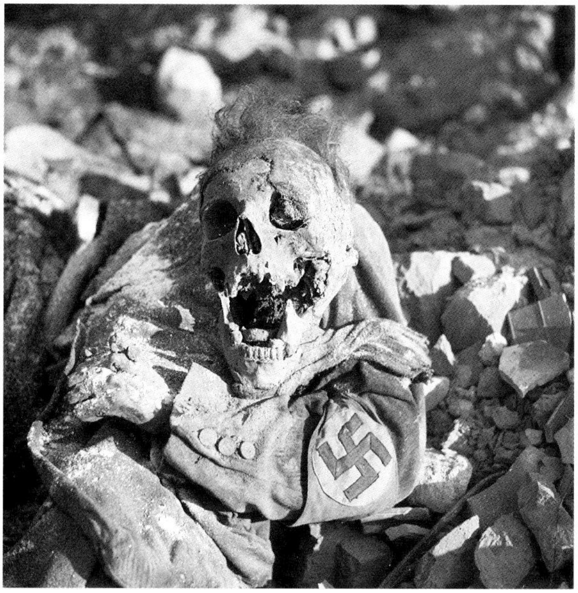

reconciliation and invention, Dresden press photographer Richard Peter descended into his city's ghostly air raid shelters, which had become tombs, and snapped uncomfortably close photographs of desiccated corpses (illus. 84). In his pictures, suffocated mothers collapse over their children's prams, a closely framed woman lies buried to her bust in rubble and a fully outfitted soldier seemingly screams from his ruin-strewn expiration. In these moments following total defeat, Germany seemed ready to confront the memory of its past with modestly innovative pictorial representations of that past's location in the present.[4]

84 Richard Peter, '. . . A Mother: Female Corpse in a Bombshelter' and 'Air Raid Warden: Skull and Body in Uniform in a Bombshelter', from the series *Dresden after the Bombing of 13–14 February 1945*, 1945, gelatin silver prints published in halftone as facing pages in Peter's *Dresden: A Camera Accuses* (1950).

Yet this moment of aesthetically fresh reflection did not last long. The subject of war crimes soon disappeared from the cinema of Germany's occupied zones, while even piles of rubble, so central to the everyday experience of urban residents, largely fell from the content of photographs by the decade's end. Instead of these lingering signs of atrocity and destruction, audiences in the West, who principally consumed their images from film, illustrated periodicals and photo books, were largely fed a standard pictorial fare. Traditional forms of narrative cinema now reigned while a conventional diet of photojournalism, touting the country's coming reconstruction (*Wiederaufbau*), fed audiences reassuring visions of the future. Particularly after the founding of the two Germanies in 1949, photographs in the Federal Republic's print media highlighted the country's quickly developing economy of plenty, such as Hannes Kilian's picture of well-stocked delicatessen shelves and the eager eyes they drew after the West German currency reform of 1948 (illus. 85). Photographs such as these lavished attention on material plenty and the new citizens who enjoyed it.

Residents in the German Democratic Republic found straightforward prints of heroic socialist reconstruction, as in an anonymous photograph from 1950 advocating 'socialist competition' (illus. 86).[5] In both West and East, most photographers avoided difficult subject matter and postponed the development of a new visual grammar that might have helped digest the lingering presence of a deeply traumatic past. Such pictorial docility stood in stark contrast to the country's pioneering encounter with photography made just two and a half

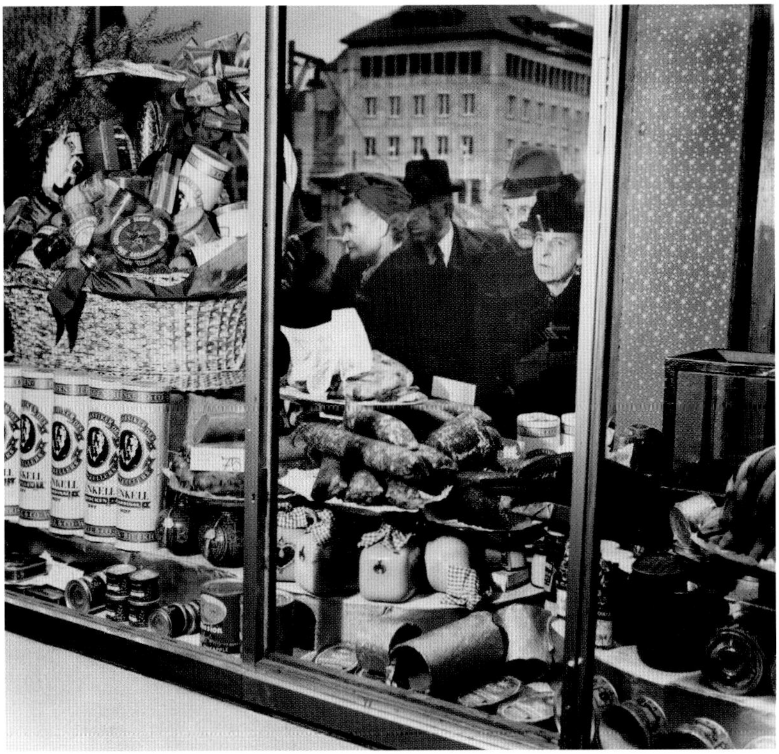

85 Hannes Kilian, 'Grocery after the Currency Reform', 1949, gelatin silver print.

decades earlier after the First World War, as discussed in Chapter Three. In these earlier years, artists in Berlin's Dada movement, along with other image makers, stressed the utter fluidity of photographic meaning and, just as importantly, the medium's inability to represent the extremes of modern experience without the aid of radical pictorial reinvention, such as photomontage.

Yet in post-war Germany between 1950 and 1960, most citizens saw photographs of smiling faces and new buildings with rarely a trace of the recent horrors that the vast majority of these same viewers had just witnessed. No single explanation can account for a discrepancy of such significance. But a number of factors help explain what was largely a post-war docility in photography. The German studies scholar Andreas Huyssen, for example, suggests that in the wake of the war's horrors, an emotional refusal overtook image making and reception in Germany. 'Confronted by the [press] photographs and films from Dachau and Buchenwald,' he explains, 'psychological image denial took over. The experience of crushing defeat and bombed-out cities, combined with a guilty conscience, produced paralysis of the visual imagination. The result was an inability to mourn the victims of Nazism both

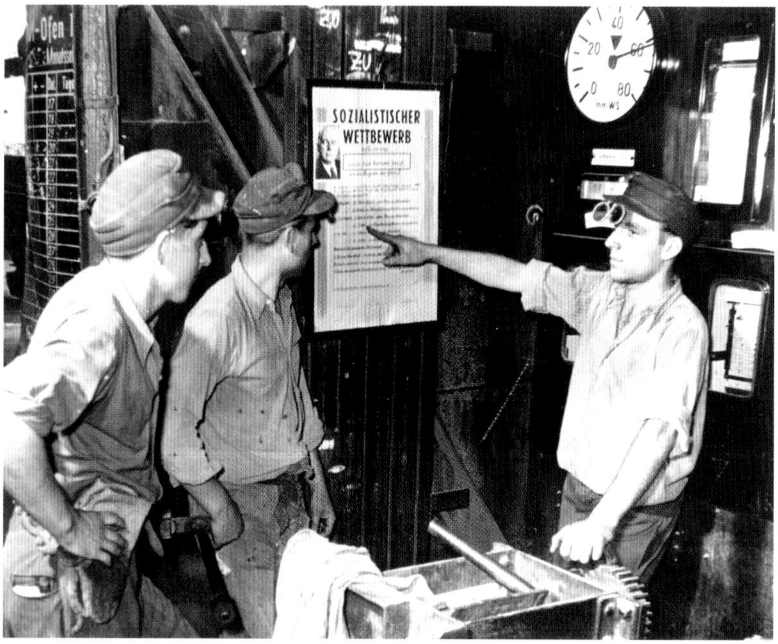

86 Unattributed, *Members of a Youth Brigade at the Henningsdorf Steel Mill*, c. 1950, gelatin silver print.

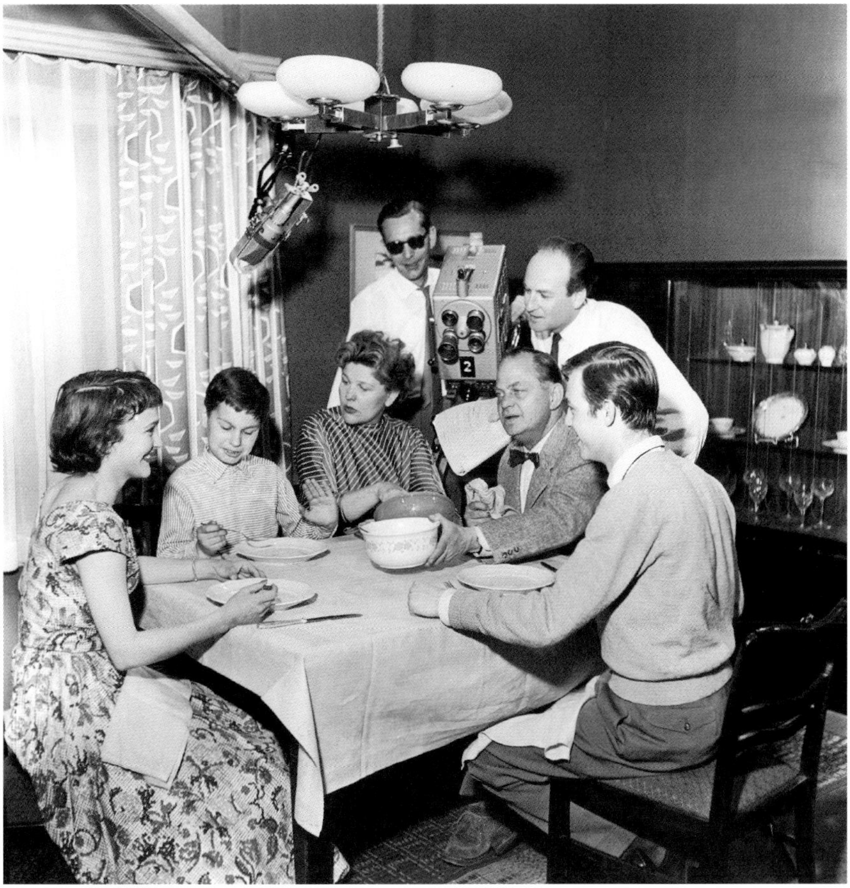

87 Max Ehlert, 'In the Studio Recording the TV series Our Neighbours This Evening – Family Schölermann, produced by NWDR' (North-West German Broadcasting), 1956, gelatin silver print.

at home and abroad.' The dearth of German photographs addressing the past, therefore, came not from a '*Bilderverbot* (prohibition of images) grounded in insight into the limits of representing extreme trauma', but in the broad refusal of that trauma's location in the present.[6] Curator Stephanie Barron adds that the Federal Republic in particular experienced an 'economically induced amnesia' as the 'economic miracle' covered emotional wounds with full employment and tantalizing consumer goods.[7] Augmenting this coddling was the rising Cold War between East and West, a conflict forcefully occupying the terrain of culture and thereby turning attention to the present as shaped by competing visions of the future, not the past.

Correspondingly, the industry of illustrated periodicals and photo books that emerged after the war and boomed following 1949 pursued cautious content that led to tame bodies of photographs. The weekly news magazine *Der Spiegel*, for example, wished to assure readers of its objectivity amid Cold War tensions, claiming that it did not want art but craftsmanship. The magazine tamped down any aesthetic experimentation that might have provided new ways of envisioning a difficult past. The photo historian Klaus Honnef has noted that the magazine's editor, Rudolf Augstein, specifically wanted 'the truth, the whole truth, and nothing but the truth', a desire partly fed by disgust with the preceding years of fascist photographic propaganda.[8] This exercise of compensation, grounded in a pictorial neutrality prized by photographers such as Max Ehlert, one of Augstein's regulars, reassuringly demonstrated no discernable artistic ambitions. One of his typical photographs from 1956 shows the making of the *Familie Schölermann* TV show. Taken at the director's eye level, it catches the production crew and staged family in action (illus. 87). Nor did this regime of photojournalism seek to address the past that it so thoroughly rejected or, in some cases, from which it wished to hide. Ehlert, as discussed in the previous chapter (see illus. 70), had been an expert in fashion and cinema photography. He was also talented at catching fascist pomp and ceremony with his camera. Through such cases of strategic forgetting and psychological denial, 'mechanisms of repression' arose that, according to Honnef, 'fostered a selective image of the immediate past . . . and a collective amnesia'.[9]

The vast majority of the photographs that arose from these conditions lay in particularly stark contrast to those snapped by American photojournalists such as Margaret Bourke-White and Lee Miller, who focused and even enhanced their signature documentary approaches while reporting on the atrocities they found in liberated death camps. Post-war German photographers were thus charged with an aesthetically stifling task. Among the static pictorial media, photography was the one most strongly associated with seamless and legible realism. Its apparently natural mode of representation essentially made it an important pictorial workhorse. In a conflicted climate of amnesia spiked by the growing cultural tension strung between Germany's West and East, the medium was often charged with the job of forgetting the past and envisioning Germany's split future. The tendency, however, was not a rule impervious to moments of disruption.

Photography and Rubble

Photography's post-war docility remained particularly unmoved in an important set of post-war photographs that called heavily on traditional photographic realism: the body of images often referred to as *Trümmerfotografie* (rubble photography). These pictures were taken in the five years following defeat but were generally not published as photo essays or books until late in the decade. In the immediate post-war years, professional photographers found that their primary means of income, such as photo studios and photo agencies, had utterly collapsed. If their cameras and equipment had survived plunder and requisition, photographers generally turned to assignments given by new photo-weeklies such as *Heute* (Today), which was set up by the American occupation forces in 1945, and a new array of photo-book publishers on the lookout for contemporary material to release. With the 1948 currency reform in the West and the subsequent declaration of both Germanies as separate states, these venues for the publication of photography began to flourish, leading to a dramatic hunger for documentary photographs, the genre that dominated Germany's mid-century.[10] At their most basic, rubble photographs practise their documentary charge in a fascination with the indescribable expanses of devastation that German cities had become. Already in these pictures, one can find a use of conventional vantage points that avoid any perceptually challenging pictorial grammar, and a reliance on pre-packaged forms of meaning that lie external to the war's direct experience.[11]

As for the first scenario, photographers avoided the disorienting points of view that were generally associated with the interwar avant-garde. Instead, the vast majority of these pictures capture the vastness of destruction within a single and traditionally structured frame. The Berlin-born and Jewish photojournalist Henry Ries, who had fled fascism and returned after the war, lavished his photographic attention on ruins that clearly surprised him. *Nollendorfplatz in Schöneberg* (*Landscape of Ruins in Nollendorfplatz, Schoenberg (Berlin)*) shows a flattened mound of rubble in the foreground and – in the middle ground – two streets merging into one, the length of which recedes along a deep orthogonal line to the left (illus. 88).[12] Along this plunge one sees a seemingly endless stretch of fragmented facades that form a background of spindly destruction. Only one man walks far down the street in what is probably an early summer morning. Berlin appears a post-apocalyptic ghost town. A rail track and slightly obscured refuse carriages constitute the only signs of clearing work. To make sense of this vast and potentially upsetting content, Ries offers a picture that fits comfortably within traditions of urban-view photography, particularly as found on postcards. Much as in these small-format pictures, an easily perceivable object or space in the foreground anchors the viewer's position within the image, as the middle and backgrounds withdraw along a diagonal urban recession. A clearly defined horizon line, then, helps frame this ravaged space from above while also giving it a sense of scale.

88 Henry Ries, *Landscape of Ruins in Nollendorfplatz, Schoenberg (Berlin)*, 1946, gelatin silver print.

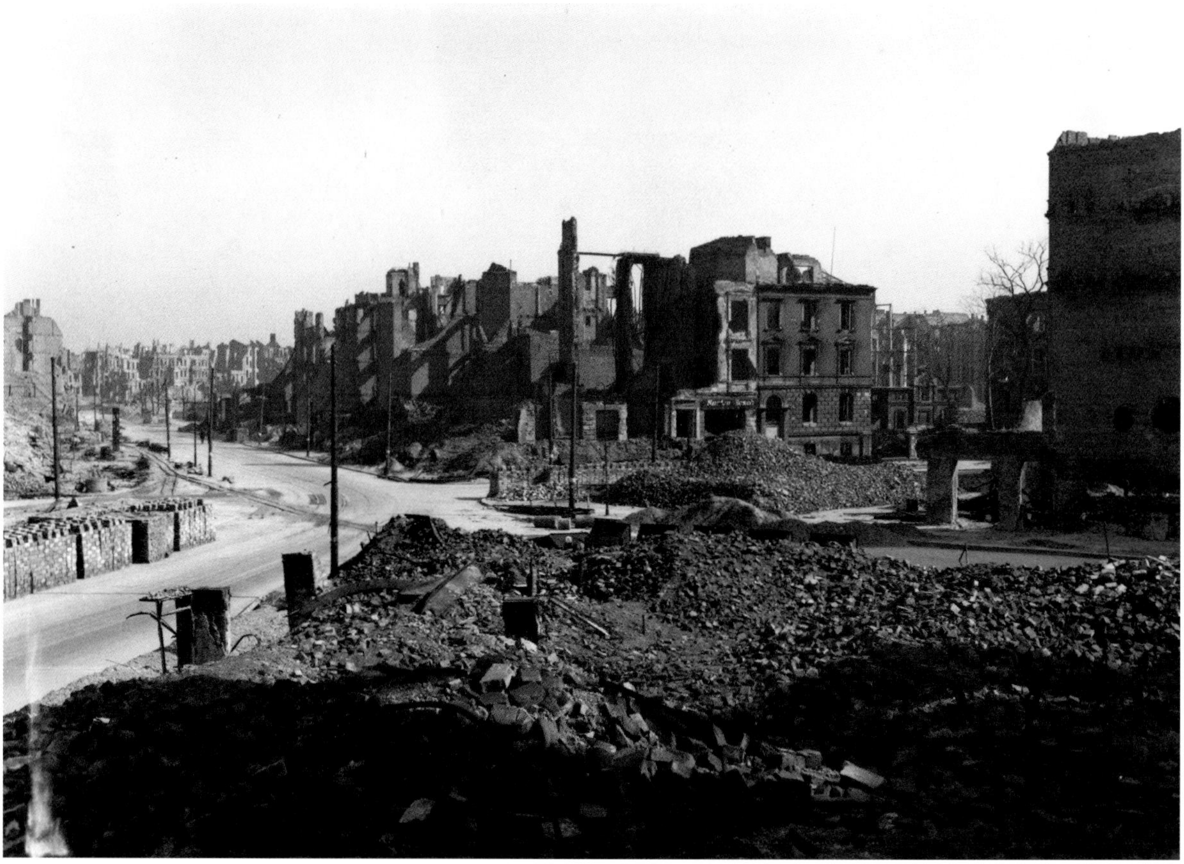

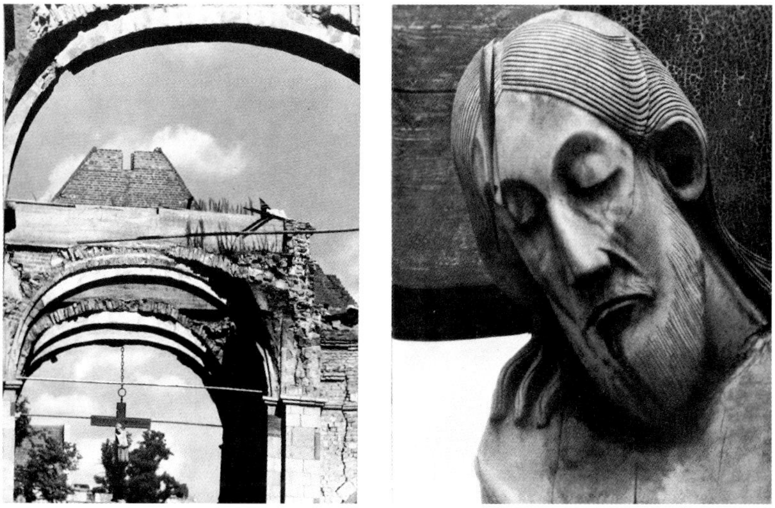

89 Hermann Claasen, halftone illustration of 'Crucified Christ in the St Georg Basilica,' in his 1947 book *Hymn in the Fiery Furnace: Cologne – Remains of an Old German City*, p. 44.

Outside this sort of press photography, a number of photo books dealing with the subject of ruins were published at the decade's close, and they also concentrated on the vastness of Germany's urban destruction. But in these more carefully produced photo series, external narratives that borrowed from Christian religion, Graeco-Roman antiquity or Cold War culture displaced attention from the actual causes of destruction and the specific trauma endured. Such is the case in one of the era's most famous rubble books, authored by Cologne-based photographer Hermann Claasen. Entitled *Gesang im Feuerofen. Köln – Überreste einer alten deutschen Stadt* (Hymn in the Fiery Furnace: Cologne – Remains of an Old German City, 1947), it offers views of destruction that have since become iconic.

Making some sense out of this catastrophic rubblescape is the religious metaphor set up by the book's very title, a reference to the Hebrew Testament's Daniel, whose three companions refuse Nebuchadnezzar's idolatrous demands and are thrown into an oven. Their 'hymn to God' leads the three to divine salvation even amid the kiln's licking flames. Of course, this reference stood uncomfortably close to the ovens in which so many death-camp inmates were incinerated. But Claasen assures his desired reading by highlighting the perseverance of Christian icons, institutions and religious practice amid his city's post-inferno-like ruins. Paired images of the destroyed St Georg Basilica, for example, show a crucifix miraculously hanging from the structure's bare arches while an adjoining shot tightly focuses on Christ's sad face, bomb damage clearly having cleaved his head (illus. 88). The great majority of the book's images are of similarly destroyed churches and their sculptures, though his panoramic 'Corpus Christi Procession' provides an exception. This two-page spread illustrates a line of black-clad nuns who process before the sort of ruined expanse featured in Ries's Berlin photographs.[13] As the historian of photography Ludger Derenthal observes, however, here 'there is no before and no after, no life amid the rubble and clearing work'.[14] Rather than manifest a historical moment in the course of twentieth-century history, these catastrophic ruins telegraph a 'rebirth of belief' in the wake of Germany's destruction. In such a manner, Claasen's pictures and the ruins they represent find meaning through religion rather than the political and historical causes of the war, or the actual human suffering experienced as these buildings came crashing down. Stressing metaphysics over physics, the book's narrative explains how Cologne's very rubble points to 'a return to the great order of God's creations', as Claasen's introductory text offers.[15] Forgetting in the face of such omnipresent and undeniable destruction required a dramatic reattribution of meaning. In Claasen's case, that reassignment occurs with an imposition of religious metaphors and an image succession that increasingly focuses on ecclesiastical symbols recovered from the ruins and placed in the support of such a reading.

In the eastern Soviet-occupied sector, one could occasionally find a more aggressive rubble photography. But here too the use of metaphors and, in some cases, allegories, became critically important. This was true of the other most notable rubble photography book to emerge next to Claasen's own. Entitled *Dresden. Eine Kamera klagt an* (Dresden: A Camera Accuses, 1950), it features the work of the Dresden-based photojournalist Richard Peter and sports what is arguably the most famous image of Germany's ruins (illus. 90).[16] Snapped from the city's town hall, it foregrounds a sculptural allegory of kindness with its left hand extended, spreading grace before a destroyed cityscape with no horizon line and therefore no visible end. Peter's camera unreservedly makes its accusation through stark juxtaposition of allegory and reality.

Many of his other pictures roughly follow the pattern seen in Claasen's work. But Peter's attention to the dead of Dresden makes for a significant

90 Richard Peter, 'View from City Hall toward the South with the Allegory of Benevolence – Bonitas, Sculpture by August Schreitmüller, from 1908–1912', from the series *Dresden after the Bombing of 13–14 February 1945*, 1945, gelatin silver prints published in Peter's *Dresden: A Camera Accuses* (1950).

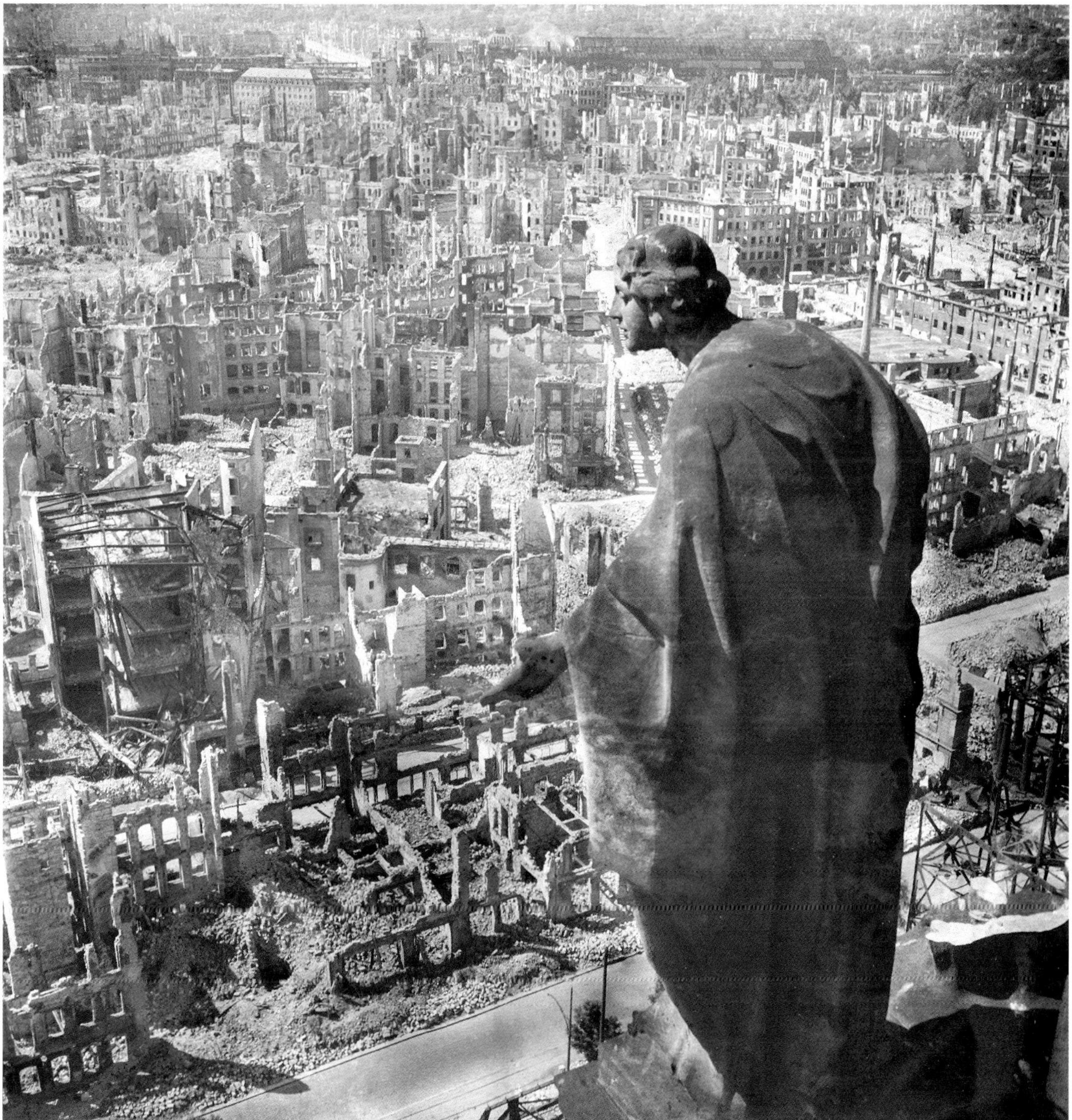

departure. He opens this subject, which is confined to a discrete section of the book, with a haunting photograph entitled 'The Tragedy of the Opened Basement' (illus. 91). This picture mercilessly closes in on a battered wall of neo-Baroque architecture where scribbles cry out for missing relatives and suggest frantic searches and personal loss. By having the scribbles stand in for the missing to whom they appeal, absence itself represents loss. The people referenced by the building's text may be the corpses that appear on the subsequent pages as Peter takes his viewers into a similar building's basement. What follows are the closely framed and starkly illuminated photos of suffocated bodies discussed earlier (see illus. 84). One of the more ghoulish aspects of these images is the degree to which the figures look stuck somewhere between life and death. Their clothes are generally intact and their hair, particularly that of the women, survives. The figures slump forwards or backwards as if caught in sleep rather than having expired in suffocation. Here it is important to remember that Peter only published this volume in 1950 after the German Democratic Republic had been founded and Cold War rhetoric had escalated significantly. It is within this context that the photographer could finally publish the haunting pictures that he had originally taken four years earlier. Within his book's framework they appear not as a confrontation with Germany's war guilt (as would be the case with one corpse still wearing his National Socialist military uniform) or with the trauma so broadly suffered by the country's citizens. Nor do they introduce the difficult subject of Germany's heavy bombing of British, Polish, Dutch and Soviet cities, for which this act was seen by the Allies as fitting retribution. Instead the text in Peter's book condemns the two Western countries responsible for Dresden's firebombing: the United Kingdom and the United States. The prologue, penned by the poet and party politician Max Zimmering, intones of the lost Dresden:

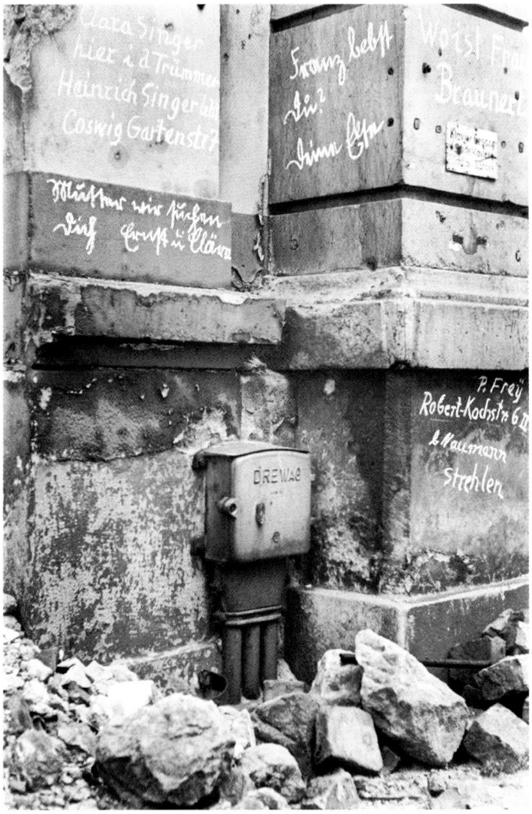

91 Richard Peter, 'Search Messages on an Apartment Building', gelatin silver print from the series *Dresden after the Bombing of 13–14 February 1945*, 1945, published as 'The Tragedy of the Opened Basement' in Peter's *Dresden: A Camera Accuses* (1950).

> The brilliance that once was in your eyes, illuminated by music and painting,
> Was made to yield to a particular shame, and that shame
> Carries the name of Wall Street.

A similar passage in Zimmering's introduction notes that surviving Dresdeners unhesitatingly embraced the Red Army soldiers who arrived with the fall of National Socialism. At the book's end, the city's rebirth is indicated through mounds of rubble being cleared away and then – in the last image pair – by the newly reconstructed city hall and a mason climbing atop an unidentified structure. In Peter's book, photography reconstructed the possibility of perceiving an unrecognizable world. And it did so by speaking in strict terms of contemporary political rhetoric while still deploying immediately recognizable allegorical relays.

Humanism and the Weimar Legacy

Deploying images of the destroyed Dresden for Cold War rhetoric, rather than for directly confronting Germany's traumatic past, became an equally regular practice for an East German state that accepted no responsibility for the preceding war and its crimes. German communists, as the state and its party regularly declared, had also suffered persecution by the Nazis, and now they were building a society that descended directly from their Weimar-era progenitors.[17] Peter's photographs thus serve less to chronicle the recent German past and more to visualize the difference between war and peace, with the GDR clearly championing the latter. In essence, these works made a political link to the Weimar past through protestations of innocence and peace, but without the aesthetic experimentation that was characteristic of the interwar period. This conservative tendency found expression in an endless flow of banal photographs showing leaders of the Sozialistische Einheitspartei Deutschlands (Socialist Unity Party of Germany) visiting factories and farms, offering what one historian has called 'the smiling face of dictatorship'.[18]

This overlooking of the Weimar era's avant-garde contributions had much to do with the Cold War moment. Within East Germany's extreme Stalinist context, photography's realist charge to represent the new socialist state had to be clearly and directly realized, lest the photographer face severe consequences. The sense that she or he had paid too much attention to the manner in which the subject had been presented could excite the disqualifying charge of 'formalism', or a related one of anti-social autonomy. As Ernst Nitsche, one of the more strident enforcers of these aesthetic restrictions, declared in 1953:

> to develop a realistic art of photography, one must naturally consider the German Democratic Republic's new social relations . . . Abstract and formal pictorial compositions that allow nothing to be recognized and that only generate a false sentimentalism, kitschy photographs of an antiquated style: these all betray isolation from the people and provide an objective help for imperialism.[19]

Faced with this threat, which could lead to publishing or exhibition bans, or worse, many photographers simply staged their shots so as to achieve complete control over the content, as in the awkwardly theatrical image of a factory worker sternly pointing to a notice about 'socialist competition' (see illus. 86). Such pictures laboured to realize the vaguely articulated category of socialist realism in photography.

Meanwhile, during this same period, the conservative tendency in the West found reinforcement with the American *Family of Man* exhibition. Curated by Edward Steichen at New York's Museum of Modern Art in 1955, it travelled the world and landed in West Berlin that same year. The vast array of professional and amateur photographs it displayed, a few of which came from the Weimar era, proffered a unity, harmony and togetherness of the world's population in a time of Cold War tension, a gesture famously condemned by the likes of Roland Barthes and Susan Sontag as mythologizing. German curator Karl Pawek followed with a remarkably similar exhibition nine years letter. Titled *Weltausstellung der Photographie* (World Exhibition of Photography, 1964), it also pursued lofty ahistorical themes such as 'What is mankind?' and 'women' with contemporary and interwar pictures. Like *The Family of Man*, Pawek's show typified West Germany's general effort to establish continuities with the pre-Nazi past and to position the country over East Germany as the true inheritor of what now appeared to be the Weimar era's humanist and democratic legacy.[20]

Parallel to a world mediated by a vast array of benevolent pictures in exhibitions and magazines was one built by artists such as Otto Steinert. His 'Subjektive Fotografie' (Subjective Photography) movement embraced techniques pioneered by the interwar avant-garde. But he and his followers used these to realize deeply personal aesthetic expressions. In the movement's art pictures, one found blurring, dramatic vantage points, close-ups, solarization and negative printing. This was one of the few places where post-war photography gave up its mimetic charge and approximated the language of avant-garde modernism. Doing so allowed these photographers to claim the Weimar-era heritage of modernism and publicly to reject the stifling socialist realism enforced in the East by the likes of Nitsche. Just as importantly, it allowed art photography to work in a language of abstraction that ambitious post-war painting now spoke. But unlike in the 1920s, photographers such as Steinert used cutting-edge techniques not to digest the recent past or the tumultuous present, but to pursue an autonomous aesthetic expression.

Persistence of Memory

Public photography addressing Germany's recent past may have been scarce in the 1950s, but it did exist, particularly outside the country and within limited circles. The Yiddish and Hebrew-language memorial tomes known as yizkor books offer an important case that shows how post-war silence about the past was in no way complete.[21] Published in the years following the Holocaust by and for Jews from individual destroyed communities, these volumes memorialize people lost to Nazi genocide, especially in the occupied territories of Poland, Russia and other parts of Eastern Europe, where Germany unleashed its most barbaric atrocities. The genre originally arose in Europe's medieval era after Crusade armies, en route to the Middle East, murdered Jewish populations in Central Europe. Both then and later, the books essentially served the liturgical purpose of listing specific names to include in prayers for Jewish mourners.

Like many post-war yizkor books, one published in South Africa in 1956 and dedicated to the destroyed six-hundred-year-old Jewish community of Chelm, Poland, functioned much like a family photo album. This memorial tome chronicled the town's Jewish history, its notable citizens, its destruction and its dead. Page after page in the necrology provides photographs of murdered citizens, often in the company of family and friends, and accompanied by short biographical sketches (illus. 91). Many of the photographs employed here had been made in photo studios. Therefore the sitters appear formal and austere, a seriousness suitable to the history that the book chronicles.

Woven through this volume and the others of its time is the historical fact that Nazi Germany committed these murders. To a certain extent, these are stories and photographs of Germany's recent history as remembered by its Eastern European Jewish neighbours. Some portions of the Chelm book state this fact outright. Consistent with the convention, the volume ends with the actual yizkor, the call to remember the dead. Among these incantations is a dedication by Miriam Fligelman-Szteinberg: 'My most beloved and dearest who perished as martyrs at the hands of the Hitlerists, may their names be erased.' It goes on to list the dead. As Daniel Magilow and Lisa Silverman note, this phrasing is a standard Hebrew-Yiddish curse originally directed against Haman in biblical antiquity and used by custom thereafter to condemn enemies. 'We see here', they explain, 'how the yizkor book represents the Holocaust through the lens of Jewish history and tailors it to a Jewish audience still coping with raw anguish.'[22]

The post-war yizkor books demonstrate that the apparent phenomenon of German historical amnesia can be addressed not by asking if the recent past was being discussed, but instead by inquiring into who was talking about it, why, and in what context. Jews in the Americas from Argentina to Canada, as well as in South Africa, commemorated and vigorously discussed the Holocaust in these years. Parallel to this, the Russian-American photographer Roman Vishniac's pictures of Polish Jewish communities before their destruction, first published in 1947, reached growing numbers of Jewish communities and beyond.[23] Conversations about the Holocaust and the war in Germany similarly took place among groups of survivors and within families of war veterans, although the latter often remained notoriously tight-lipped about their participation in atrocities.

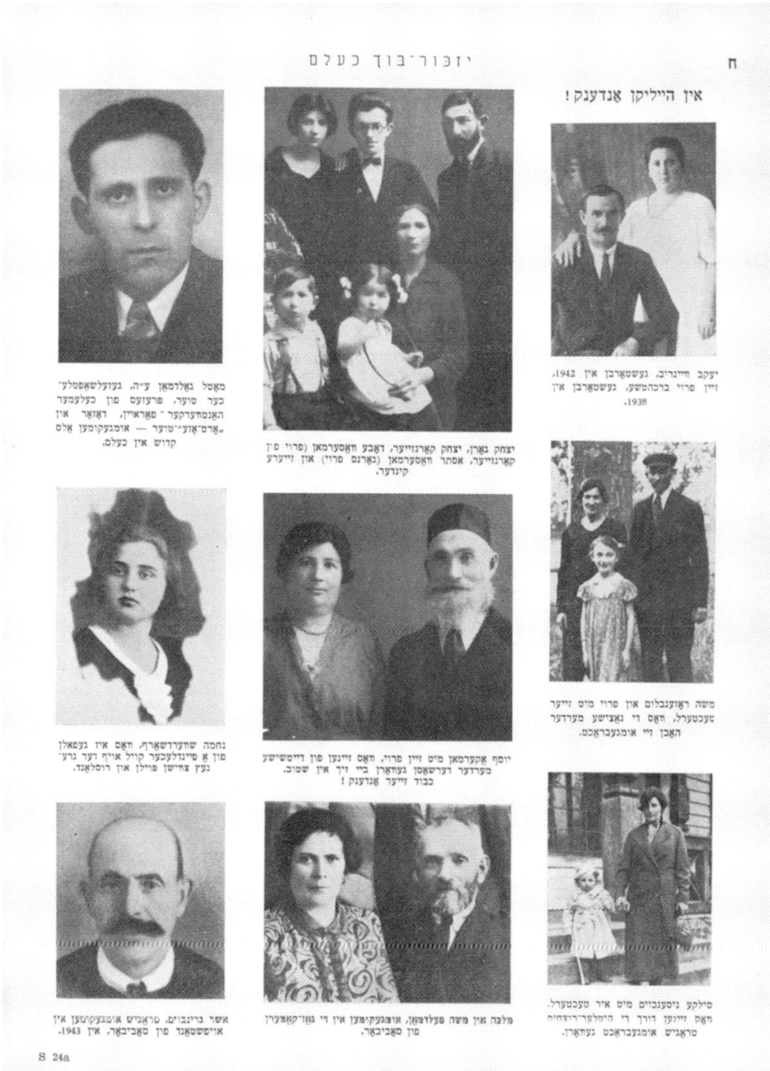

92 Page of portraits from yizkor book of Chelm, Poland, assembled and published in South Africa, 1954, likely halftone print.

Public debate in Germany unmistakably broke out with the publication in 1960 of Gerhard Schoenberner's comprehensive photographic account of the Holocaust, *Der gelbe Stern* (The Yellow Star), which reintroduced pictures that had scarcely been seen in Germany since just after the war. The capture of Adolf Eichmann on 11 May that same year, followed by his trial and execution in Israel over the following two years, also forged a new iconography of international German accountability, summed up by the image of the accused, sealed in a glass box before judges in Jerusalem. This container was ostensibly meant to protect him but it also rendered his trial participation a spectacle. Back in Germany and to great controversy, Alexander Kluge and Peter Schamoni reintroduced the overlooked presence of fascist-era architecture as *Brutalität in Stein* (Brutality in Stone, 1961), a short film that offered photographic-like details of major Nazi-era buildings overlaid with sound from period newsreels. The presence of the past as seen in the present had most definitely returned, at least in post-war West Germany's public visual culture.

Photographic Disruptions

The broader coercion and conformity that helped sustain a stifling post-war cultural climate was regularly disrupted, even before this point in the early 1960s, by subtle acts of photographic resistance on both sides of the Iron Curtain. Many of these were derived from the documentary approaches of the interwar era that had been forged by worker photographers in Europe and by American photographers around the Farm Security Administration, whose Depression-era images inspired post-war Germans. Ursula Arnold, who had studied photography in Leipzig in the 1950s, took pictures on her own initiative as a nonconformist artist in East Germany. Her shot of a Leipzig magazine vendor (illus. 93) shows the old woman bent steeply forward as she mounts a public stairway with her paper burden. One of the magazines she holds, the satirical *Eulenspeigel*, contrasts in tone with the seriousness of her meagre life, made starker by the apparent prosperity of the woman behind her. As Arnold later explained, 'My sympathies belong to those who don't count among the powerful.'[24] Her work expresses this sentiment by highlighting the discrepancy between the rhetoric of heroic 'living socialism', as the government described its society, and actual lived conditions. Unfortunately, because she had no way of disseminating her work at the time, her oeuvre was only later discovered as an alternative voice of the time.

93 Ursula Arnold, *Leipzig, Magazine Vendor*, 1956, gelatin silver print.

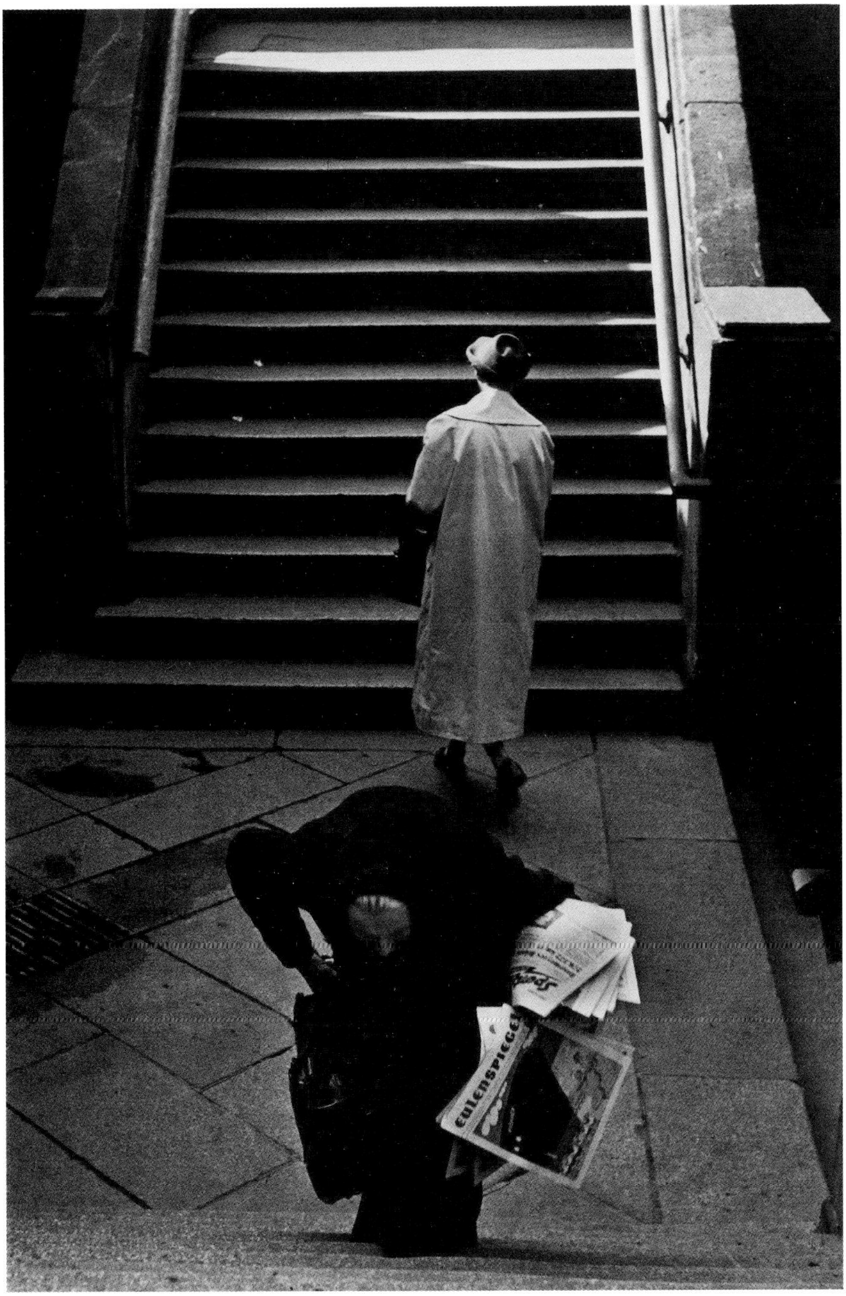
Eulenspiege

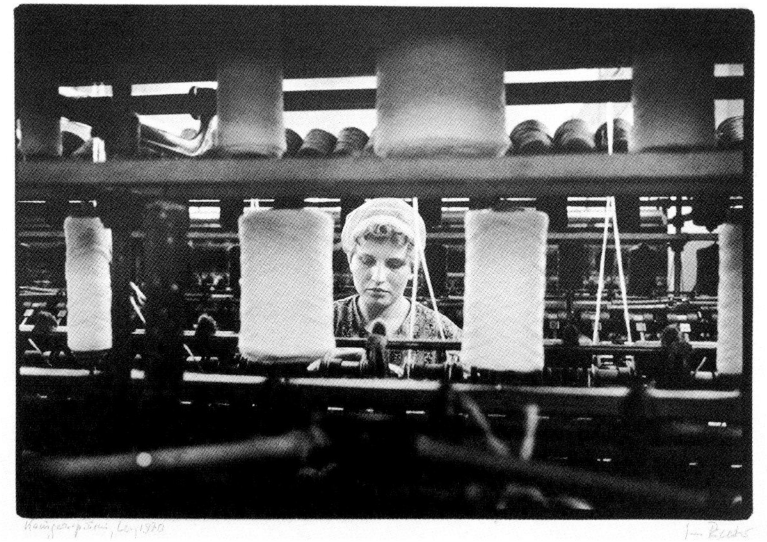

94 Evelyn Richter, *Worsted Mill, Leipzig*, 1970, gelatin silver print.

More public was the work of Arno Fischer, who took seemingly banal and unremarkable pictures of life in his city of Berlin, such as his *East Berlin* of 1959. In this picture four people sit aimlessly aside an empty lot, surely the site of a bombed building. Fischer became a prized photographer in the East and his work was published widely. Inspired by *The Family of Man* and its universal humanism in the documentary mode, the photography professor Evelyn Richter focused her work on women and machines, and the contact that she, as an intellectual, could make with industrial workers, the oft-pronounced heroes of socialism. But her pictures are often melancholic, as one of a woman before a worsted mill in 1970 (illus. 94). Framed by heads of yarn on what seems an endless extent of racks, she looks down as if in a stupor, deadened psychologically by her repetitive work and dreary life. Despite the subtly critical posture of this and other photographs, Richter's work was recognized and celebrated in its time.

Contrasting with these refreshingly critical images were not just the approved photographs of party leaders and parading crowds, the balance of the GDR's public visual culture, but photography's hidden use by East German governmental agencies. The Staatssicherheitsdienst, known derisively as the Stasi, served as the official state security service. It notoriously ensnared a vast portion of the country's population into acting as informants against 'enemies of socialism', even if the person of interest were a spouse or parent. Obsessive to the point of being ridiculous, its agents used the camera to conduct surveillance into even the blandest corners of a suspect's life. Contemporary artist Simon Menner has pulled from this now-open archive to reveal such things as domestic surveillance focusing on a citizen's stash of foreign liquor or conspicuous use of a Western coffee maker. He also found photographs from a guidebook instructing in the use of disguises with techniques so absurd that one would essentially be recognized immediately as a Stasi agent (illus. 95). Such violations and undercover strategies were essentially open secrets that produced the sense that one was being watched by a Stasi lens all the time.

The West also saw photographers who broke with conformity, and state agencies that used the camera for alternative forms of surveillance. Herbert Tobias had served on the Eastern Front during the war and thereafter became a fashion photographer who lived openly as a gay man, even though Nazi-era laws still on the books criminalized homosexuality. His *Good Friday* of 1954 depicts him as a handsome young man playing the crucified Jesus. The image both mocks organized religion and comments on his treatment by a state that had publicly renounced the persecution of what the Nazis termed 'degenerates'.

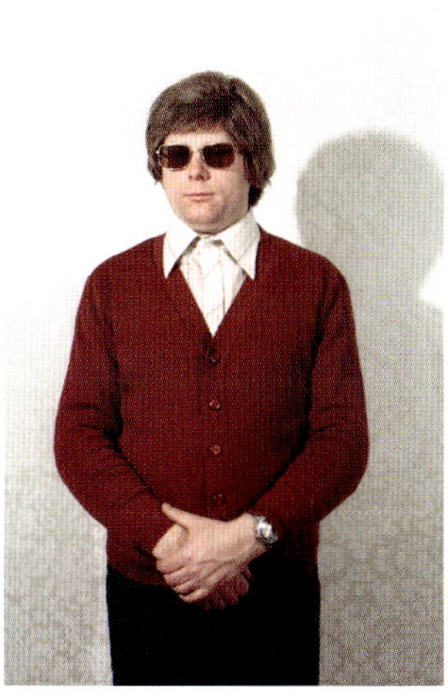

95 Simon Menner, *Untitled: From a Disguise Seminar*, 2013, format undetermined.

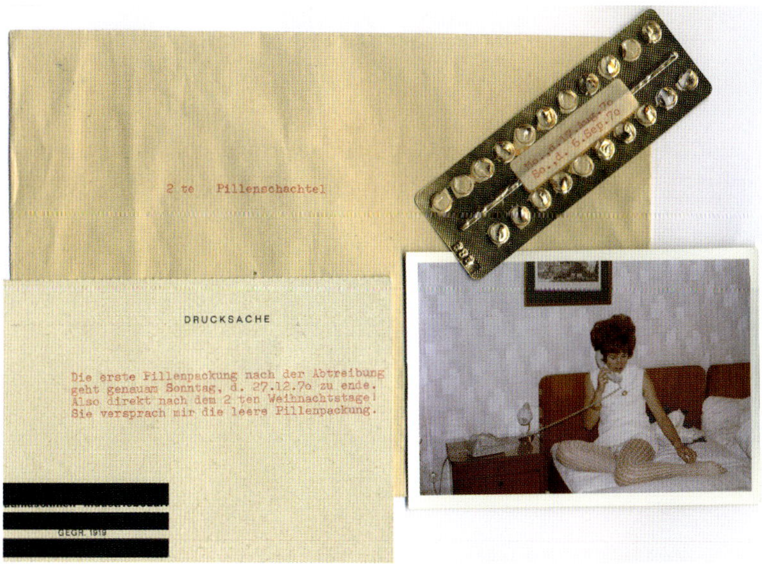

96 From the 2015 exhibition *Margret: Chronicle of an Affair – May 1969 to December 1970*.

In 1950 he had been denounced under the anti-gay law and thereafter moved to Paris, only to be repatriated to Germany three years later after being caught up in a raid on a gay bar. He had been metaphorically crucified by Europe's remaining fascist-era moral order and he now wished to visualize just this destiny.

Similarly working against this moral order, albeit it in a clandestine and sexist manner, was a Cologne businessman now known as Günter K., who fetishistically documented an affair with his secretary Margret S. from May 1969 to December 1970. In typewritten and stereotypically Teutonic efficiency, he labelled samples of her hair – from both her head and pubis – and fingernails, along with empty birth-control-pill packets, restaurant receipts and more (illus. 96). These accompany graphic descriptions of their sex acts. As part of this archive of desire he included hundreds of colour and black-and-white photographs he took of Margret in endless positions and contexts, her pile of red hair often the focus for his camera's lens. Such alternate breaking of the era's social and sexual mores ran parallel to the upheavals of 1968 but worked firmly within the bureaucratic language of the professional middle class. This archive and others he built from further love affairs would have remained secret had they not been found decades later in a briefcase abandoned in an apartment.

More ironically subversive were the paintings by Gerhard Richter based on photographs. These works formed part of a genre that he and his art partner Jörg Immendorf, both exiled artists from East Germany, mockingly termed Capitalist Realism. Richter's style has varied wildly both then and now. In these early photo-based works, he generally borrowed from West Germany's booming commercial culture and its photographic expression, focusing on fashion advertising and on pornography. He also drew directly from his vernacular family photographs, such as for his haunting painting *Uncle Rudi* (illus. 97). Standing rigidly with his hands at his side, the smiling uncle wears his Nazi-era military uniform not long before he died on the Eastern Front during the war. Richter's technique of dragging a dry brush across the freshly painted canvas muddles the image. But his moderated touch allows this blur to seem more characteristic of a photograph than a painting. Reading as the product of a camera lens out of focus, the visual fog signals allegorically the recession of the relative into time and memory, territories of the historical and mnemonic with which many

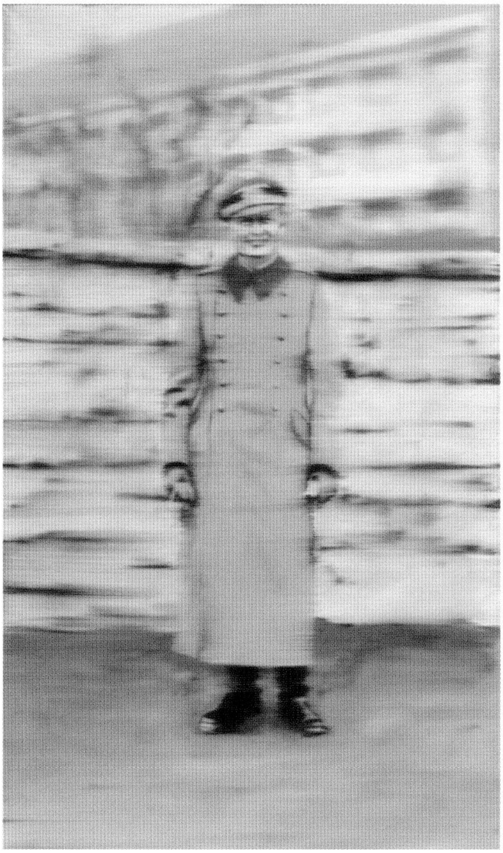

97 Gerhard Richter, *Uncle Rudi*, 1965, oil on canvas.

Germans on both sides of the Iron Curtain had difficulty reconciling themselves.

Painter Anselm Kiefer offered a far more aggressive reckoning with recent history in his *Occupations* project (1969). In this series of photographs, he had himself pictured in his father's military uniform offering the *Hitlergruss*, the once ubiquitous fascist salute. He largely took these pictures at politically or aesthetically significant sites, such as European monuments or the sea, the second of which evoked the Romantic paintings of Caspar David Friedrich, which originally inspired the iconography of German nationalism. Though breaking the pictorial silence on fascist-era symbology, Kiefer's work met with great controversy on the Left. The very act of making this gesture was and remains illegal in the Federal Republic of Germany. 'Who is this fascist who thinks he's an antifascist?' complained the Belgian conceptual artist Marcel Broodthaers to the editor of the art magazine *Interfunktionen*, which published the photographs in 1975.[25] To a significant degree, such pictures highlight the extent to which photography and twentieth-century German history met over violent terrain.

Photography as Art

Within these photographic conditions made tense by the medium's post-war realist charge and the recent history on which it often failed to report, another development was taking place. The West's booming economy generated an extraordinarily sophisticated advertising culture that stressed photography, while the East's non-conformist practices led to an art photography that actually gained popular – if not always official – acceptance, perhaps on account of its aesthetic of deep ambivalence that spoke for many discontented citizens. As for the former, West German advertising firms followed on Subjective Photography's partial recovery of interwar

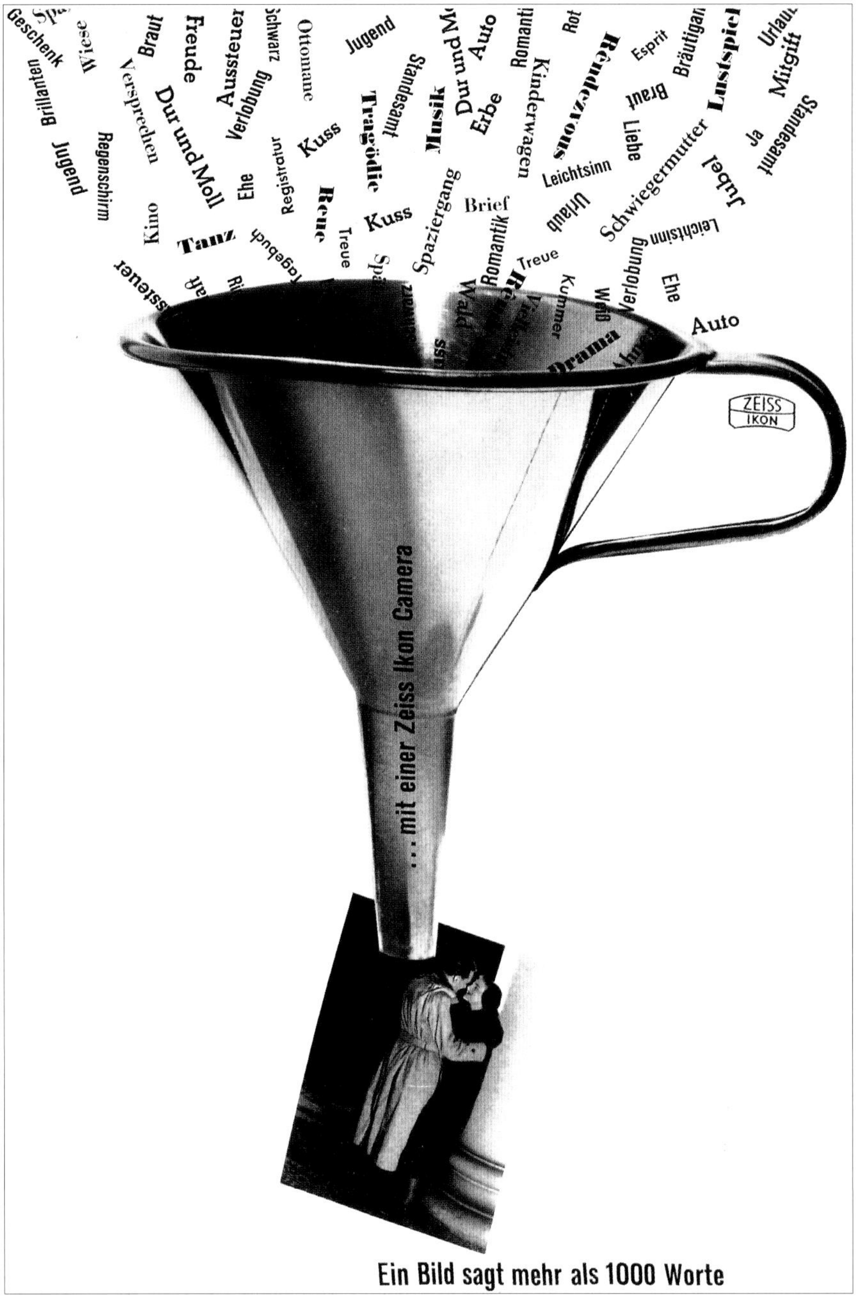

98 Franz Hubmann, 'A Picture Says More than 1,000 Words . . . with a Zeiss Ikon Camera', in *Magnum*, no. 12 (1957), likely halftone print.

99 Bernd and Hilla Becher, *Cooling Towers Wood-Steel*, 1959–77, 9 gelatin silver prints.

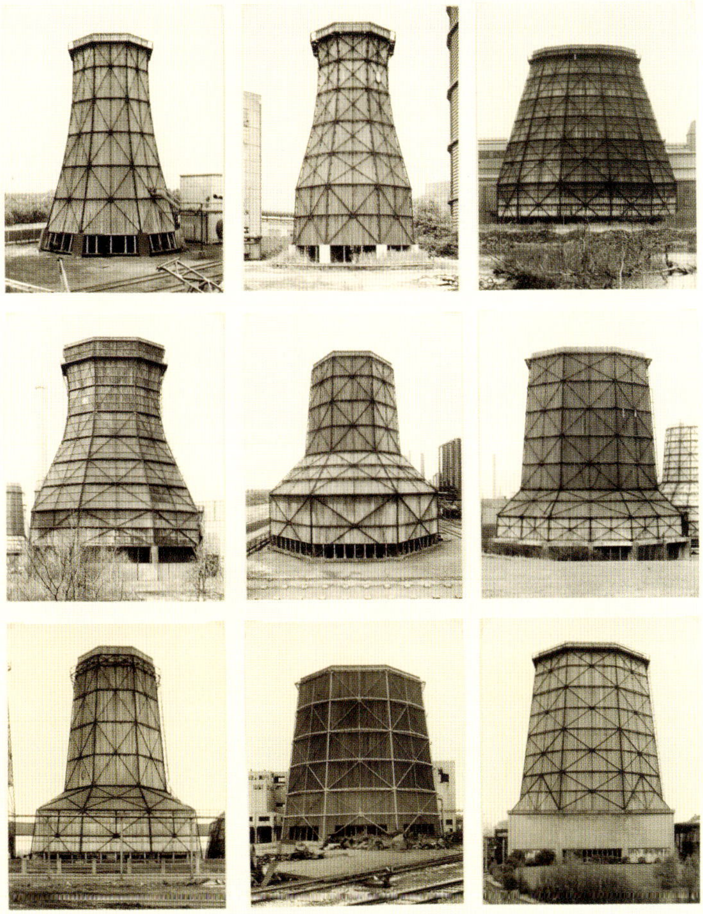

avant-garde techniques by employing similar strategies in their campaigns. A 1957 ad for the Zeiss camera corporation borrowed from Dada montage to visualize the expression that 'a picture says more than 1,000 words', in this case a canted Zeiss snapshot that blares words such as 'kiss' and 'dance' in multiple type through a metal funnel montaged above an embracing couple (illus. 98). Similarly, a photograph by Willi Moegle from 1959 for the

Jena Glass corporation mines Bauhaus photo strategies to emphasize the pure clarity of the company's products, visible almost only by their edges. Essential here was the ability of these photographers to reduce their products to recognizable typologies, such as the classic snapshot for the Zeiss ad and the purest crystal for the Jena Glass campaign.

Working in an advertising agency in Düsseldorf during these same years, Hilla Wobeser and Bernd Becher absorbed these lessons, incorporating them into their subsequent training in fine and applied art at the city's art academy. Soon working only in photography, they sought subject matter in the vast industrial zones of the Ruhr valley just northeast of Düsseldorf, much as Albert Renger-Patzsch had in the 1920s. There they found what they termed the anonymous sculptures of pre-war industries, the colossal plants and related buildings of the country's steel industry. They began taking photographs of these buildings following a predetermined system that grouped the structures by architectural typologies, offering dry and objective matrixes of the region's inventory of industry typologies (illus. 99). They specifically opposed this documentation of pre-Nazi architecture to the Subjective Photography movement of Otto Steinert. As Wobeser later explained: 'Steinert and the people of his generation did not want to look back, they did not even want to look into the present, they just looked towards the future. It was a kind of escape.'[26] This focus on objects and typologies that they had partially learned in advertising constituted their reckoning with history, a recovery of the vernacular architecture and strict style of objective photography that they also rediscovered in photography of the Weimar era. In turn, contemporary photographers have meditated on the ongoing influence of the couple's work worldwide, such as in the series *Yogurt Pots, an Homage* by the Dutch artists Hester Keijser and Norman Beierle, who go by the group pseudonym Beierle + Keijser (illus. 100). Their pictures poke fun at the literal meaning of the word *Becher*, which means cup/container in German, by monumentalizing empty yogurt pots, depicting them as anonymous sculptures that, as a group, betray an industrial typology.

The German couple married and Bernd Becher became a professor at the Düsseldorf Art Academy, where he and Hilla trained a generation of highly successful art photographers.[27] What they asked their charges to do is find a typology and pursue it until a specific relationship between

100 Beierle + Keijser, *Yoghurt Pots, an Homage*, 2011, 9 c-type Lambda prints.

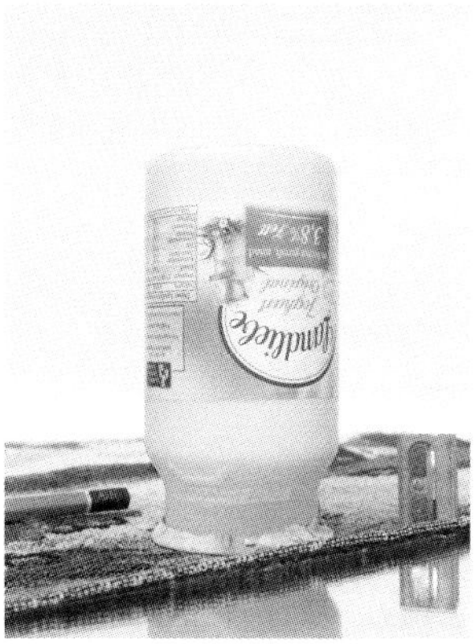
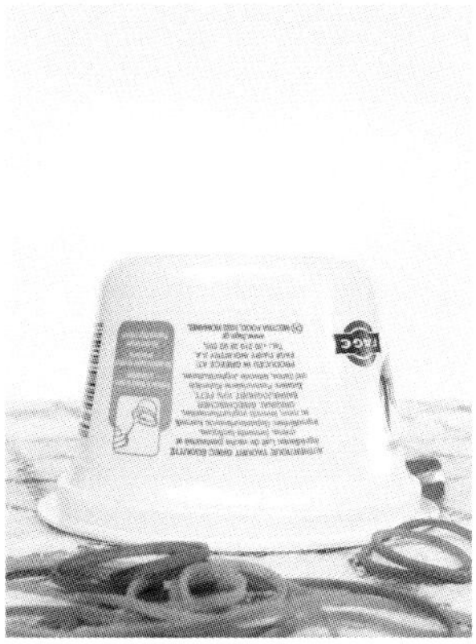
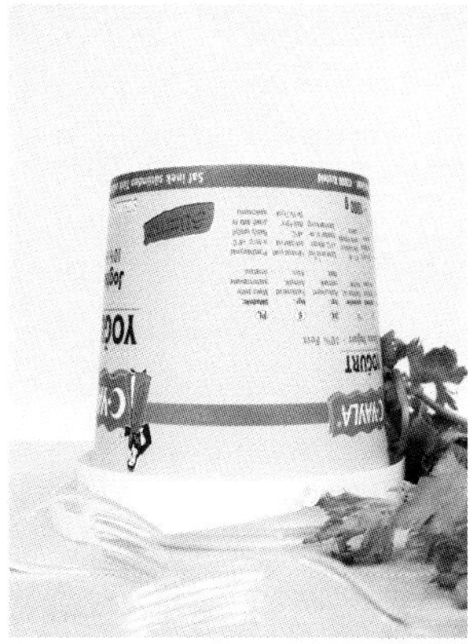
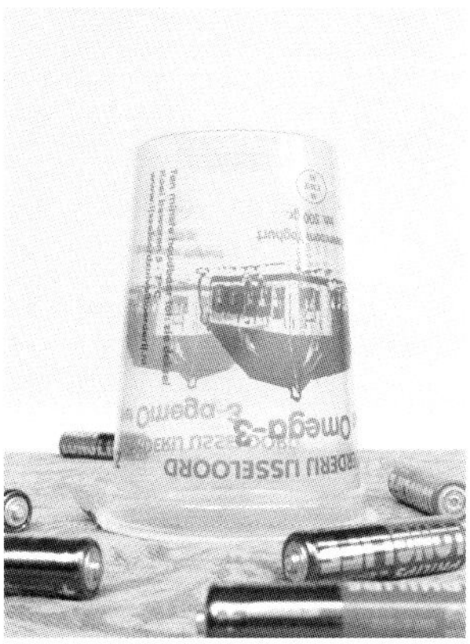
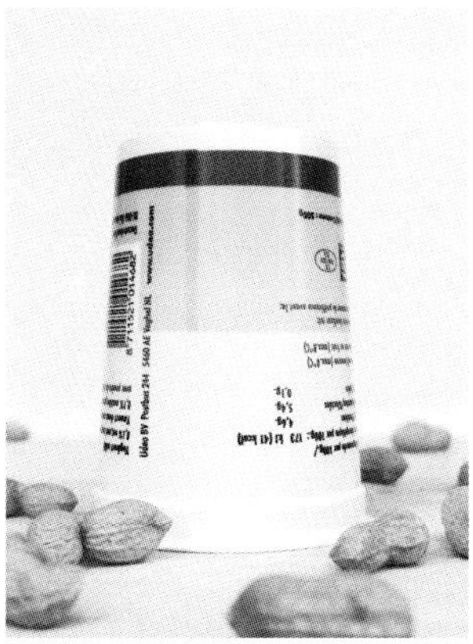
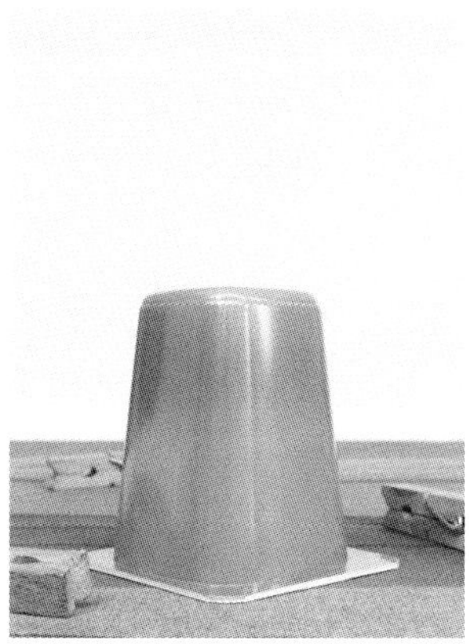
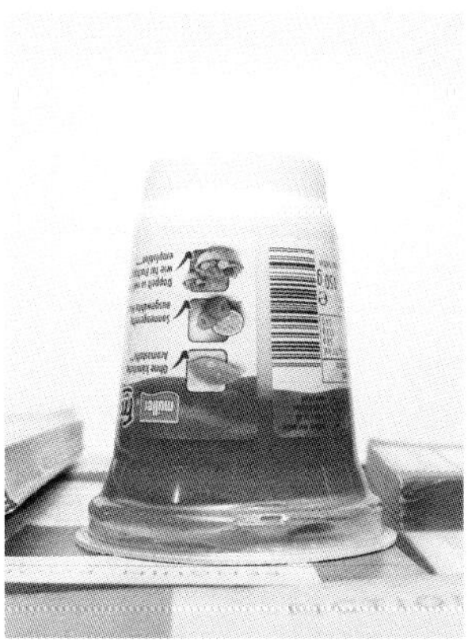

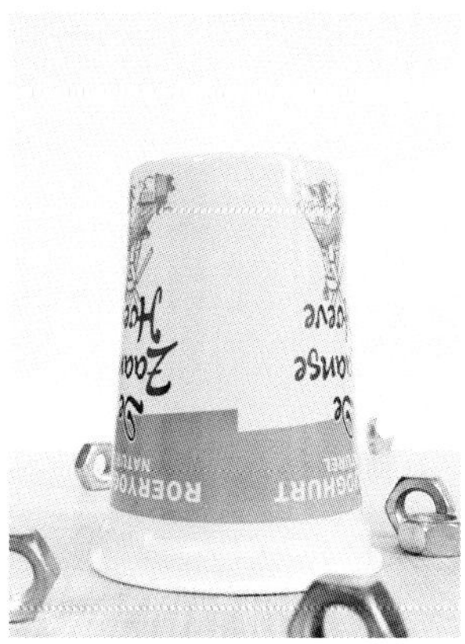

method and aesthetic emerged. Thomas Struth, for example, began photographing the length of streets while Candida Höfer and Thomas Ruff took shots of interiors. In the case of Höfer, projects such as *Turks in Germany* (illus. 101) later developed into her typology of monumental interior spaces, which she realized through the 1990s. These photographers were recovering the strategies of the New Objectivity and New Vision, but they applied the logic of form and vision to the objects and spaces of the century's end. They had, in other words, made their lessons in historical avant-garde photography attentive and relevant to their day.

In the East, photography as art won slow recognition beyond smaller circles of nonconformist photographers and the handful of professionals who taught at the country's art academies. In 1982, for instance, the annual GDR Art Exhibition in Dresden included photographs for the first time. In the same period, semi-independent display venues as well as art and fashion magazines began to flourish in a more permissive environment. A diverse number of themes, subjects and techniques found attention in this widening world of art photography, though most photographers employed historical documentary approaches to reflect on the country's evolving society. Sibylle Bergemann,

102 Sibylle Bergemann, *All-Kinds-of-Fur*, Independent Fashion Design Group, Kathi, 1988, East Berlin, GDR.

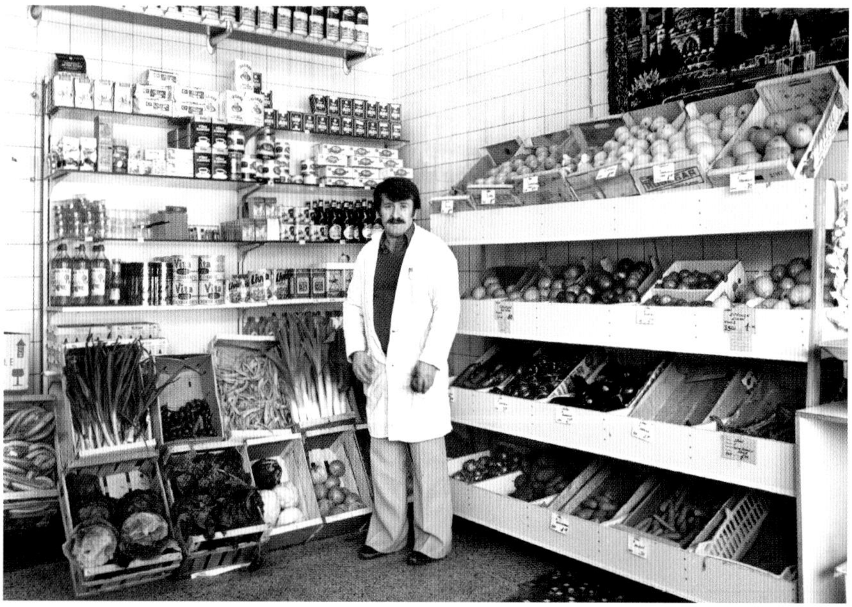

101 Candida Höfer, 'Ulmenstrasse Düsseldorf 1978', from the series *Turks in Germany*, gelatin silver print.

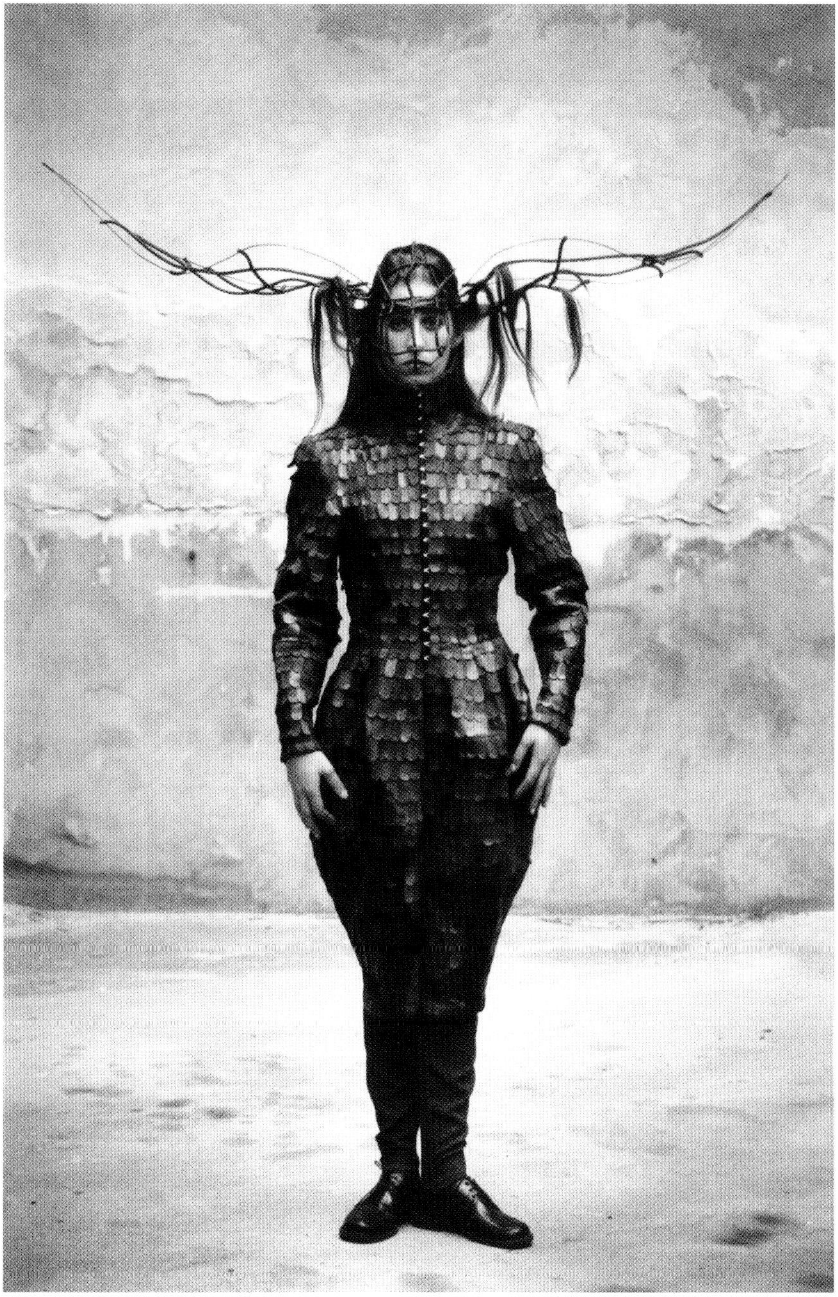

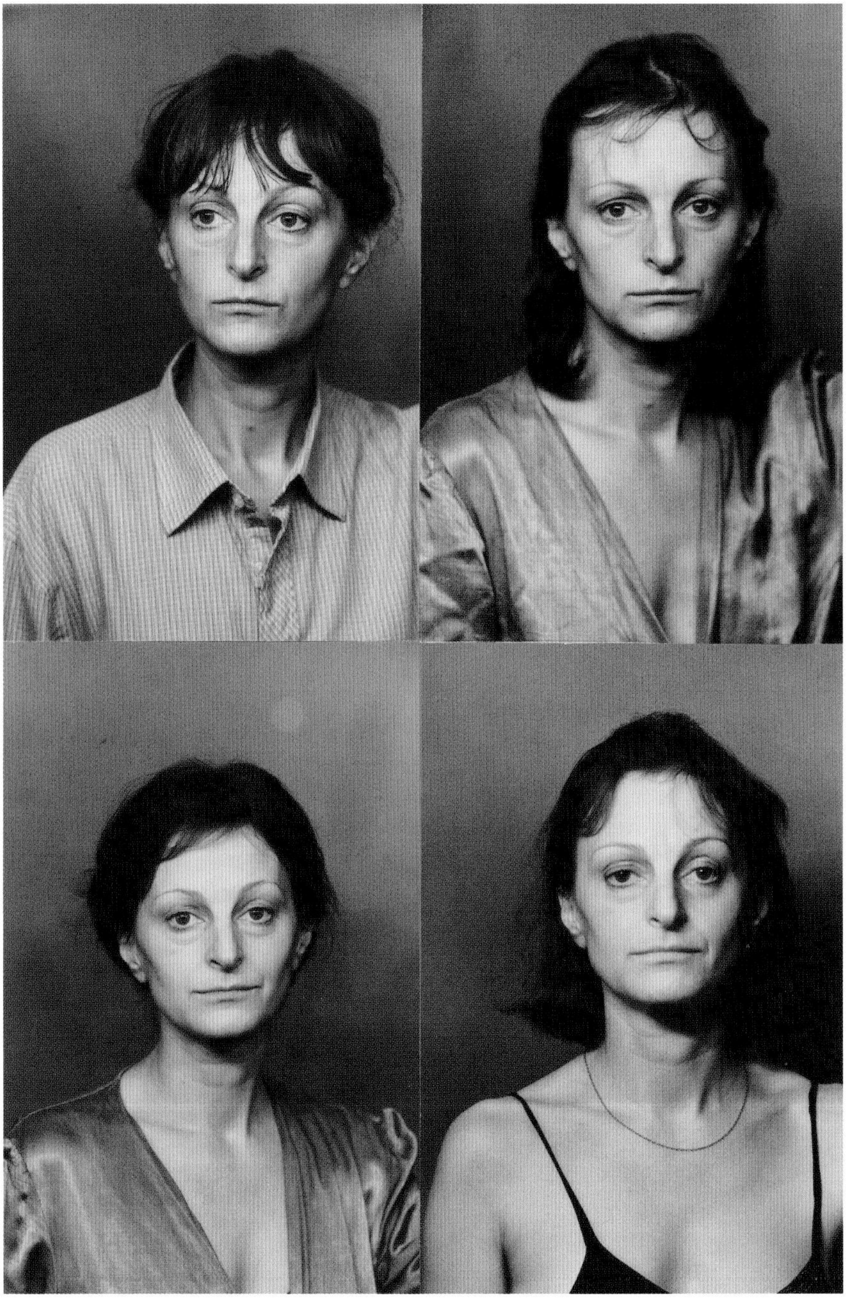

103 Helga Paris, *Self-portraits I–IV* (1981–9), gelatin silver prints on paper.

who had trained with Arno Fischer and later married him, pursued a form of fashion photography that she called 'literary reportage'. It teased out the moods and fantasies of her subjects, such as in her *All-Kinds-of-Fur* of 1988 (illus. 102). This reference to a Brothers Grimm fairy tale has the main character Heike Krohne, eyes fixed on the viewer, channelling the story's beautiful princess with an otherworldly headdress and a tight, scaly dress, both of which reflect the medieval past and the East German punk fashion of the day at once. Ulrich Wüst developed a mode of landscape photography that stressed the grey and sterile spaces of the country's cities, particularly where new and soulless construction met empty lots. The more veteran Helga Paris created a long series of self-portraits that showed both the possibilities and limits of self-fashioning in the East German state, each variation changing only in hairstyle and clothing (illus. 103). Particularly fascinating are the pictures of Jens Rötzsch, which use the existing but faulty colour film technology of his country to photograph state ceremonies, rallies and other public events. The inaccuracy of the colour and the brightness of his daytime flash render his subjects oddly surreal, as in his *1989 Pentecost Meeting of the FDJ* [Freie Deutsche Jugend – Free German Youth] *in the World Youth Stadium* (see illus. 82). These young women, prepared to march onto a field and perform synchronized formations, seem too individualized to merge into the mass ornament of socialist performance, and too colourful to be participating in anything short of a carnival. Such nuanced and ambivalent approaches to documentary now strike many former East Germans as flat or even embarrassingly kitschy, but they would go on to colour the photography of a unified Germany after 1989.

The increasingly permissive society that made these pictures possible would come to a sudden end when the wall separating East and West Berlin came down in November of 1989, an event that alone generated a massive new photographic iconography of unification. East and West German citizens sitting astride the wall signalled a new age, and provided significant inspiration for other Eastern European nations seeking to throw off the yoke of one-party rule. These events generated what American historian Francis Fukuyama controversially pronounced as 'the end of history', the conclusion of mankind's sociocultural development in liberal democracies with neoliberal economies.[28] Germany, at least for the moment, seemed to have an entirely different recent history to digest with photography.

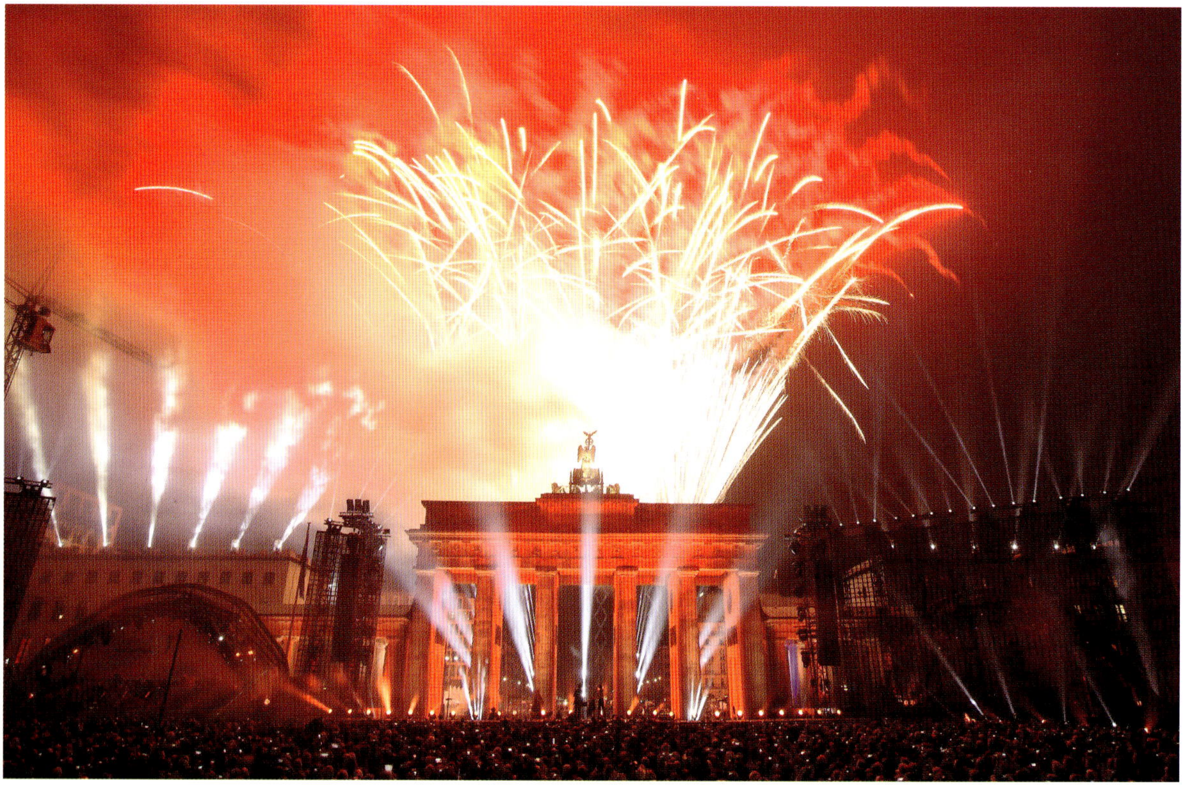

six

Photographic Promiscuity, 1990–2016

In November 1989, the Berlin Wall fell and the two Germanies began their rapid course toward reunification. In the following year, the first version of Photoshop was released, making the digital processing of photography available to just about anyone who had access to a computer. While these two events may seem unrelated, in Central Europe they occasioned an explosion in the number of photographs that dealt with a difficult past, a quickly changing present and an uncertain future. *Die Wende* (The Turnaround), as the events of '89 and their aftermath have come to be called, stimulated a broad public conversation about Germany's twentieth-century history. Debates roiled over revelations about one-party rule in the GDR (German Democratic Republic) just as a new frankness emerged about the fascist era. After periods of hushed speaking or outright silence, people suddenly could not shut up about the past. With this new loquaciousness came a flood of photographs that inundated the public sphere through controversial exhibitions, books and more. Meanwhile, the development of new technologies such as the Internet and Photoshop made discovering, sharing and even composing these potent pictures far easier. Germany has since become a photo-mad country where images are not just plentiful in number, as elsewhere in the world. They also speak promiscuously about the past, present and future in ways that place the medium squarely at the centre of discussions about national identity in a still newly united country. One of the important consequences of these developments has been an extraordinary rise in the country's art photography. Photographers east of the Rhine now play an outside role in the medium's contemporary aesthetic practice worldwide. Germany and photography are now regularly thought of as a natural conjunction.

104 Sean Gallup, *Germany Celebrates 25th Anniversary of the Fall of the Berlin Wall*, 2014, format undetermined.

Physically Engaging the Past

Germany completed its reunification on 3 October 1990 by pulling the defunct GDR into an existing framework of the West's federal states. Citizens of the newly merged country celebrated with extraordinary displays of acclaim that have since been restaged at each important anniversary. These occasions generally take the Brandenburg Gate as their principal site of festivity, each time repeating the fireworks and speech making that accompanied the original event, as at the twenty-five-year mark (illus. 104). A photographically mediated iconography of unity has emerged, one that has successfully reassigned the grim associations of the Brandenburg Gate away from Wilhelmine- and fascist-era pomp toward a new, democratic and cautiously proud nation. The reconstruction of the Pariser Platz to the east of the Gate seems to have been completed with the camera in mind. Many of the buildings recreate the original space, but in photogenic, modernist architectural terms that allow a celebration of nation that is both proximate to and distanced from the difficult past.

Similarly, in advance of the fifth anniversary of unification, the artists Christo and Jeanne-Claude wrapped the equally historically rich Reichstag building in silvery cloth tied down with blue ropes. They also designed this installation with the camera in mind, enabling this former and future seat of government to re-enter the public imagination as a place aligned with modernity, particularly a modernity defined by international art. Extraordinary photographs circulating the planet showed this beautifully sheathed building standing next to architectural symbols of old (illus. 105). The press photographer Wolfgang Kumm realized one of the best images of the installation with this repurposing of history's architectural material as his goal.

Just as artists, photographers and government officials performed this post-unification work of reattribution, other people and institutions turned with increasingly intense scrutiny to the past as mediated through photography. To no small degree of contention, for example, the Hamburg Institute for Social Research opened an exhibition in 1995 that reassessed the role of the Nazi-era armed forces in war atrocities. The historical consensus until then had been that the SS committed the balance of the period's war crimes. But the show titled *Vernichtungskrieg. Verbrechen der Wehrmacht 1941 bis 1944* (War of Annihilation: Crimes of the Wehrmacht, 1941–1944) employed a

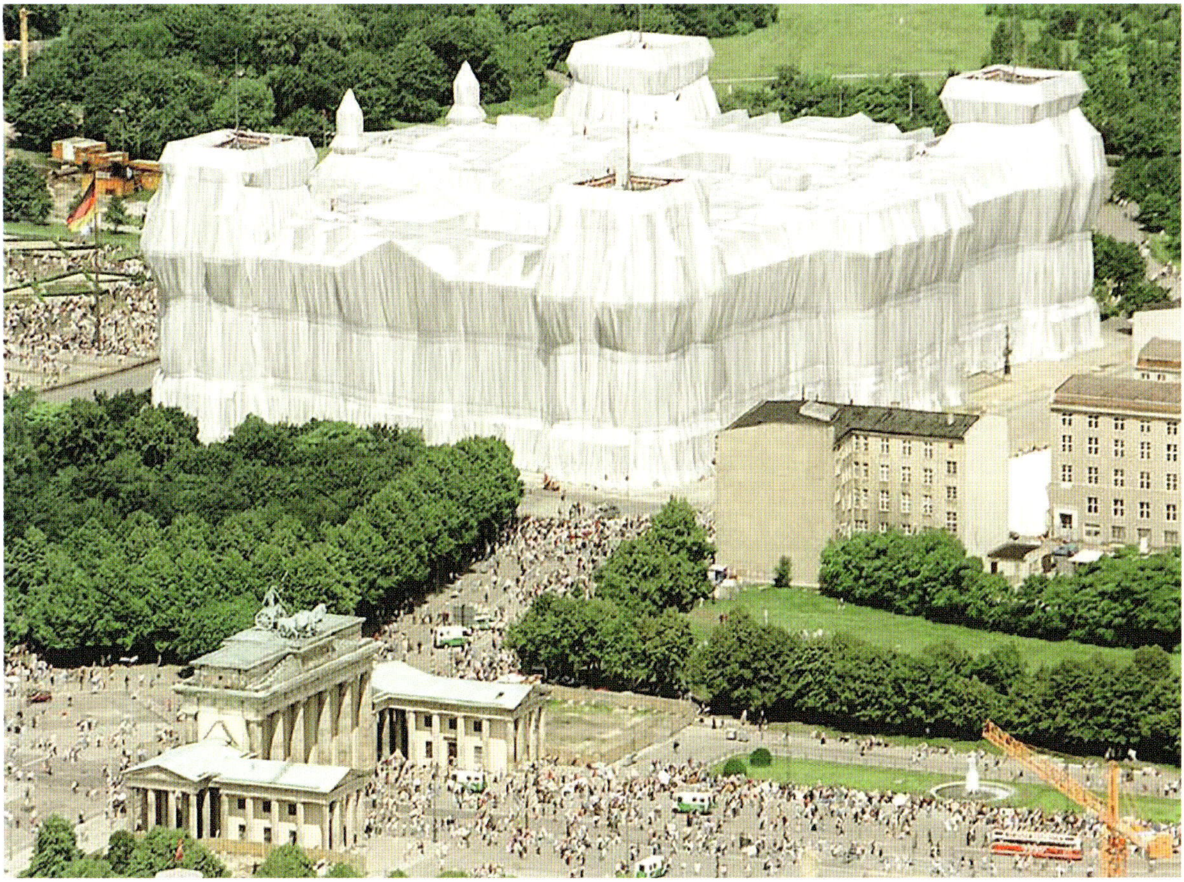

105 Wolfgang Kumm, *Germany/ Reichstag*, 1995, format undetermined.

wealth of documents, ephemera and most especially photographs to establish otherwise. Though it travelled to many German cities and received over 1.2 million visitors in total, it met with tremendous controversy and was even bombed by neo-Nazis during its second iteration in 1999. During its long run, a motif of spectatorship emerged that showed important politicians and everyday visitors pointing at the arrays of atrocity photographs and examining them closely. The country, it seemed, had not just turned toward its difficult past. It was now prepared to engage at close proximity with the photographic evidence of the most horrific of the atrocities committed in its name, even if those responsible were previously deemed safe from accusation.

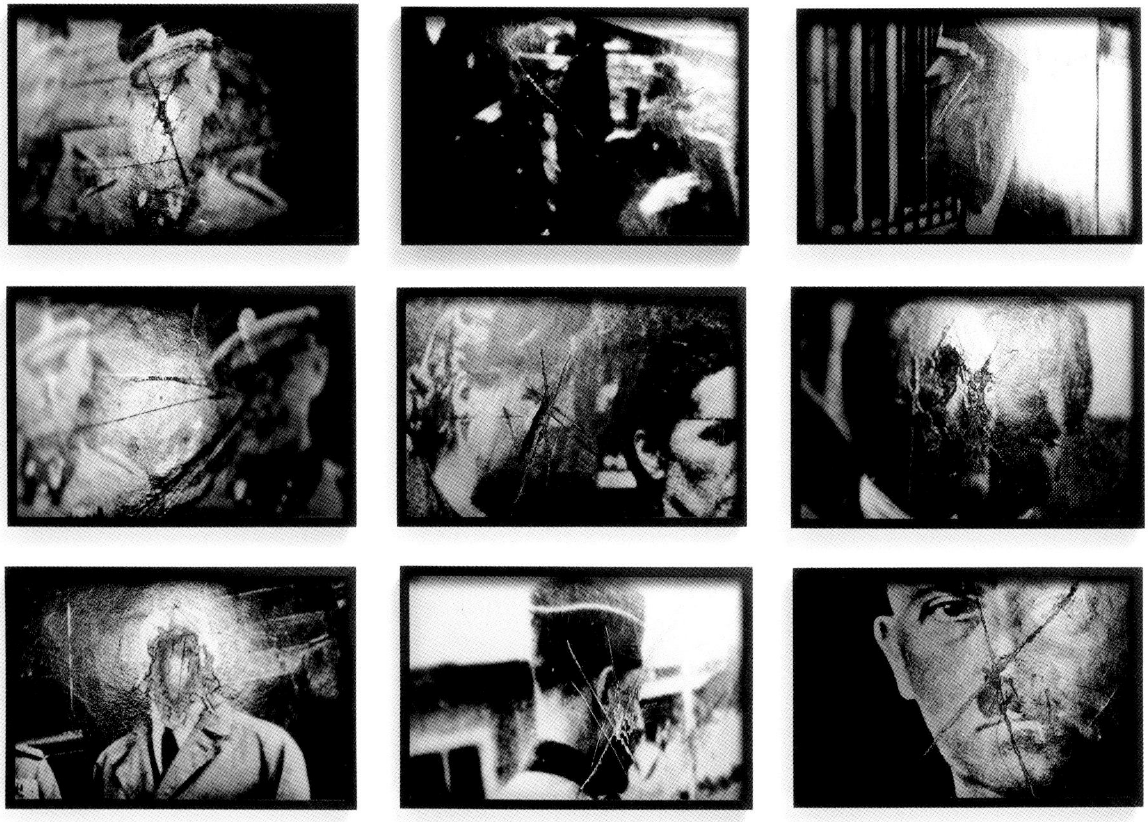

106 Rudolf Herz, *Museum Photographs, Dachau, 1976–80*, 1990, gelatin silver prints.

Photography historian and artist Rudolf Herz documented a similar physical engagement with photographs of the past in his 1996 work *Museum Photographs, Dachau, 1976–80* (illus. 106). To create the raw material for this matrix of nine images, Herz photographed many of the official photographs on display at the museum of the former Dachau concentration camp near Munich. His harsh flash, extreme enlarging and careful post-production work captured and emphasized the damage that visitors made to these museum pictures, highlighting how a confrontation with the site can include an iconoclastic attack on the images of those responsible for this atrocity. His artwork becomes the defacement itself, a pictorial foregrounding of the physical engagement with history made by the site's international visitors.

In his 'Zugzwang' (1995), Herz paired a once ubiquitous portrait of Hitler with a remarkably similar likeness of Marcel Duchamp, the latter taken over a decade earlier (illus. 108). Both, it turns out, were snapped by the man who became Hitler's personal photographer, Heinrich Hoffmann. Herz pasted innumerable silkscreen reproductions of these portraits along a grid – much like wallpaper from floor to ceiling – in a museum room with the Duchamp and Hitler prints alternating vertically and horizontally. With this striking all-over covering, he wished to underscore the role these men played as primary antagonists of twentieth-century art, Duchamp

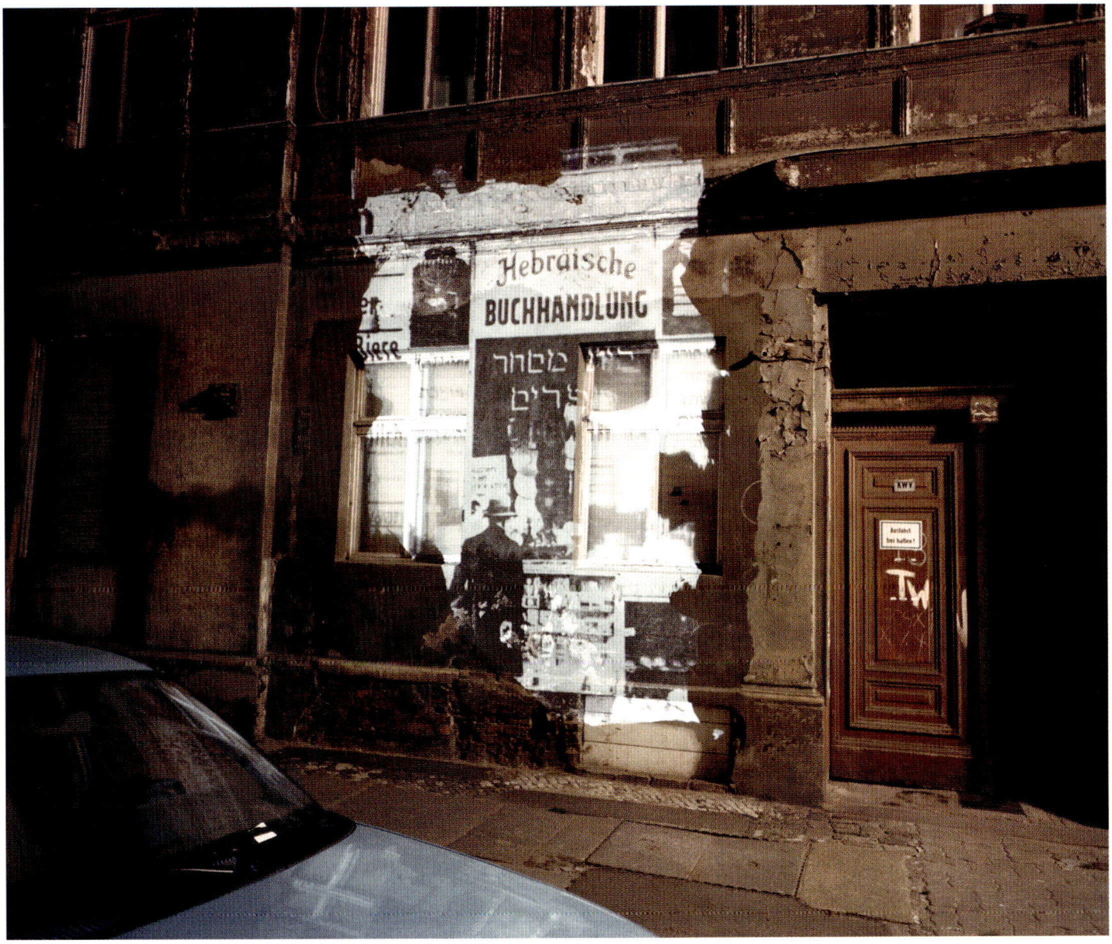

107 Shimon Attie, '43 Almstadt Street (formerly 7 Grenadier Street)': slide projection of former Hebrew bookstore, Berlin, 1991 (1930), from the series *Writing on the Wall*, 1991–2, chromogenic print.

advocating an intellectual art and Hitler a Nazi Pop and, more broadly, the violent elimination of modernism. In adapting the contemporary practices of conceptual and installation art to the task of collective memory making, Herz introduced a new and forceful way to process the traumatic past through photography.[1]

The American artist Shimon Attie dug through photo archives and business registers to stage a similar historical reckoning with the medium. His 1991–2 night-time installations throughout Berlin projected the interwar facades of Jewish businesses onto the modern-day buildings they once occupied (illus. 107). Similar to what Herz would later do, Attie used the medium to restage and rethink Germany's difficult past through physical engagement, in this case with the immaterial light signposting an absence one could touch and inhabit in the buildings themselves.

Recently, the national effort to guarantee the location of the past in the present has led not just to a flood of photographs with which citizens and visitors can physically engage, but also new memorials and landmarks that have sometimes lost significance through their very ubiquity. In 2013 a mild controversy erupted when it turned out that users of the gay male dating and hook-up app Grindr were posting photographs of themselves at Berlin's Holocaust Memorial near the Brandenburg Gate. In these pictures, men showed themselves smiling in seductive poses amid the site's columns. The app's founder initially voiced approval of this trend, noting that 'As a Jew and an Israeli, I'm deeply moved by how users are coming together as a community on Grindr to share and inspire others [to] take part in [the] memory of the Holocaust.'[2] He later backed away from this praise and asked for greater reverence from his users. Intriguingly, some of the posts were made by Israelis, a fact showing the degree to which physical encounters with the German past can now take individual and seemingly inappropriate form.

Something comparable could be said of Simon Menner's ironic and humorous recovery of photographs from the photo-rich Stasi archives, as discussed in the previous chapter (see illus. 95). This East German secret police agency menaced the country's citizens in ways that were, at the time, far from amusing. But here too domestic and international audiences demonstrate that these exceptional histories have been sufficiently digested

108 Rudolf Herz, 'Zugzwang', installation at the exhibition *The 20th Century: A Century of Art in Germany* at the Nationalgalerie Berlin/Hamburger Bahnhof, 1999, silkscreen reproductions.

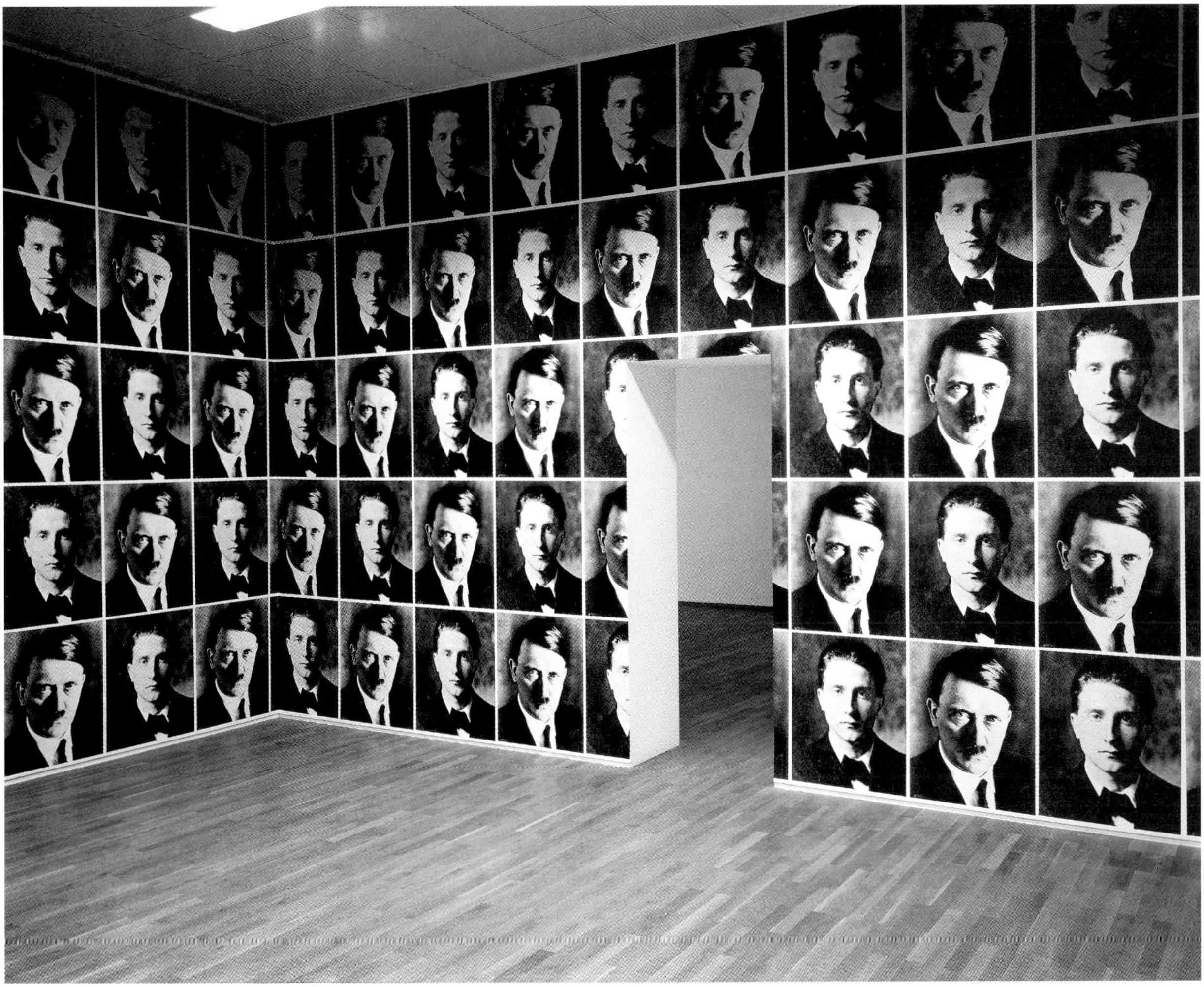

in and through photography to now provoke innumerable individual reactions. With contemporary eyes looking back, pictures from the East German past may mean something quite different from what was originally intended. Sibylle Bergemann, for example, famously took pictures of GDR-era statues of Karl Marx and Friedrich Engels in what now seem to be various states of dismantlement (illus. 109). It is as if she caught the symbolic break-up of the socialist ideology that the state had encoded in these heroic representations.

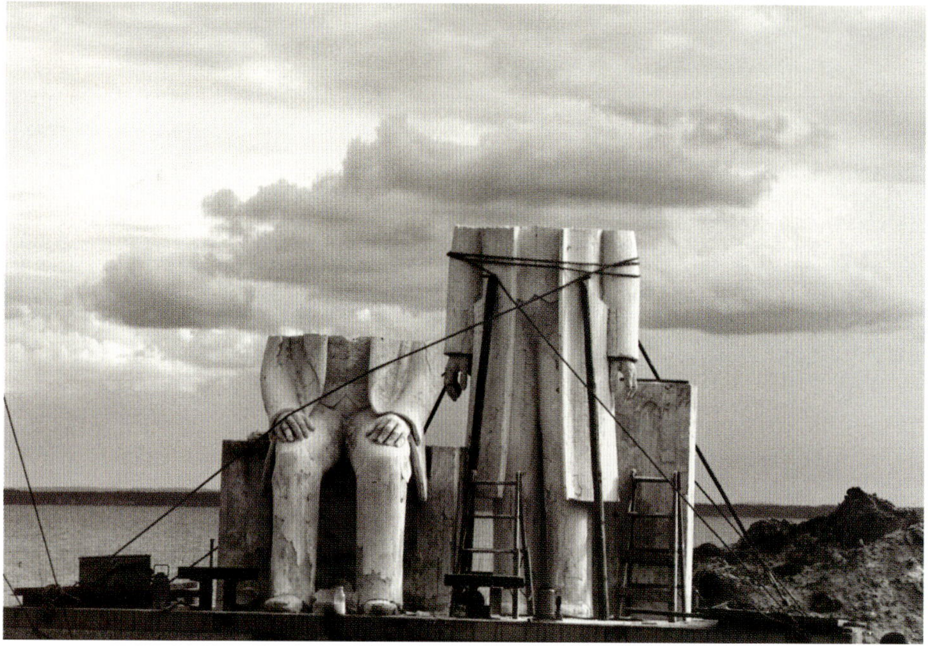

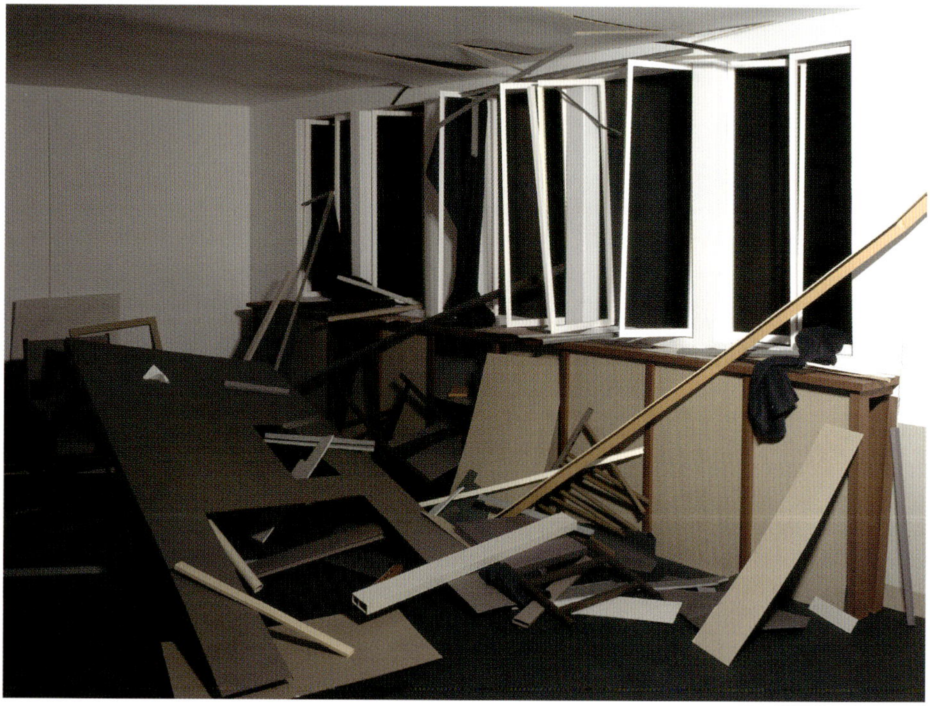

109 Sibylle Bergemann, 'Untitled – Gummlin' from the series *The Monument*, 1975–86, gelatin silver print.

110 Thomas Demand, *Room*, 1994, c-print/Diasec.

She published her photographs in a 1990 book co-authored by poet and playwright Heiner Müller and titled *A Spectre Is Leaving Europe*, punning on the first line of Marx and Engel's *Communist Manifesto* (1848), 'A spectre is haunting Europe.' But in fact, Bergemann originally took these pictures as part of an official commission to cover the making and installation of these statues through the late 1970s and early '80s. The varying textures of German history have come to allow new and sometimes surprising meanings from photographs taken in the past. Pictures from the East German and the fascist eras now play an ever-changing role in mediating what Germany was and has become.

Equally talented art photographers have produced pictures that specifically mediate on this function of the medium. Thomas Demand, who studied architecture before turning to photography, painstakingly constructs three-dimensional models based on historically significant photographs from the recent and more distant twentieth-century past. He then takes pictures of these coloured paper constructions and thereafter destroys the models, leaving only the photograph as his final work. His *Room*, from 1994 (illus. 110), seems to show the work of a hurricane or of rampaging hellions. But viewers with a historical memory for news photography will recognize this space as the room in which Hitler survived an assassination attempt in 1944. The bomb may have destroyed the space, but the dictator survived. Devoid of the figures present in the original picture, Demand's photograph transforms this important memory of the fascist past into a space haunted by the evacuation of its important actors. He fills it instead with the artist's concentrated effort to materially construct the likeness of a pregnant moment. How, he asks, can he and his audience digest these images of the difficult past?

The New New Vision

Other contemporary artists have adopted an array of techniques to confront German history, often with the aid of Photoshop. Beate Gütschow developed a method that allows her to photographically reconsider the tradition of German Romantic landscape painting, which played such a heavy role in the fascist imaginary. Using a view camera, she took analogue photographs in the countryside and then scanned them digitally. Using her computer, she then composed these files into new pictures based on paintings by artists such as Caspar David Friedrich. Her *LS#3* (the letters denoting *Landscape* [*Landschaft*], illus. 111) presents an early nineteenth-century ideal. Foliage frames the left- and right-hand sides of the picture while a central tree provides the primary point of interest, which is being admired by two small figures to the right. This composed photograph closely resembles Friedrich's famous *Solitary Tree* of 1833 while it also remains, much as the painting, attentive to writings of the conservative eighteenth-century art critic Basilius von Ramdohr. In his art treatise, which included the chapter 'On Landscapes and Sea Pieces' of 1793, von Ramdohr advised that

111 Beate Gütschow, *LS#3*, 1999, c-print.

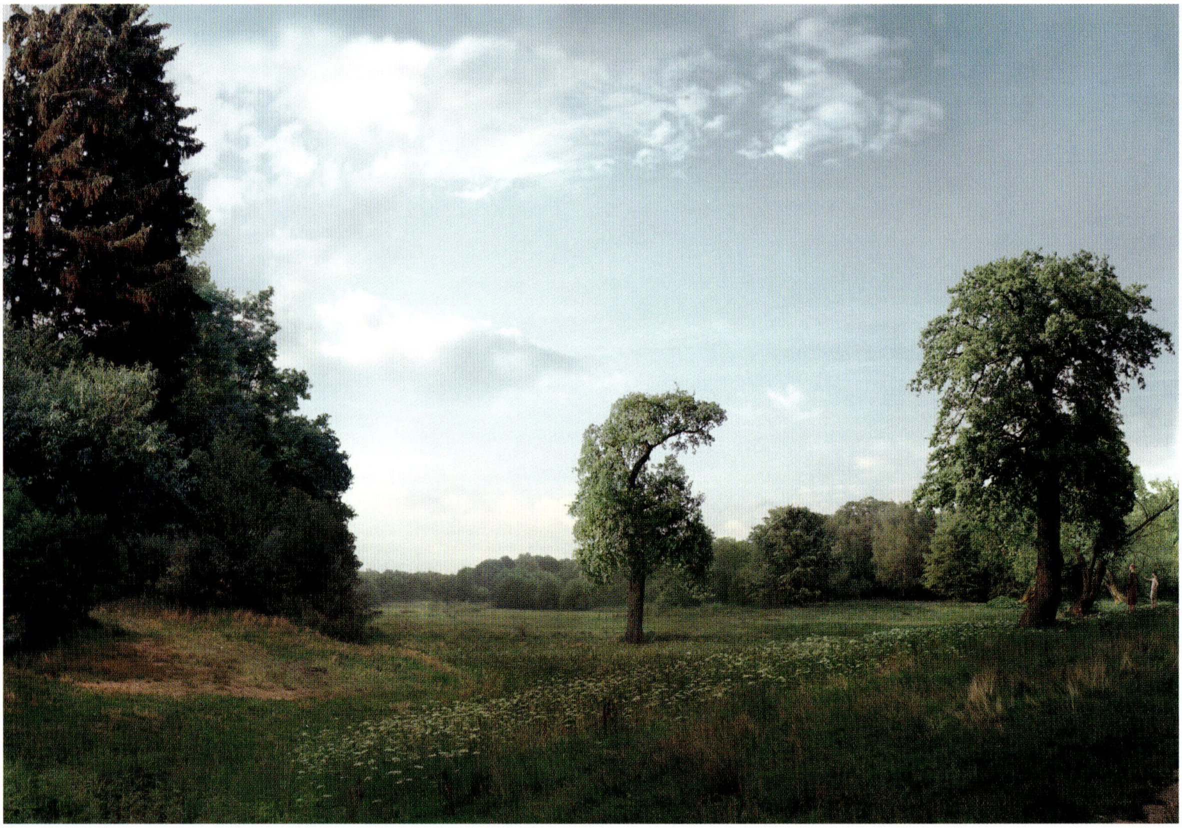

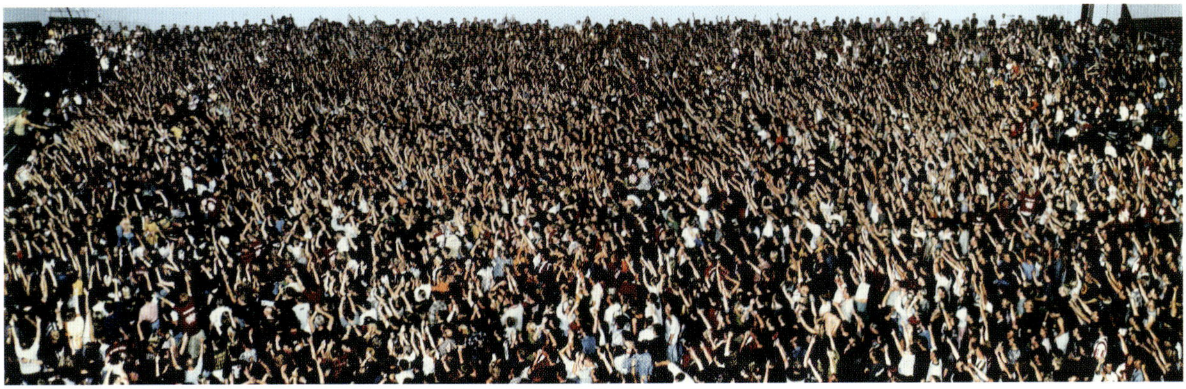

112 Andreas Gursky, *Tote Hosen*, 2000, chromogenic colour print.

> The profiles of the foreground, the middle ground, and the background must clearly be distinguished from one another to form bands along which the eye runs gladly . . . Particular care must be taken over aerial perspective, so that we believe that we can walk deep into the place depicted.[3]

In this photographic series, Gütschow distances the Romantic aesthetic from its painterly expression and asks her audience to consider its deeply fabricated nature anew, particularly as it depicted a German landscape that never actually existed outside of certain ideologies.

While Gütschow rehearses the nineteenth-century aesthetic past in her *LS* series, many other photographers have turned once more to the avant-garde heritage of the Weimar era to reconsider these classic strategies of objectivity for the new century. Andreas Gursky, who studied with Bernd and Hilla Becher in Düsseldorf, initially found himself challenged to generate the sort of productive typology that his professors wanted (see Chapter Five). He ultimately hit upon the all-over composition that had no beginning and no end, such as an unvarying view of the Rhine River or an endless trade floor in Chicago. These pictures approximate the copious details and formal repetitions made famous by *Neue Sachlichkeit* and *Neues Sehen* photography. But with the advent of Photoshop, Gursky could digitally enhance this all-over effect by, for example, digitally stitching together numerous views of a rock concert so as to create a flat expanse of cheering youth that seems to extend from the stage at left all the way to the photograph's right edge (*Tote Hosen*, illus. 112). Though a perfectionist regarding technical detail and

113 Julian Faulhaber, *Staircase*, 2007, lambda print.

formal precision, Gursky would also be conscious of the historical resonance of a mass crowd with raised arms cheering this famous German rock band, Die Toten Hosen. In any case, he and other former students of the Bechers have effectively realized the implications of Weimar-era New Objectivity and New Vision by fine-tuning its formal effects digitally. Julian Faulhaber achieves a similar result not with Photoshop but with the best analogue technologies available. He chooses freshly completed buildings as his subjects, before they have been sullied by use, and then exposes their surfaces and spaces to his film for long durations of time (illus. 113). The result bears the highly focused realism made famous by Albert Renger-Patzsch. But Faulhaber accelerates the pictorial terms of this realism so intensely that precision produces the unreal, leading one to ask whether this is analogue reality or digital fiction. More recently, Andrea Grützner has taken a similar approach to document the spaces of her youth, which she spent in the former East. In a series concentrating on an old rural inn in Saxony, she aims her camera at the building's nooks and crannies to call on her experience of these spaces (illus. 114). The strong flash and reduction

114 Andrea Grützner, 'Guesthouse 16', from the series *Guesthouse*, 2013–14, inkjet print on paper.

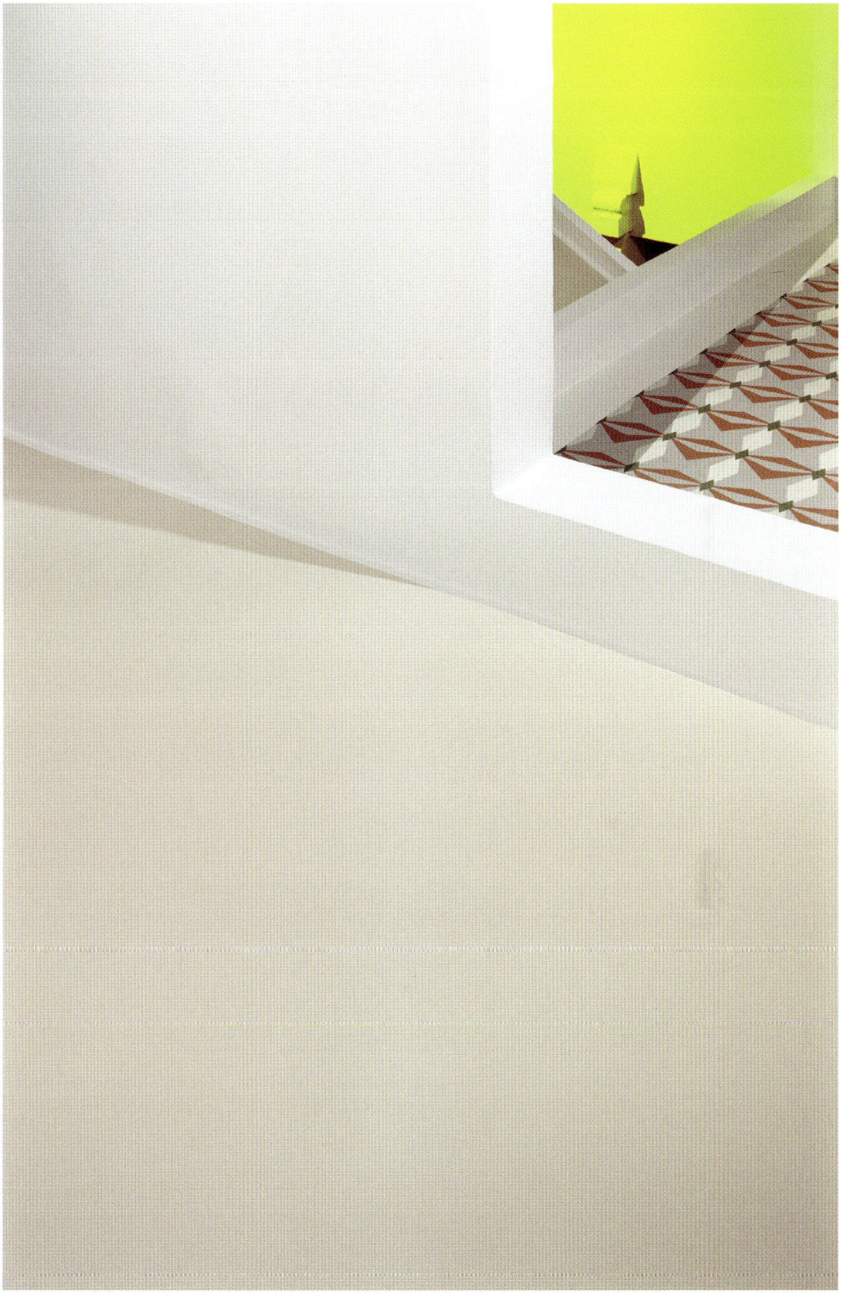

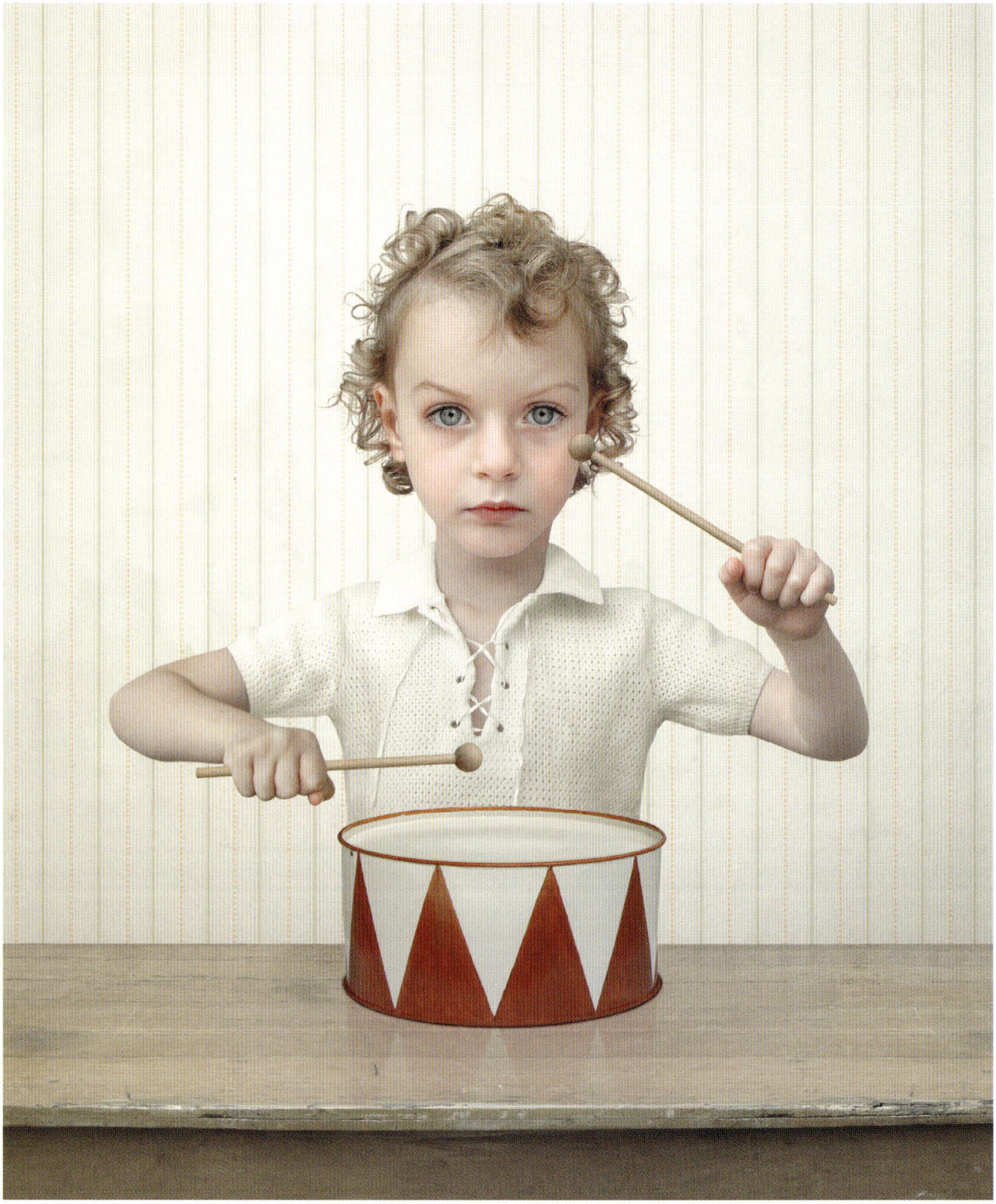

115 Loretta Lux, *The Drummer*, 2004, ilfochrome print.

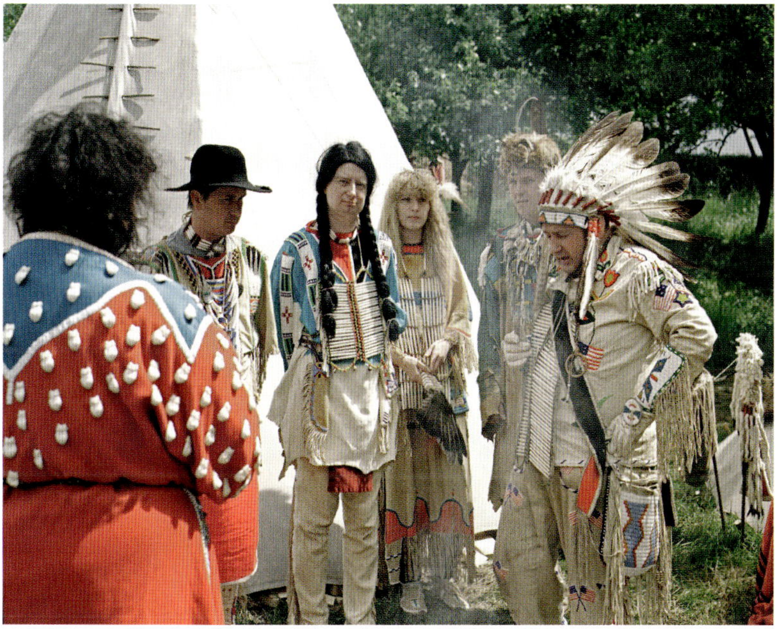

116 Andrea Robbins and Max Becher, 'German Indians: Meeting', from the series *Karl May Festival*, 1997–8, archival inkjet print.

of shadow that produce the alienating effects of Faulhaber's pictures here reproduce the alterations of memory.

Loretta Lux riffs on the detail-rich Weimar-era portrait in a way comparable to Gursky. Over a period of months, she will pose her child subject and tirelessly work with the resulting image in Photoshop by enlarging his or her head, widening the eyes and removing all blemishes such that an oddly adult quality emerges (illus. 115). Lux was born in Dresden, where she spent time admiring the masterpiece paintings that make the city's museums famous. She later studied painting in Munich before turning to photography, preferring its less physical engagement with colour and canvas. Her portraits correspondingly recall classic painting and modernist photography at once, just as they can tease themes of German history. The Drummer seems to reference the tin drum of Günter Grass's famous novel of the same name, one of the most prominent reconsiderations of the Nazi past.

The photography duo Andrea Robbins and Max Becher, the latter being the son of Bernd and Hilla Becher, reconsider the photo-essay format first made famous in Germany between the wars by focusing their lens on the

'German Indians'. These groups of largely former East German citizens idealize Native Americans as famously presented in the German-language novels of Karl May around the turn of the last century. The 'tribes' regularly meet in modern-day powwows, socializing as their alter egos in what they specifically understand as an escape from modernity (illus. 116). Robbins and Becher attend to this sociability and the laboriously constructed costumes of the participants. Focused more on the cosmopolitan margins of society, Wolfgang Tillmans famously shot odd photographs of his friends in the 1990s as they made love, took drugs or simply posed in fetish gear (illus. 117). Following in the wake of Nan Goldin's visits to Berlin, Tillmans worked out a German inflection of the photography of intimacy first popularized by the American.

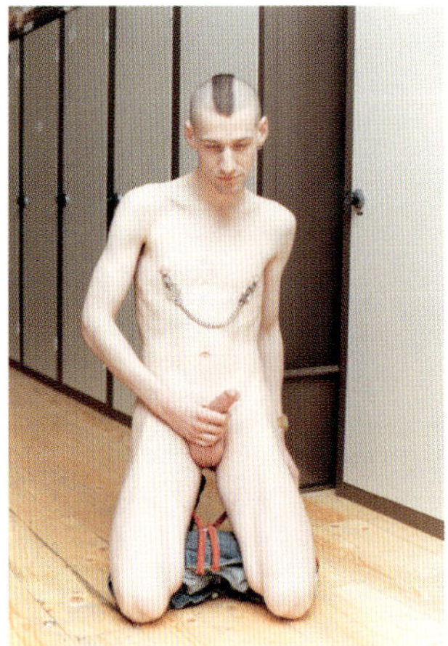

117 Wolfgang Tillmans, *Kneeling Nude*, 1997, c-print.

The vast expansion of the Internet has made the collection of photographs such as these possible for large groups of consumers. The Berlin-based artist Joachim Schmidt has specifically worked with this new era of digital availability by assembling books between 2005 and 2010 that he titles *Other People's Photographs*. One of them, *Currywurst*, consists of nothing more than photographs culled from the Web of this basic Berlin dish, consisting of sausage, ketchup and curry powder (illus. 118). Through appropriation, Schmidt visualizes a typology much as the Becher students might. Even with such new modes of dissemination and collection, the photo book continues to play an enormous role in the Central European photography scene, in part because of publishers such as Steidl and Hatje Cantz. The finely polished volumes issued by these presses have given visibility not just to Germans but to important photographers from around the world, such as the Korean-American Niki Lee and members of the famous Helsinki School. Germany's recent obsession with the past, along with the nation's desire to have photography mediate this compulsion, has produced a photo-mad country of promiscuous makers and users. In the process, it has also reconfigured the relationship between photography and Germany. Whereas in the nineteenth century, the medium played an important role in defining the identity of Germany and the German, now it critically re-digests those terms on a mass scale for a global audience.

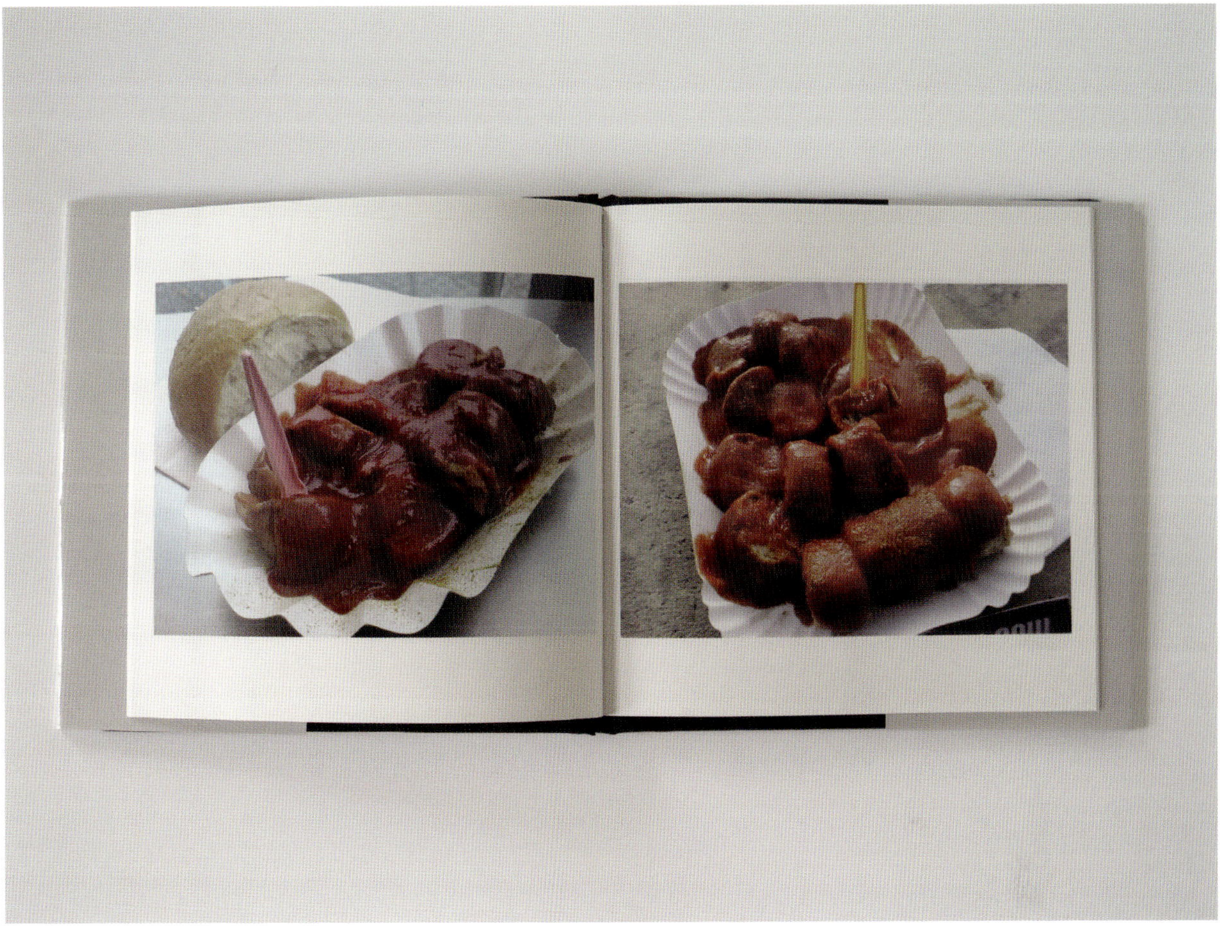

118 Joachim Schmidt, from the book *Currywurst*, in the series *Other People's Photographs*, 2008–11.

References

All translations are the author's except where otherwise indicated.

Introduction

1 Klaus Honnef, Rolf Sachsse and Karin Thomas, *Deutsche Fotografie. Macht eines Mediums 1870–1970* (German Photography: Power of a Medium, (1870–1970)), exh. cat., Kunst- und Ausstellungshalle der Bundesrepublik Deutschland, Bonn (Cologne, 1997).

one: Belated Photography, 1839–1870

1 Erich Stenger, 'Aus der Frühgeschichte der Photographie. Die Erfindung der Fräulein von Wunsch', *Photographische Korrespondenz*, LXV/10 (1929), pp. 284–90. I borrow this evocation of von Wunsch from Bodo von Dewitz's superlative work on early German photography, particularly his *Silber und Salz. Zur Frühzeit der Photographie im deutschen Sprachraum 1839–1860*, exh. cat., Museum Ludwig (Cologne, 1989), on which this book heavily draws.

2 Eder was Austrian, but before unification in 1871, this Central European empire was considered a great German power, much like Prussia.

3 Erich Stenger, *The March of Photography* [originally *Die Photographie in Kultur und Technik*, 1938], trans. Edward Epstean (London, 1958), pp. 13–14.

4 Johann Wolfgang von Goethe, 'Von deutscher Baukunst' [1772], *Goethes Werke, hg. im Auftrag der Großherzogin Sophie von Sachsen (Weimarer Ausgabe)*, 1/37 (Weimar, 1896), pp. 137–51.

5 A short biography in Ulrich Pohlmann, ed., *Zwischen Biedermeier und Gründerzeit. Deutschland in frühen Photographien 1840–1890 aus der Sammlung Siegert*, exh. cat., Münchner Stadtmuseum (Munich, 2012), p. 349.

6 Johann Gottlieb Fichte, *Address to the German Nation*, ed. Gregory Moore (Cambridge, 2008).

7 Douglas Nickel, 'Talbot's Natural Magic', *History of Photography*, XXVI/2 (2002), pp. 132–40.

8 David Blackbourn, *History of Germany, 1780–1918: The Long Nineteenth Century*, 2nd edn (London, 2003), p. 11.

9 Leopold von Ranke, 'Über die Trennung und die Einheit von Deutschland', *Sämmtliche Werke*, XLIX/L (Leipzig, 1887), p. 172. Cited from James Sheehan, 'What is German History? Reflections on the Role of the *Nation* in German History and Historiography', *Journal of Modern History*, LII (March 1981), p. 1–23, text taken from p. 1.

10 Heinrich Heine, 'Über Ludwig Börne' [1840], *Werke*, ed. M. Greiner (Berlin and Cologne, 1962), 2, pp. 752–3. Cited from Sheehan, 'What is German History?', pp. 1–2.

11 Sheehan, 'What is German History?, pp. 8–9.

12 Ignaz Paul Keller, 'Über Daguerres Entdeckung', in *Neues Licht: Daguerre, Talbot und die Veröffentlichung der Fotografie im Jahr 1839*, ed. Steffen Siegel (Paderborn, 2014), p. 162.

13 On the flurry of claims to photography's invention and the discursive construction of photography on which these claims relied, see Geoffrey Batchen, *Burning with Desire: The Conception of Photography* (Cambridge, MA, 1997).

14 Bodo von Dewitz, 'Daguerre oder Talbot? Zu Konkurrenz der Verfahren im deutschen Sprachraum', in von Dewitz, *Silber und Salz*, p. 24.

15 Von Dewitz, 'Daguerre oder Talbot?', p. 25.

16 The text attributed to Johann Heinrich von Mädler is reprinted as 'Über die Erfindung des Hrn. Daguerre', in Siegel, *Neues Licht*, pp. 57–60.

17 Josef Maria Eder, *Johann Heinrich Schulze. Der Lebenslauf des Erfinders des ersten photographischen Verfahrens und des Begründers der Geschichte der Medizin* (Vienna, 1917).

18 Von Dewitz, *Silber und Salz*, p. 32. See his footnote 49 for the animated debate about this award among interwar historians of photography.

19 Although Daguerre enforced a patent in the UK.

20 Dominique François Arago, 'Report', in *Classic Essays on Photography*, ed. Alan Trachtenburg (New Haven, CT, 1980), p. 24.

21 Ludwig Pfau, in Siegel, *Neues Licht*, p. 252.

22 See von Dewitz, *Silber und Salz*, p. 28.

23 Stephen Pinson, *Speculating Daguerre: Art and Enterprise in the Work of L.J.M. Daguerre* (Chicago, IL, 2012), pp. 202–3. The images, still in Munich, were damaged in cleaning after 1936 and are no longer visible.

24 Bodo von Dewitz, '"... die Ehre der schönen Entdeckung, die Bilder der Camera obscura zu fixieren ..." Zur allgemeinen Entwicklung der frühen Photographie im deutschen Sprachraum', in *Zwischen Biedermeier*, ed. Pohlmann, pp. 11–12.

25 Ludwig Hoerner, 'Die Einführung der Photographie in den Metropolen und in der Provinz (1839–1860)', in von Dewitz, *Silber und Salz*, pp. 88–96.

26 Laurie Stein, 'A Culture of Harmony and Memory', in *Biedermeier: The Invention of Simplicity*, ed. Hans Ottomeyer and Laurie Winters, exh. cat. (Milwaukee, WI, 2006), p. 72.

27 Detlef Hoffmann and Ute Wrocklage, 'Die daguerreo-typisierten Männer der Paulskirche. Parlamentarierportraits der ersten

deutschen Nationalversammlung in Frankfurt 1848/49', in von Dewitz, *Silber und Salz*, pp. 404–37.

28 See Detlef Hoffmann, 'Deutschland als Reiseland', in *Zwischen Biedermeier*, ed. Pohlmann, pp. 114–21.

29 Hoffmann, 'Deutschland als Reiseland', pp. 119–20, and Wilhelm Heinrich Wackenroder, *Herzensergießerungen eines kunstliebenden Klosterbruders* (Berlin, 1797), p. 109.

30 Hoffmann, 'Deutschland als Reiseland', p. 120.

31 Francis Frith, *Gossiping Photographer on the Rhine* (London, 1864), p. 25.

32 Ibid., p. 13.

two: Photography and Nation, 1871–1918

1 Franziska Windt, 'Majestätische Bilderflut. Die Kaiser in der Photographie', in *Die Kaiser und die Macht der Medien*, ed. Generaldirektion der Stiftung der Preußische Schlösser und Gärten Berlin-Brandenburg (Berlin, 2005), pp. 70–71.

2 Walter Benjamin, 'The Work of Art in the Age of Its Technological Reproducibility' (2nd version), in *Walter Benjamin: Selected Writings*, vol. III: *1935–1938*, ed. Howard Eiland and Michael Jennings (Cambridge, MA, 2002), pp. 115–16.

3 David Blackbourn, *History of Germany, 1780–1918: The Long Nineteenth Century* (London, 2003), pp. 199–200.

4 *Deutsche Hellas*, *c.* 1900, quoted in *Wir sind nackt und nennen uns du*, ed. Michael Andritzky and Thomas Rautenberg (Giessen, 1989), p. 39.

5 See Eva Giloi, '"So Writes the Hand That Swings the Sword": Autograph Hunting and Royal Charisma in the German Empire, 1861–1888', and Martin Kohlrausch, 'The Working of Royal Celebrity: Wilhelm II as Media Emperor', in *Constructing Charisma: Celebrity, Fame, and Power in Nineteenth-century Europe*, ed. Edward Berenson and Eva Giloi (Oxford, 2010), pp. 41–51 and pp. 52–66.

6 Most of the following account is taken from Giloi's anthology chapter cited in the previous and following endnotes.

7 Geheimes Staatsarchiv Preussischer Kulterbesitz, I HA Rep. 89 Nr. 2318, Nicolaas K. v. Cammenga to Wilhelm I, 13 June 1876, Blatt 172. Taken from Giloi, '"So Writes the Hand"', p. 41.

8 Kohlrausch, 'The Working of Royal Celebrity', p. 53.

9 For more on the picture culture of Kaiser Wilhelm II, see Saskia Asser and Liesbeth Ruitenberg, *Das Kaiser im Bild. Wilhelm II. und die Fotografie als PR-Instrument* (Doorn, 2002).

10 Eva Giloi, 'Copyrighting the Kaiser: Publicity, Piracy, and the Right to Wilhelm II's Image', *Central European History*, XLV (2012), p. 428.

11 Tanya Sheehan, *Doctored: The Medicine of Photography in Nineteenth-century America* (University Park, PA, 2011), and Heinz K. Henisch and Bridget A. Henisch, *The Photographic Experience, 1839–1914: Images and Attitudes* (University Park, PA, 1993).

12 On the collecting of postcards, see Naomi Schor's foundational essay, '*Cartes Postales*: Representing Paris 1900', reprinted in *Postcards: Ephemeral Histories of Modernity*, ed. Jordana Mendelson and David Prochaska (College Park, PA, 2010), pp. 1–23.

13 Robert Bosshard, Ute Eskildsen and Robert Knodt, eds, *Erinnerung an die Dienstzeit. Fotografien der Jahrhundertwende*, exh. cat., Museum Folkwang (Essen, 1993). For a discussion of similar American compositions, see 'The Camera at War' in Henisch and Henisch, *The Photographic Experience*, pp. 364–94.

14 Deac Rossell, *Faszination der Bewegung. Ottomar Anschütz zwischen Photographie und Kino* (Frankfurt am Main, 2001).

15 Rossell, *Faszination der Bewegung*, p. 23.

16 Ibid., p. 27.

17 Clément Chéroux, 'Photographs of Fluids: An Alphabet of Invisible Rays', in *The Perfect Medium: Photography and the Occult*, exh. cat., Metropolitan Museum (New York, 2005), p. 119.

18 Elizabeth Cronin, *Heimat Photography in Austria* (Vienna, 2015).

19 Geoffrey Batchen, 'Taking and Making', in *Each Wild Idea: Writing, Photography, History* (Cambridge, MA, 2002), pp. 82–106.

20 Albert Kohn, *Unsere Wohnungs-Enquête* (1909), republished in Gesine Asmus, '"Mißstände . . . und das Licht des Tages zerren." Zu den Photographien der Wohnungs-Enquête', in *Hinterhof, Keller und Mansarde. Einblicke in Berliner Wohnungselend 1901–1920. Die Wohnungs-Enquête der Ortskrankenkasse für den Gewerbebetrieb der Kaufleute, Handelsleute und Apotheker*, ed. Gesine Asmus (Reinbek bei Hamburg, 1982), p. 35.

three: The Weimar Era and Photo-consciousness, 1919–1932

1 Willi Münzenberg, 'Aufgaben und Ziele der internationalen Arbeiter-Fotografen-Bewegung', *Der Arbeiter-Fotograf*, V/5 (1930), p. 99.

2 Johannes Molzahn, 'Nicht mehr lesen! Sehen!', *Das Kunstblatt*, XII/3 (1928), pp. 78–82.

3 Alfred Heller, 'Zum Geleit', *Die Kultur der Reklame*, I/1 (1919), p. 82.

4 Ferdinand Avenarius, *Das Bild als Verleumder. Beispiele und Bemerkungen zur Technik der Volker-Verhetzung. Flugschrift des Dürerbundes* (Munich, 1915).

5 Mia Fineman, *Faking It: Manipulated Photography before Photoshop* (New York, 2012).

6 See Andreas Hallen and Diethart Kerbs, *Revolution und Fotografie, Berlin* (Berlin, 1989), and Rudolf Herz, *Revolution und Fotografie, München* (Munich, 1988).

7 Felix Stössinger, 'Wie das deutsche Volk belogen wurde', *Die freie Welt*, II/5 (1920), pp. 2–3.
8 *Die freie Welt*, I/1 (1919), p. 2. Translated in Sherwin Simmon, 'Photo-caricature in the German Popular Press, 1920', *History of Photography*, XX/3 (1996), p. 258.
9 John Heartfield interviewed in 1966, in *John Heartfield. Der Schnitt entlang der Zeit. Selbstzeugnisse. Erinnnerungen. Interpretationen*, ed. Roland März and Gertrud Heartfield (Dresden, 1981), p. 11.
10 Wieland Herzfelde, 'Zur Einführung' (Introduction) in the catalogue to the Erste Grosse Dada Messe (First Great Dada Fair), 1920.
11 Hugo Ball, *Flight Out of Time: A Dada Diary*, ed. John Elderfield, trans. Ann Raimes (Berkeley, CA, 1996), p. 56.
12 Richard Huelsenbeck, *En Avant Dada. Eine Geschichte des Dadaismus* (Hanover, 1920), p. 41.
13 *Die neue Sachlichkeit* can also be translated as 'New Sobriety' or 'New Matter-of-Factness'. Stephanie Barron and Sabine Eckmann, eds, *New Objectivity: Modern German Art in the Weimar Republic, 1919–1933*, exh. cat., Los Angeles County Museum of Art (Los Angeles, CA, 2015).
14 Gustav Hartlaub, 'Introduction to "New Objectivity": German Painting since Expressionism', in *The Weimar Republic Sourcebook*, ed. Anton Kaes et al. (Berkeley, CA, 1994), pp. 491–3.
15 Helmuth Lethen, *Cool Conduct: The Culture of Distance in Weimar Germany*, trans. Don Reneau (Berkeley, CA, 2001).
16 H. Wieynck, 'Die künstlerische Bildgestaltung in der Fotografie', *Fotografische Rundschau* (1926), p. 227. Taken from Ute Eskildsen, 'Photography and the Neue Sachlichkeit Movement', in *Germany: The New Photography, 1927–33*, ed. David Mellor (London, 1978), p. 106.
17 Albert Renger-Patzsch, 'Photographie und Kunst.' *Das Deutsche Lichtbild*, 1929. Translated by Barry Lane and reprinted in *Germany: The New Photography*, ed. Mellor, p. 15.
18 Pepper Stetler, 'The Object, the Archive and the Origins of *Neue Sachlichkeit* Photography', *History of Photography*, XXXV/3 (2011), p. 281.
19 See Stetler for more on the subtleties of the category *sachlich*, and Daniel Magilow, *The Photography of Crisis: The Photo Essays of Weimar Germany* (University Park, PA, 2012).
20 Hanako Murata, 'Material Forms in Nature: The Photographs of Karl Blossfeldt', www.moma.org/interactives/objectphoto, 13 June 2016.
21 On physiognomy as a form of cultural self-diagnosis, see Sabine Hake, 'Zur Wiederkehr des Physiognomischen in der modernen Photographie', in *Geschichten der Physiognomik. Text, Bild, Wissen*, ed. Rüdiger Campe and Manfred Schneider (Freiburg im Breisgau, 1996), pp. 475–513.
22 Walter Benjamin, 'Little History of Photography', in *Walter Benjamin: Selected Writing*, vol. II: *1927–1934*, ed. Michael Jennings, Howard Eiland and Gary Smith (Cambridge, MA, 1999), pp. 511–12.
23 László Moholy-Nagy, 'Produktion-Reproduktion' [1922], translated as 'Production-Reproduction' in *Photography in the Modern Era: European Documents and Critical Writings, 1913–1940*, ed. Christopher Phillips (New York, 1989), pp. 79–82.
24 The attribution of these early images is contested. They were probably the work of a collaboration between Moholy and Schulz. See Herbert Molderings et al., eds, *László Moholy-Nagy: The Photograms. Catalogue Raisonné* (Ostfildern, 2010).
25 Tim Gidal, *Jews in Germany: From Roman Times to the Weimar Republic* (Cologne, 1988).
26 The *Arbeiter-Illustrierte Zeitung* was earlier published as *Sichel und Hammer* (*Sickel and Hammer*) and, before that, *Sowjet-Russland im Bild* (*Soviet Russia in Pictures*).
27 See Walter Benjamin, 'The Work of Art in the Age of Its Technological Reproducibility' (second version), in *Walter Benjamin: Selected Writings*, vol. III: *1935–1938*, ed. Howard Eiland and Michael Jennings (Cambridge, MA, 2002), pp. 101–33.
28 See Daniel Magilow, 'The Illustrated Press and the Photo Essay' (Chapter 2), *The Photography of Crisis*, pp. 34–62.
29 Paul Westheim, 'Bildermüde?', *Das Kunstblatt*, XVI/3 (1932), pp. 20–22, and Wilhelm Hausenstein, 'Photo-Inflation?', *Rhein-Mainische Volkszeitung* (29 January 1930).
30 Olivier Lugon, '"Photo-Inflation": Image Profusion in German Photography, 1925–1945', *History of Photography*, XXXII/3 (2008), pp. 219–34.

four: The Alluring Surface, 1933–1945

1 Angela Schönberger, *Die neue Reichskanzlei von Albert Speer. Zum Zusammenhang von nationalsozialistischer Ideologie und Architektur* (Munich, 1981).
2 Albert Speer, *Inside the Third Reich* (New York, 1971), p. 291.
3 Anson Rabinbach, '*Staging Antifascism*: The Brown Book of the Reichstag Fire and Hitler Terror', *New German Critique*, XXXV/1 (Spring 2008), pp. 97–126.
4 Adolf Hitler, *Mein Kampf* (Munich, 1940), p. 116. Recently republished as a new critical volume: Christian Hartmann et al., eds, *Hitler, Mein Kampf. Eine kritische Edition* (Berlin, 2016).
5 So too did the leader's relationship with Eva Braun begin through this connection in 1926. She was working as Hoffmann's assistant.
6 Rolf Sachsse, *Die Erziehung zum Wegsehen. Fotografie im NS-Staat* (Dresden, 2003), p. 34. See also Heinrich Hoffmann, *Das Hitler-Bild. Die Erinnerungen des Fotografen Heinrich Hoffmann* (St Pölen, 2008).
7 Sachsse, *Erziehung zum Wegsehen*, p. 34.

8 The A-I-Z circulation in Prague exile was much reduced from what it had been in Berlin before February 1933.

9 See Rolf Sachsse, 'Fotografie als NS-Staatsdesign. Ein Medium und sein Mißbrauch durch Macht', in *Deutsche Fotografie. Macht eines Mediums 1870–1970*, ed. Klaus Honnef, Rolf Sachsse and Karin Thomas (Bonn, 1997), p. 84.

10 Sachsse, *Erziehung zum Wegsehen*, p. 63.

11 Bayer designed the catalogue for *Die Kamera*. Jorge Ribalta, *Public Photographic Spaces, Exhibitions of Propaganda, from Pressa to The Family of Man, 1928–55* (Barcelona, 2008).

12 The designer of these spaces, Winfried Wendland, was an ecclesiastical architect. See the upcoming book, *Nazi Exhibition Design and Modernism* by Michael Tymkiw.

13 Reprinted as abridged text in Sachsse, *Erziehung zum Wegsehen*, pp. 319–20.

14 *Die neue Reichskanzlei* (Munich, *c.* 1940).

15 See Despina Stratigakos, *Hitler at Home* (New Haven, CT, 2015).

16 I thank Daniel Magilow for suggesting this angle on the stereo cards.

17 Adolf Hitler, 'Speech at the Opening of the Great German Art Exhibition', in *The Third Reich Sourcebook*, ed. Anson Rabinbach and Sander L. Gilman (Berkeley, CA, 2013), p. 498. Text runs pp. 494–500.

18 What have come to be known as the 'Nazi Olympics' were held in Berlin in the summer of 1936. Riefenstahl released her two-part film two years later.

19 Hitler, 'Speech at the Opening of the Great German Art Exhibition', p. 498.

20 Erna Lendvai-Dircksen, *Das deutsche Volksgesicht* (Berlin, *c.* 1931).

21 Those two books were *Die Puppe* (1934) and *Les Jeux de la poupée* (1936).

22 See Sachsse, 'Fotografie als NS-Staatsdesign', p. 93.

23 Judith Levin and Daniel Uziel, 'Ordinary Men, Extraordinary Photos', www.yadvasehm.org, 13 June 2016.

24 For more about this album, see Alex Wilkinson, 'Picturing Auschwitz', www.newyorker.com, 17 March 2008.

five: History, the Future and Photography, 1946–1989

1 W. G. Sebald, *Luftkrieg und Literatur* (Munich, 1999). This adapted translation is taken from Todd Samuel Presner, '"What a Synoptic and Artificial View Reveals": Extreme History and the Modernism of W. G. Sebald's Realism', *Criticism*, XLVI/3 (2004), p. 353.

2 Recently the phenomenon of 'the hierarchy of memory' has sometimes placed the German suffering in the war on a par with that of the country's victims. See Aleida Assmann, 'On the (In)Compatability of Guilt and Suffering in German Memory', *German Life and Letters*, LIX/2 (2006), pp. 187–200.

3 See Jeffrey Herf, *Divided Memory: The Nazi Past in the Two Germanys* (Cambridge, MA, 1997).

4 David Crew (History, University of Texas, Austin) has recently suggested that these bomb-shelter pictures by Peter may have been partially staged. He is currently working on a publication to address the subject.

5 Josef Heinrich Darchinger and Klaus Honnef, eds, *Wirtschaftswunder. Deutschland nach dem Krieg 1952–1967* (Cologne, 2008), and Klaus Honnef, Rolf Sachsse and Karin Thomas, eds, *German Photography, 1870–1970: Power of a Medium* (Cologne, 1997).

6 Andreas Huyssen, 'Figures of Memory in the Course of Time', in *Art of Two Germanys: Cold War Cultures*, ed. Stephanie Barron and Sabine Eckmann, exh. cat., Los Angeles Museum of Art (Los Angeles, CA, 2009), p. 227.

7 Stephanie Barron, 'Blurred Boundaries: The Art of Two Germanys between Myth and History', in Barron and Eckmann, *Art of Two Germanys*, p. 17.

8 Rudolf Augstein, 'Lieber Spiegelleser', *Der Spiegel*, XXIX (July 1953), taken from Klaus Honnef, 'From Reality to Art: Photography between Profession and Abstraction', in Honnef et al., *German Photography*, p. 139.

9 Ibid., p. 140.

10 Ludger Derenthal, *Bilder der Trümmer- und Aufbaujahre. Fotografie im sich teilenden Deutschland* (Marburg, 1999), pp. 99–265.

11 A notable exception here is the painter and photographer Edmund Kersting, who used double exposures, solarization and other darkroom techniques to build allegories of death in his personal photos of the destroyed Dresden. At the time, however, only his standard photographs were published.

12 Ezard Reuter and Janos Frescot, eds, *Henry Ries. Photographien 1946–1949* (Berlin, 1998).

13 The panorama actually consists of two photographs taken at slightly different intervals. This is apparent in the central group of ruins, which is repeated.

14 Derenthal, *Bilder der Trümmer*, p. 48.

15 Introductory words in Hermann Claasen, *Gesang im Feuerofen. Köln – Überreste einer alten deutschen Stadt* (Düsseldorf, 1947), p. xii.

16 Richard Peter, *Dresden. Eine Kamera klagt an* (Dresden, 1950).

17 See Herf, *Divided Memory: The Nazi Past in the Two Germanys*.

18 Stefan Wolf, 'The Smiling Face of Dictatorship: On the Political Iconography of the GDR', in Honnef et al., *German Photography*, pp. 107–38.

19 Ernst Nitsche, 'Realismus und Formalismus in der Fotografie', *Die Fotografie*, VII/4 (1953), p. 113. Heavily policed debates on

the role of photography in the East after 1949 were played out in this journal.

20 Sarah James, *Common Ground* (London, 2013).

21 The following summary is drawn from Daniel Magilow and Lisa Silverman, 'Yizker-Bukh Khelm', in *Holocaust Representation in History: An Introduction* (London, 2015), pp. 31–41.

22 Ibid., p. 40.

23 Roman Vishniac, *Polish Jews: A Pictorial Record* (New York, 1947).

24 Gabriele Muschter, ed., *DDR Frauen fotografieren. Lexicon und Anthologie* (Berlin (West), 1989), p. 28.

25 Christine Mehring, 'Continental Schrift: The Legacy of *Intetfunctionen*', *Artforum* (May 2004).

26 Hilla Becher, in 'Conversation with Jean-Francois Chevrier, James Lingwood, Thomas Struth', in *Un'Altra Obiettivitá/Another Objectivity*, exh. cat., Centre National des Arts Plastiques (Paris, 1989), p. 58.

27 Bernd was appointed professor in 1976. School policy on spousal hires prevented Hilla from being given a simultaneous appointment, though they taught as a team.

28 Francis Fukuyama, *The End of History and the Last Man* (New York, 1992).

six: Photographic Promiscuity, 1990–2016

1 Georg Bussmann and Peter Friese, eds, *Rudolf Herz: Zugzwang* (Essen, 1995).

2 Meredith Bennett-Smith, 'Grindr Users Post "Sexy" Pictures from Holocaust Memorial in Bizarre, Ironic Trend', www.huffingtonpost.com, 31 January 2013.

3 Friedrich Wilhelm Basil von Ramdohr, 'Landschaften und Seestücke' [Chapter 18], *Charis Über das Schöne und die Schönheit in den nachbildenden Künsten*, vol. II (Leipzig, 1793), p. 124.

Select Bibliography

Asser, Saskia, and Liesbeth Ruitenberg, *Das Kaiser im Bild. Wilhelm II und die Fotografie als PR-Instrument* (Doorn, 2002)

Avenarius, Ferdenand, *Das Bild als Verleumder. Beispiele und Bemerkungen zur Technik der Volker-Verhetzung. Flugschrift des Dürerbundes* (Munich, 1915)

Barron, Stephanie, and Sabine Eckmann, eds, *New Objectivity: Modern German Art in the Weimar Republic, 1919–1933*, exh. cat., Los Angeles County Museum of Art (Los Angeles, CA, 2015)

Batchen, Geoffrey, *Burning with Desire: The Conception of Photography* (Cambridge, MA, 1997)

—, 'Taking and Making', in *Each Wild Idea: Writing, Photography, History* (Cambridge, MA, 2002), pp. 82–106

Benjamin, Walter, 'Little History of Photography', in *Walter Benjamin: Selected Writing*, vol. II: *1927–1934*, ed. Michael Jennings, Howard Eiland and Gary Smith (Cambridge, MA, 1999), pp. 507–30

—, 'The Work of Art in the Age of Its Technological Reproducibility (second version), in *Walter Benjamin: Selected Writings*, vol. III: *1935–1938*, ed. Howard Eiland and Michael Jennings (Cambridge, MA, 2002), pp. 101–33

Berenson, Edward, and Eva Giloi, *Constructing Charisma: Celebrity, Fame, and Power in Nineteenth-century Europe* (Oxford, 2010)

Blackbourn, David, *History of Germany, 1780–1918: The Long Nineteenth Century*, 2nd edn (London, 2003)

Bosshard, Robert, Ute Eskildsen and Robert Knodt, eds, *Erinnerung an die Dienstzeit. Fotografien der Jahrhundertwende*, exh. cat., Museum Folkwang (Essen, 1993)

Bussmann, Georg, and Peter Friese, eds, *Rudolf Herz: Zugzwang*, exh. cat., Kunstverein Ruhr (Essen, 1995)

Chéroux, Clément, ed., *The Perfect Medium: Photography and the Occult* (New Haven, CT, 2005)

Claasen, Hermann, *Gesang im Feuerofen. Köln – Überreste einer alten deutschen Stadt* (Düsseldorf, 1947)

Derenthal, Ludger, *Bilder der Trümmer- und Aufbaujahre. Fotografie im sich teilenden Deutschland* (Marburg, 1999)

Dewitz, Bodo von, ed., *Silber und Salz. Zur Frühzeit der Photographie im deutschen Sprachraum 1839–1860*, exh. cat., Museum Ludwig (Cologne, 1989)

Eder, Josef Maria, *Johann Heinrich Schulze. Der Lebenslauf des Erfinders des ersten photographischen Verfahrens und des Begründers der Geschichte der Medizin* (Vienna, 1917)

Fichte, Johan Gottlieb, *Address to the German Nation*, ed. Gregory Moore (Cambridge, 2008)

Fineman, Mia, *Faking It: Manipulated Photography before Photoshop*, exh. cat., Metropolitan Museum of Art (New York, 2012)

Frith, Francis, *Gossiping Photographer on the Rhine* (London, 1864)

Fukuyama, Francis, *The End of History and the Last Man* (New York, 1992)

Generaldirektion der Stiftung der Preußische Schlösser und Gärten Berlin-Brandenburg, ed., *Die Kaiser und die Macht der Medien* (Berlin, 2005)

Giloi, Eva, 'Copyrighting the Kaiser: Publicity, Piracy, and the Right to Wilhelm II's Image', *Central European History*, XLV (2012), pp. 407–51

Goethe, Johann Wolfgang von, 'Von deutscher Baukunst [1772]', in *Goethe's Werke, hg. im Auftrag der Großherzogin Sophie von Sachsen (Weimarer Ausgabe)*, I/37 (Weimar, 1896), pp. 137–51

Hallen, Andreas, and Diethart Kerbs, *Revolution und Fotografie, Berlin* (Berlin, 1989)

Hartmann, Christian, et al., eds, *Hitler, Mein Kampf: Eine kritische Edition* (Berlin, 2016)

Hausenstein, Wilhelm, 'Photo-Inflation?', *Rhein-Mainische Volkszeitung* (29 January 1930)

Henisch, Heinz K., and Bridget A. Henisch, *The Photographic Experience, 1839–1914: Images and Attitudes* (University Park, PA, 1993)

Herf, Jeffrey, *Divided Memory: The Nazi Past in the Two Germanys* (Cambridge, MA, 1997)

Herz, Rudolf, *Revolution und Fotografie, München* (Munich, 1988)

Hoffmann, Heinrich, *Das Hitler-Bild. Die Erinnerungen des Fotografen Heinrich Hoffmann* (St Pölen, 2008)

Honnef, Klaus, Rolf Sachsse and Karin Thomas, eds, *Deutsche Fotografie. Macht eines Mediums 1870–1970* (Bonn, 1997), published in English as *German Photography, 1870–1970: Power of a Medium* (Cologne, 1997)

Huelsenbeck, Richard, *En Avant Dada. Eine Geschichte des Dadaismus* (Hannover, 1920)

James, Sarah, *Common Ground* (London, 2013)

Lendvai-Dircksen, Erna, *Das deutsche Volksgesicht* (Berlin, *c.* 1931)

Lethen, Helmuth, *Cool Conduct: The Culture of Distance in Weimar Germany*, trans. Don Reneau (Berkeley, CA, 2001)

Lugon, Olivier, '"Photo-Inflation": Image Profusion in German Photography, 1925–1945', *History of Photography*, XXXII/3 (2008), pp. 219–34

Magilow, Dan, *The Photography of Crisis: The Photo Essays of Weimar Germany* (University Park, PA, 2012)

Mellor, David, ed., *Germany, the New Photography, 1927–1933* (London, 1978)

Molderings, Herbert, et al., eds, *László Moholy-Nagy: The Photograms. Catalogue Raisonné* (Ostfildern, 2010)

Münzenberg, Willi, 'Aufgaben und Ziele der internationalen Arbeiter-Fotografen-Bewegung', *Der Arbeiter-Fotograf*, V/5 (1931), p. 99

Ottomeyer, Hans, and Laurie Winters, eds, *Biedermeier: The Invention of Simplicity*, exh. cat., Milwaukee Art Museum (Milwaukee, WI, 2006)

Peter, Richard, *Dresden. Eine Kamera klagt an* (Dresden, 1950)

Pohlmann, Ulrich, ed., *Zwischen Biedermeier und Gründerzeit. Deutschland in frühen Photographien 1840–1890 aus der Sammlung Siegert*, exh. cat., Münchner Stadtmuseum (Munich, 2012)

Presner, Todd Samuel, '"What a Synoptic and Artificial View Reveals": Extreme History and the Modernism of W. G. Sebald's Realism', *Criticism*, XLVI/3 (2004), pp. 341–60

Rabinbach, Anson, and Sander L. Gilman, eds, *The Third Reich Sourcebook* (Berkeley, CA, 2013)

Ranke, Leopold von, 'Über die Trennung und die Einheit von Deutschland', in *Sämmtliche Werke*, XLIX-L (Leipzig, 1887)

Reuter, Ezard, and Janos Frescot, eds, *Henry Ries: Photographien 1946–1949* (Berlin, 1998)

Rossell, Deac, *Faszination der Bewegung. Ottomar Anschütz zwischen Photographie und Kino* (Frankfurt am Main, 2001)

Sachsse, Rolf, *Die Erziehung zum Wegsehen. Fotografie im NS-Staat* (Dresden, 2003)

Sebald, W. G., *Luftkrieg und Literatur* (München, 1999), published in English as *On the Natural History of Destruction*, trans. Anthea Bell (New York, 2003)

Sheehan, James, 'What is German History? Reflections on the Role of the *Nation* in German History and Historiography', *Journal of Modern History*, LII (1981), pp. 1–23

Simmon, Sherwin, 'Picture as Weapon in German Mass Media, 1914–1930', in *Art and Journalism on the Political Front*, ed. Virginia Hagelstein Marquardt (Gainesville, FL, 1997), pp. 142–82

Speer, Albert, *Inside the Third Reich* (New York, 1971)

Stenger, Erich, 'Aus der Frühgeschichte der Photographie. Die Erfindung der Fräulein von Wunsch', *Photographische Korrespondenz*, LXV/10 (1929), pp. 284–90

—, *The March of Photography*, trans. Edward Epstean (London, 1958)

Stetler, Pepper, *'Stop Reading! Look!': Modern Vision and the Weimar Photographic Book* (Ann Arbor, MI, 2015)

Stössinger, Felix, 'Wie das deutsche Volk belogen wurde', *Die freie Welt*, II/5 (7 February 1920), pp. 2–3

Vishniac, Roman, *Polish Jews. A Pictorial Record* (New York, 1947)

Wackenroder, Wilhelm Heinrich, *Herzensergießerungen eines kunstliebenden Klosterbruders* (Berlin, 1797)

Westheim, Paul, 'Bildermüde?', *Das Kunstblatt*, XVI/3 (1932), pp. 20–22

Acknowledgements

Covering such a vast expanse of photography in a critical fashion requires the insight of many more minds and eyes than a single author can provide. For this help I thank Tanya Sheehan, Geoffrey Batchen, Antonella Pelizzari, Steffen Siegel, Sabine Kriebel, Maria Gough, Noam Elcott, Bettina Gockel, Ulrich Pohlmann, Anne McCauley, Elizabeth Cronin and Susan Sidlauskas. I offer particularly heartfelt thanks to Daniel H. Magilow who provided tireless feedback from the initial stage of proposal all the way to the completed manuscript. Sara Miovic aided as a research assistant, and Tanja Rommelfanger performed the heroic task of securing nearly 120 images and permissions from frequently recalcitrant German collections. Vivian Constantinopoulos enthusiastically accepted the idea of a volume on photography and Germany, and then patiently awaited the full draft. Harry Gilonis beautifully edited the copious images, and Martha Jay the ample text. To all these friends and colleagues I express my gratitude.

Photo Acknowledgements

From *A-I-Z* [*Arbeiter-Illustrierte-Zeitung*]: 59 (VI/14, 10 April 1927), 64 (XII/18, 10 May 1933); Agfa Foto-Historama, Köln (Museum Ludwig) – photos © Rheinisches Bildarchiv: 2, 3, 7, 18, 19, 31, 34; photo Akademie der Künste, Berlin, Kunstsammlung, Inv.-Nr.: JH 2195 © The Heartfield Community of Heirs/Artists Rights Society (ARS), New York/VG Bild-Kunst, Bonn, 2016: 64; Archive of the Auschwitz-Birkenau State Memorial and Museum, Oświęcim, Poland: 78; © Artists Rights Society (ARS), New York/VG Bild-Kunst, Bonn, 2016: 65; © Shimon Attie, courtesy of the artist and Jack Shainman Gallery, New York: 107; collection of the author: 25, 29, 42, 44; from Ferdinand Avenarius, *Das Bild als Verleumder. Beispiele und Bemerkungen zur Technik der Volker-Verhetzung. Flugschrift des Dürerbundes* (Munich, 1915): 42; from Winfried Bade, *Deutschland Erwacht – Werden, Kampf und Sieg der NSDAP* (Hamburg, 1933): 68; Bauhaus Archiv, Berlin; Artists Rights Society (ARS), New York/VG Bild-Kunst, Bonn, 2016: 42; © Sibylle Bergemann/Ostkreuz: 102, 109; from *Berliner Illustrirte Zeitung*, XLIV/3 (17 January 1935): 70; Berlinische Galerie, Berlin: 47 (photo © bpk – Bildagentur für Kunst, Kultur und Geschichte/Berlinische Galerie, Landesmuseum für moderne Kunst, Photographie und Architektur, Berlin; Artists Rights Society (ARS), New York/VG Bild-Kunst, Bonn, 2016): 47; Berlinische Galerie Landesmuseum für Moderne Kunst, Fotografie und Architektur, Berlin: 93; © bpk – Bildagentur für Kunst, Kultur und Geschichte/Julius Braatz: 24; photos © bpk – Bildagentur für Kunst, Kultur und Geschichte/Heinrich Hoffmann: 66; © bpk – Bildagentur für Kunst, Kultur und Geschichte /Staatsbibliothek zu Berlin: 28, 59; Bundesarchiv, Koblenz: 76; Pay Christian Carstensen, Hans Hitzer and Friedrich Richter, *Deutschland* (Berlin: Der Volk und Reich Verlag, 1936), vol. II: 71; from Hermann Claasen, *Gesang im Feuerofen. Köln – Überreste einer alten deutschen Stadt* (Düsseldorf, 1947) – photo © Artists Rights Society (ARS), New York/VG Bild-Kunst, Bonn, 2016: 89; photo © DEFA-Stiftung/Eugen Klagemann: 83; courtesy Delmes & Zander, Berlin + Cologne: 96; © Thomas Demand, Artist Rights Society (ARS)/VG Bild-Kunst, Bonn, 2016: 110; from *Der Deutsche Fürstentag in Frankfurt am Main im August 1863* (Frankfurt am Main, 1863): 14; photo Deutsches Historisches Museum, Berlin: 86; photo Deutsches Literaturarchiv Marbach: 35; Deutsches Röntgen Museum, Remscheid: 36; from Ilya Ehrenburg, *Die heiligsten Güter: Roman der grossen Interessen* (Berlin, 1931): 57; Evelyn Richter Archiv der Ostdeutschen Sparkassenstiftung im Museum der bildenden Künste Leipzig – photo Harald Richter, Hamburg: 94; © Julian Faulhaber/Artist Rights Society (ARS)/VG Bild-Kunst, Bonn, 2016: 113; from *Die freie Welt*: 44 (II/29, 8 August 1920), 45 (II/17, 15 May 1920); from Francis Frith, *Gossiping Photographer on the Rhine* (Reigate, 1864): 17; photo Galerie Bassenge, Berlin, © Artists Rights Society (ARS), New York/VG Bild-Kunst, Bonn, 2016: 57; courtesy of Galerie Buchholz, Berlin/Köln: 117; photo © Getty Images, 2016: 62, 67, 75, 79, 104, 105; photos Getty Research Institute, Los Angeles 45, 46; Werner Gräff, *Es kommt der neue Fotograf!* (Berlin, 1929): 61; © Andrea Grützner: 114; © Andreas Gursky/The Broad/Artist Rights Society (ARS)/VG Bild-Kunst, Bonn, 2016: 112; © Haus der Geschichte Baden-Württemberg, Sammlung Kilian: 85; Haverford College Fine Art Photography Collection – photo © Artists Rights Society (ARS), New York/VG Bild-Kunst, Bonn, 2016: 51; photo Markus Hawlik/Berlinische Galerie, © Helga Paris: 103; courtesy of the photographer (Rudolf Herz), © Rudolf Herz: 106, 108; Historisches Museum, Frankfurt – photo Horst Ziegenfusz: 11; photo Hochschule Fulde, University of Applied Sciences © *Der Spiegel*/Max Ehlert, 2016: 70; courtesy of the photographer (Candida Höfer), © Candida Höfer, Köln/VG Bild-Kunst, Bonn 2017: 101; from Heinrich Hoffmann, *Hitler wie ihn keiner Kennt* (Berlin, 1932), *Jugend um Hitler* (Berlin, 1934), *Hitler: Abseits vom Alltag* (Berlin, 1937), *Hitler baut Grossdeutschland*, *Hitler befreit Sudentenland*, *Hitler in seinen Bergen*, *Hitler in seiner Heimat* (all Berlin, 1938), *Hitler: ein Volk ehrt seinen Führer* (Berlin, 1939), *Mit Hitler im Westen* (Berlin, 1944): 72; Institut für Grenzgebiete der Psychologie und Psychohygiene, Freiburg im Breisgau: 37; photo International Center of Photography, New York (gift of Mr. Herbert Lust, 1987) – photo © Artists Rights Society (ARS), New York/VG Bild-Kunst, Bonn, 2016: 74; from *Jedermann sein eigner Fussball*, no. 1 (15 February 1920): 46; KAB Deutschlands bzw. KAB St. Josef Rees – © KAB Rees: 23; from Albert Kohn, *Unsere Wohnungs-Enquête im Jahr 1911* (Berlin, 1912): 40; photo © Lee Miller Archives, Chiddingly, East Sussex: 80; from Erna Lendvai-Dircksen, *Das deutsche Volksgesicht* (Berlin, 1932): 73; Lidice Collection, Lidice, Czech Republic – Lidice Memorial (photo Martin Homola): 97; from *Magnum* no. 12 (1957): 98; from *Meggendorfers Humoristischen Blättern* no. 506, XIII/10 (1900): 33; courtesy of the artist (Simon Menner), © Simon Menner: 95; The Metropolitan Museum of Art (Ford Motor Company Collection [gift of Ford Motor Company and John C. Waddell, 1987 (1987.1100.460)]) – photo © ringl + pit, courtesy of Robert Mann Gallery, New York: 55; from *Münchner Illustrierte Presse* (13 March 1932): 60; courtesy Musée National d'Art Moderne, Paris; Artists Rights Society (ARS), New York/VG Bild-Kunst, Bonn, 2016: 53; photo Musee National d'Art Moderne, Paris © CNAC/MNAM/Dist. RMN-Grand Palais/Art Resources NY: 48; Museum für Kunst und Gewerbe, Hamburg: 5, 12; Museum für Kunst und Kulturgeschichte der Hansestadt Lübeck: 4; The Museum of Modern Art, New York, NY – digital image © The Museum of Modern Art/Licensed by SCALA/Art Resource, NY: 39; The Museum of Modern Art, New York (Thomas Walther Collection, gift of Thomas Walther) – digital images © The Museum of Modern Art/Licensed by SCALA/Art Resource, NY: 50, 56; The Museum of Modern Art, New York (Thomas Walther Collection purchase) – digital image © The Museum of Modern Art/Licensed by SCALA/Art Resource, NY; Artists Rights Society (ARS), New York/VG Bild-Kunst, Bonn, 2016: 49; from *Die neue Reichskanzlei: Architekt Albert Speer* (Munich, 1940): 63; photos New York Public Library: 17 (the Miriam and Ira D. Wallach

Division of Art, Prints and Photographs – Photography Collection), 92; from Richard Peter, *Dresden – Eine Kamera klagt an* (Dresden, 1950): 84, 90, 91; Photographische Sammlung/SK Stiftung Kultur – August Sander Archiv, Köln: 52; Princeton University Art Museum, Princeton, New Jersey (museum purchase, anonymous gift [x1990-68 a-i.]) – photo Bruce M. White, © Princeton University Art Museum/Artists Rights Society (ARS), New York/VG Bild-Kunst, Bonn, 2016: 99; photo Gerald Raab: 13; from Henry Ritter, *Der politische Struwwelpeter: Ein Versuch zur Einigung Deutschlands* (Düsseldorf, 1849): 13; courtesy of the photographers (Andrea Robbins & Max Becher), © Andrea Robbins & Max Becher 1997/98: 116; photo © Jens Rötzsch: 82; Sammlung Christian Brandstätter (Vienna) – photo © IMAGNO/Austrian Archives: 9, 10; photo Sammlung Deutsches Historisches Museum, Berlin: 88; photo San Francisco Museum of Art: 58; Schloss Babelsberg and Wehrgeschichte Museum, Rastatt – Stiftung Preußische Schlösser und Gärten Berlin-Brandenburg/Bildarchiv – photo Daniel Lindner: 21; courtesy of the artist (Joachim Schmid) © Joachim Schmid: 118; from Johann Anselm Heinrich Schnäbeli, *Album der Proklamierung des deutschen Kaiserreiches im Schlösse zu Versailles 18. Januar 1871* (Berlin, 1871): 21; from *Simplicissimus*, VIII/42 (1903/04): 35; photo © SLUB/Deutsche Fotothek/Richard Peter: 84, 90, 91; courtesy Sonnabend Gallery, New York © Beate Gütschow, VG Bild-Kunst, Bonn 2016: 111; photo © *Der Spiegel*/Max Ehlert, 2016: 87; photo Staatsbibliothek zu Berlin/Preußischer Kulturbesitz, Berlin, © bpk – Bildagentur für Kunst, Kultur und Geschichte/Heinrich Lichte: 40; photo Staatsbibliothek zu Berlin/Preußischer Kulturbesitz, Berlin, © bpk – Bildagentur für Kunst, Kultur und Geschichte/Staatsbibliothek zu Berlin: 42; Stadtmuseum, Munich: 1, 6, 8, 14, 15, 16, 20, 22, 65, 69; photos Steidl Verlag: 68, 71, 72; from Ullstein Verlag, *50 Jahre Ullstein 1877–1927* (Berlin, 1927): 32; from *Unfallgefahren und Unfallschutz in der Holzindustrie. Verhandlungen der Konferenz der Maschinenarbeiter, Schneidermüller und Säger am 12., 13., u. 14. Nov. 1911 in München* (Berlin, 1911): 42; U.S. Holocaust Memorial Museum, Washington, DC: 77, 81; photo Universitätsbibliothek Heidelberg: 33; University of Michigan Museum of Art, Ann Arbor, photo © Artists Rights Society (ARS), New York/VG Bild-Kunst, Bonn, 2016: 54; Wien Museum, Vienna: 26; photo Wittenbergische Landesbibliothek Stuttgart: 60; courtesy Yosi Milo Gallery, New York, © Loretta Lux/Artist Rights Society (ARS)/VG Bild-Kunst, Bonn, 2016: 115. *Joghurtbecher (eine Hommage)* was published under the artist names Beierle + Keijser – © photography Norman Beierle, © text Hester Keijser: 100.

Index

Illustration numbers are in *italic*